Palliser's New Cottage Homes, 1887

Palliser, Palliser & Co.

DOVER PUBLICATIONS, INC.
Mineola, New York

Bibliographical Note

This Dover edition, first published in 2003, is a slightly abridged reprint of *Palliser's New Cottage Homes and Details,* first published by Palliser, Palliser & Co., New York, in 1887. Some ads that appeared in the original book have been omitted

International Standard Book Number: 0-486-42816-8

Manufactured in the United States of America
Dover Publications, Inc., 31 East 2nd Street, Mineola, N.Y. 11501

"Ah, to build to build!
That is the noblest art of all the arts.
Painting and Sculpture are but images,
Are merely shadows, cast by outward things.
On stone or canvas, having in themselves
No separate existence.   Architecture,
Existing in itself, and not in seeming
A something it is not, surpasses them
As   substance shadow."

                              Longfellow.

Palliser, Palliser & Co, Arch'ts

SKETCH OF A HOUSE ERECTED AT WATERBURY, CONN.

PALLISER, PALLISER & CO., ARCHITCTS, 24 E. 42D ST., N. Y..

FRONTISPIECE.

PALLISER'S
NEW COTTAGE HOMES

AND

DETAILS,

CONTAINING

Nearly Two Hundred & Fifty New & Original Designs in all the Modern Popular Styles,

SHOWING

Plans, Elevations, Perspective Views and Details of low-priced, medium and first-class

Cottages, Villas, Farm Houses, Town and Country Places, Houses for the Seashore, the South, and for Summer and Winter Resorts, etc., etc.

CITY BRICK BLOCK HOUSES,

Farm Barn, Stables and Carriage Houses,

AND

1500 DETAIL DRAWINGS,

Descriptive and Instructive Letter Press, also Specifications and Form of Contract.

Elevations and Plans to Scale of 1-16 inch to the Foot.

Details to Scale of 3-8 inch to the Foot.

Making in all a most practical book for Architects, Builders, Carpenters, and all who are interested in the subject of Building, and those who contemplate building, or the improvement of Wood, Stone or Brick Buildings.

NEW YORK:

PALLISER, PALLISER & CO.,

24 East Forty-Second Street.

DEDICATED

To those, who happy homes have always known,
To those, who plan and work such homes to own;
To all, who building homes would bless mankind,
To all, who in their homes a refuge find.

To youth, whom wedded life will soon employ,
To children dear, each day their parents' joy;
To all who favor honor, truth and love,
To all whose virtues promise homes above.

" Architecture is delightful in itself, and valuable to society, in proportion to its power of exalting the soul and refining the intellect."
—SIR S. FERGUSON.

PREFATORY.

Some years ago when there was but one building journal in existence in the United States and that published but once a month, and when Architectural books were comparatively scarce and sold at $10 to $15 each and a circulation of 700 to 1,000 copies was considered a big thing, the authors of this work published "Palliser's American Cottage Homes," "Palliser's Model Homes" and "Palliser's Useful Details," at prices bringing them within the reach of everyone, which, as soon as they were presented to the Building community of the country, met with a rapid sale, and judging from the number of editions through which they have passed, and the immense circulation reached—50,000 copies of "Palliser's Useful Details" alone having been issued—they have, without doubt, met the approval of those most interested in practical Architectural works, and must have filled, in a measure, a want before unsupplied.

As a result of their popular teachings we find in the rural districts among the buildings erected at the present day almost an entire absence of the vulgar, meaningless, square-box like or barnesque style of Architecture, sometimes pretentious and therefore jig-sawed and ginger-breaded to the death, which years ago was the rule rather than the exception with white lead for exterior painting and the regulation green blinds. It is also worthy of note that the idea is no longer prevalent that good taste in Architectural design should be exercised only in regard to the erection of the more costly structures built for people of means, but on the contrary, more thought and attention is now paid to the design and erection of the smallest Cottages and Villas than has been given in the past to the more ornate and costly dwellings.

The success achieved by the above mentioned books—brought about by their own merit and their reasonable price, together with the help of our many friends, and the friends of Architectural taste and its development, to whom we tender our many thanks not forgetting that most potent power in the land, The Public Press, which has been most liberal in praising and extending our efforts—has induced the authors to publish another to take their place, and which is now presented to the public, and in its pages will be found a more extensive collection of designs of modern domestic Architecture of low and medium cost than ever appeared in a single volume before, all fully drawn out and explained, and with Detail Drawings illustrating the features which go to make up structures such as are needed to meet the wants of the American people, and the materials at hand for construction in this country, which are principally of wood.

All the designs given are new and original, and have never before been produced in any Architectural work, and what is aimed at in this instance is to present a mass of practical Architectural designs and details, easy of construction, pleasing in form, and generally of an inexpensive though artistic and tasteful character, which cannot fail to interest and help all who are in any way connected with improvement in building, and there are thousands of cities, towns and villages in all the States of the Union in which the wants of the people continually demand the erection of buildings such as are represented in this book, which we trust will prove more than suggestive to them by assisting their judgment and decision as to their plans and character of the buildings they will erect so as to obtain the best results, as it should not be forgotten that there is a commercial value to be attached to a well arranged plan and carefully studied grouping of the exterior of a house, for it is evident that a dwelling built on these principles require no more material or labor, but is simply a scientific rendering to produce harmony and convenience, and the difference between a house of this kind and one of ordinary construction when placed in the market is at once apparent. Then again, in the matter of constructing the work material is economized in these days of modern ideas and progress, the old principles, which were to use large timbers and cut them all to pieces by morticing and notching down to levels, being discarded and smaller timbers used, but so put together and constructed as to give greater strength without wasting material and labor.

To attempt to give here a table of contents or list of illustrations and all the details contained in this book would require considerable room and—in our opinion—entail a waste of space, therefore it is omitted.

We have felt some hesitation in giving the actual cost of building the different dwellings described, as many people forget to consider that time, site, fluctuations in prices, various localities, style of finish, and business management will affect the cost very materially. We can give but one cost of the construction and finishing of a house exactly as it has been built from our plans, etc., and that is the sum total of the actual amount of money expended, but as to what is the best method to adopt in building so as to have it done in a good manner, and with the least expenditure of money and saving of time and trouble, can only be settled on after a careful consideration of all the circumstances connected with each individual case. It would be manifestly absurd for us to make the statement that it is cheapest and best in every instance for an owner to buy materials and have the work done by the day, dispensing with a contractor, as it is certainly not true and by far the greater number of buildings are erected by contract, sometimes under one general contract, or sub-divided amongst the different trades. Another method is that of the owner buying the materials and giving out the labor to the various mechanics for lump sums. All these several modes of doing work have been employed by our many clients, and ourselves too, on buildings of our own, and as a general rule building by contract in one form or another has the preference, although we know instances where good management in building by day's work has proved advantageous. The designs here presented have been carefully selected from a very large number in our office with a view of giving the best results at as small an expense as possible.

We also desire to state here that we do not publish these designs in any other form, giving costs of constructing each on an increased scale, or separate from the designs for the use of builders only, as we understand has been done in other quarters. The costs given on the one hand stated to be in the interest of the public to protect them against the demands of dishonest builders, and to be the actual cost of structures, not the cost and a contractor's profit added, which was alleged might be all the way from the honest ten to fifteen per cent. to the dishonest forty, fifty or a hundred per cent., which they assert some builders try to get, while on the other hand printing the designs on single sheets for builders to show parties intending to build, giving no costs, that information being reserved for the builder, and so that if it were possible he might monopolize his customer and get an exorbitant price. We beg to say most emphatically that we resort to no such means to try and serve our customers, and in connection with our work have but one side to present to the entire public, whether Architects, Carpenters and Builders, or people intending to build, and we believe that all may find many valuable hints, while at the same time we are confident of its kind reception and success in all that it aims to accomplish.

24 EAST 42ND STREET, NEW YORK.   THE AUTHORS.

INTRODUCTORY.

We present on the following pages American Homes of to-day, not, however, of any well defined style of Architecture, except what may be termed our National style, for it would be folly for us, who live in the nineteenth century, a nation noted for its inventive genius, to undertake to transplant to this new country any foreign style which was perfected centuries ago, and which, though eminently fitted for the age in which it flourished, is not adapted to our wants and times. There has been enough attempts and failures in this direction the past half century, and the evidences are to be plainly seen in many directions even to-day in existing classical tubs, the Italian villas and Mansard roofed boxes of all grades and sizes, to say nothing of numerous nondescript extravagances, all of which have been found wanting for this people, and instead there is springing up a National style which is becoming more distinctive in character and unlike that of any other nation, as the American climate, life, economy of time and labor, requiring greater facility and conveniences, with snug and comfortable quarters for Winter and shady porches and verandas for Summer. This style of design in building is usually stamped by the genius and individuality of its author, the conditions he has to meet, and the materials used. Some time in the future it is probable that there will be a multitude of styles adapted from the Classic, each possessing more or less merit.

The designs illustrated in this book are of a varied character, some of them indicate work of an expensive kind, but the greater number are for that of a cheap kind, or of a moderate cost, and all are such as may be readily executed.

The ornament used in nearly every design is of a plain, but at the same time effective order, and easy of execution. Very little carved ornament is introduced, and that may be readily produced by any ordinary mechanic.

The scale on which the detail drawings are made is large enough to render them perfectly plain to enable any good mechanic to put the same into execution without the least difficulty, and full-size detail drawings can be made for the work very easily. The plans and elevations, or designs, are drawn to a scale of $\frac{1}{16}$ inch to the foot, and the details to a scale of $\frac{3}{8}$ inch to a foot.* Where any other scale is used the fact is mentioned on the plates.

Since the issue of our first book on building homes, some 10 years ago, in addition to a large local practice we may be said to have been the first to organize a system by correspondence for furnishing people everywhere about to build with working plans, specifications, &c., &c., to meet all their requirements, and more especially people in the country where Architects had done but little business and the people had been obliged to plan their own houses, or copy from their neighbors, and it seems to have gotten into the minds of many people that we sell ready-made plans to suit all the different ideas of persons who intend building, the amount of money to be expended, or their depth of pocket, their families, climate, soil, views, winds and storms, seasons the house will be occupied, water supply, drainage, and all the other numerous and varied details connected with building. This, of course, is impossible, if it is to be done correctly, and we must treat each individual case separately, as Architects should.

Another thing, as we anticipated, there has sprung up during the past five or six years in many directions several persons and firms imitating that part of our business referred to above. Most of them, however, put out designs that are very crude, and offer services that would apparently be of a very inferior order and clap-trap generally. Their methods are of the worst order of quackery, making deliberate calculations to mislead the public by issuing pictures, sketches of the imagination, never built, and with impossible costs of construction, given to catch the ignorant, only to prove disappointing to them when tried. Rumor has it that one of these quacks has been scheming to close up all the Architects' offices in the country so as to have a monopoly of the plan business himself, though he is not an Architect, but claims to know more than them all.

An Architectural journal, which has been supported by Architects furnishing for it, free of cost, designs, &c., for publication, wishes to draw plans, and inserts the following: "Should any of our readers desire to procure plans and specifications for building, whether churches, schools, dwellings, stores, carriage houses, homes, &c., or if they desire plans made for alterations, enlargements or additions of any kind to existing buildings, erection of porches, bay windows, extensions, wings, &c., they are reminded that all business of the kind will receive prompt attention at this office on very moderate terms. Address ———." A well known building monthly commenting on this says: Doubtless the very "moderate terms" prove quite effective, and while the regular skilled practitioner may by these terms be enabled to "take a rest" young draftsmen and would-be Architects will have excellent opportunities to pick up a few ideas at the expense of the persons caught by the moderate terms.

Others in the field issue catalogues of plans, giving a few dimensions, and the same matter on every page, about furnishing plans and urging people to pay from $25 to $250 for a set of ready-made plans of the design they may select, although that would probably never be what could be used to meet their wants. These venders of ready-made plans will tell you that it is much the best for you to order plans, &c., of designs in the catalogue that suit you, or nearly so, without having alterations made in the plans, as all changes can be indicated to the Builder when the plans are turned over to him. Now, anyone with common sense would ask in such cases what can be the good of these plans but to make trouble between owners and builders, changes and extras followed by a law suit, which is frequently the result of half prepared plans, specifications and contracts.

We were once shown by a client plans and specifications for an 18 room house, for which he paid $15. It was all contained on a sheet of paper two feet square, specifications and everything, but this plan being useless to the owner he employed us as Architects to draw up proper plans, details, &c., and have the works executed, which cost $3,800, and cheerfully paid us properly for our services.

* The plates in this Dover edition have been reduced to 92% of their original size.

If one writes these venders of plans, asking if a design can be executed for the amount asked they will answer yes, it can be done if our plans and specifications are followed. If so much can be done why don't they complete the thing and deliver the house itself at any point for a stated price? But their great object is to sell you plans, etc. The costs given in the catalogue are stated to be the actual cost of the structures just such as will be secured by buying the materials and hiring the labor performed by day's work. And it is further stated that the plans are practical, having stood the test of construction, many of them under their own superintendence ; and in another place that the cost is figured from prices of material and labor in the neighborhood of ———— on such a date just one month before the catalogue is issued. Therefore it would appear that a great deal of building is done in that locality by the day, and awful cheap and quick, which, however, is a delusion and a snare. A builder once remarked : " Why, at such prices the material must all be stolen. How can it be accomplished otherwise, I cannot understand?"

These venders advertise that they alone inform owners fully and accurately about actual costs and all other things that should be known, instead of being like others giving information to Architects, or plainly in the interest of builders, and they conjure the public that the way to avoid trouble in building is to have plans and specifications, and advise them not to trust untried plans made by amateurs, but be sure and get theirs, that they make no mistakes, and sell them for a quarter what an Architect charges. They state that in all their specifications good materials are called for, that it is poorest economy to expend the labor in working up inferior materials, and yet, look at the costs given for completed buildings—often less than the best materials can be bought for that is required in the building. Beware of persons offering to do more than they or anyone can possibly accomplish.

We know of a gentleman, thinking of building him a Cottage Home, saw in a newspaper a cut and advertisement of a handsome house, cost $1,500, giving a glowing description of the interior finish, its beauties in the way of Queen Anne stairs, mantels, &c. He wrote and asked the advertisers if it had ever been built for the money, and if so where and for whom. In reply he was referred to two parties in the same State, but at different towns, and he communicated with them and received replies, stating that they cost very much more, and then were not built according to the description in the advertisement. One of the parties had received a letter from the advertisers saying that the house should certainly be built for $2,000, but finding they were cornered, they finally had to acknowledge to him that no builder would build it for less than $2,800 to $3,000, and this they stated after some of their own builders had figured it up, and this in view of the fact that the advertised cost is $1,500, figured according to material and labor in that locality in which the two parties had built, whose names were given as reference. The advertised $1,200 house by same parties has cost in like manner to build in a cheap way $2,100. Many more such instances could be recited, but we think enough has been given to enable anyone to form their own opinion as to the adoption of such methods and their certain results, and there are many victims, some of whom, rather than acknowledge they were taken in, allow their names to be printed as references, but if closely questioned will generally admit the truth. The moral is a common one and as old as history : "Fear the Greeks bearing gifts."

Please bear in mind that we are not in the ready-made plan business, and in all our experience, serving as we have upwards of two thousand clients all over the United States by correspondence, we have not found two persons wanting to build just the same house ; in fact, every person's location and wants differ, and their ideas and everything connected with the subject must be considered and taken into account, and this we do to arrive at a proper and practical solution of each problem presented.

In Architecture there is a method to follow in all cases presenting themselves, but no receipts or procedures. This method is none other than the application of one's reasoning power to each special case ; for what is good in one case is not available in another. It is then on the observation of these circumstances, facts, habits, climate and sanitary conditions that one's reasoning will rest before conceiving the design and drawing out the plan.

So little does the public appreciate the difference in the skill and labor of one Architect and another, that they often allow a paltry difference in charges of one-half per cent. of cost—a difference which he would think trivial in comparing the merits of two existing buildings if he were purchasing—determine the choice between Architects, without regard to the qualification on which the whole success or failure of the building will depend. It should be borne in mind that it requires from seven to ten years of study and close application to be reasonably admissible to practice, and for this time and cost of preparation the Architect is entitled to as fair a return as any investment of time and money can be. If you get cinders in your iron, it is because there are cinders in the pay ; there is always good iron to be had.

It is the legitimate claim of an Architect that his skill enables him not only to contribute his own ideas of comfort and beauty, but to satisfy the special wants of his client—to carry out his wishes, and even whims, if need be, more successfully than another, provided he is made fully acquainted with these wants and wishes ; and the Architect's claim is pretty generally acknowledged now-a-days wherever his profession is well established.

That the American people are taking up with great vigor the question of home building for themselves goes without saying, and each one should be stamped with more or less individuality so as to fit into and harmonize with the lives to be spent under its roof, and this may be readily accomplished by calling in the services of a skilled Architect and making him your confidential and responsible adviser, and a single suggestion from him is often worth his fees. Not a single building, no matter how inexpensive, should be attempted without having first a properly studied and prepared set of plans and specifications setting forth the work to be done so that after regrets may be avoided. Any one who cannot afford this certainly cannot afford to build.

Speaking of Home, what tender associations and infinite meanings cluster around that blessed word ! Home—the temple of love, the nursery of virtue, the circle of loving hearts, the play-ground of children, the dwelling of manhood, and the retreat of old age. It is the place on earth where health can best enjoy its pleasures, wealth revel in its luxuries, poverty bear its sharp thorn, sorrow nurse its grief, and dissolving nature expire.

PALLISER, PALLISER & CO., ARCHITECTS.

24 EAST 42ND STREET, NEW YORK.

PLATE I.

The large house represented on title page by first floor, second floor and roof plans, together with general perspective view, is a fair sample of the American country house, devoid of all nonsensical features tending to belittle the character of the general design, and illustrates one of the most sensible homes it has been our lot to plan. This house is built of red croton brick, with trimmings of buff brick, terra cotta and brown stone. The face of gables are tiled, roofs slated and ridges covered with terra cotta. It was recently built at Peekskill, N. Y., at a cost of about $9,000, and is said to be the most attractive house yet built in the place although several erected there have cost many times what it did. The entrance hall is eleven feet wide, and contains fireplace, stair case, seat, closet, alcove, etc., is very finely finished in oak, a rich dark color, giving an impression that is sure to be pleasing to the incomer. The parlor, to left, and sitting room, at right of hall, are connected by wide sliding doors, as are also the library and sitting room. Thus the three rooms and front entrance hall can be opened up as one room—a most desirable feature in a house of this class. The angle bay in sitting room, and location of fireplaces, are especially happy in their relation to each other. The library connects with a spacious toilet room, which in turn opens into back hall, a large closet being provided in each of these, as will be seen by a careful study of the plan. The back hall is very conveniently arranged for free and easy access to all parts of the house, and the Porte Cochere, in connection with the side veranda or porch, is a feature that cannot well be dispensed with in a country home. The dining room is a fine one, replete with conveniences, having fireplace on one side and a sideboard built in opposite ; also a spacious china closet is here provided, in which to lock up rare and costly china, and the passage way, or butler's pantry, from dining room to kitchen, is fitted up with tables, presses, drawers, etc., and is well lighted from the pantry by means of a glass slide in the partition, which is also convenient for passing dishes through. There is also a door from this passage way to cellar stairs—as well as one from kitchen —a feature essential to all first-class houses, as it often occurs that it is necessary for members of the family to pass to cellar-way, and they dislike to go through kitchen to get there. The laundry is placed on the first floor, and contains the wash tubs and refrigerator ; also a clothes closet for dirty clothes, with shute from floor above.

The second floor contains six fine chambers, a sewing room over front hall, bath room, and well lighted halls, closets in abundance, and the rooms are so connected together as to be very desirable for family use in suite as may be required.

The attic contains two finished rooms and a large amount of storage accommodation. There is a cellar under the whole house, containing storerooms, partitioned off, and the house throughout is warmed by a large portable hot air furnace, fed with cold air taken from a point about ten feet above grade level, the cold air duct or inlet being built in with the brick work behind parlor chimney. This is considered an excellent arrangement when the construction is such that it can be adopted, as it takes the cold air supply from a point where the air is more pure than is usually the case at the ground level.

The first story of the house is finished in hard woods, principally cherry and oak, the kitchen and back hall parts of yellow pine ; second story rooms all of white pine, the whole of the woods being filled and then finished with two coats of superior varnish, rubbed down to a true, even, dead finish. The transom lights to first story windows are of art glass, as are also the top panels in front entrance and vestibule doors. The staircase windows are also of art glass.

Such a house as this requires a large lot on which to build it, so as to show it up to the best advantage, and is a good sample of what the homes of many successful business men ought to be who appreciate their spare moments and desire to spend them in enjoyment and social intercourse with the family, free from the cares and restraints of the business world. Such homes as this are wanted all over our country, and it is the business men of fair means who can live in them, and who, by so doing, will educate the public taste to appreciate the sensible and artistic treatment that is so satisfying and pleasing to the mind through the eye, cultivating the taste for something honest and simple in construction, and leading the desire away from that which is pernicious and in and taste, made only to gratify the whims and caprices of the ignorant and uneducated, as is too often the case where houses of considerable pretension are sometimes executed and built by impracticable and selfish builders, whose great boast is generally that they planned this and that, and it was awful expensive ; in fact, costing in many instances double what a carefully studied design in harmony with the requirements would have done had the parties building exercised the same care and judgment in so doing that they would in any other business matter involving a like outlay.

The style of this house would be termed by many an adaptation of the so-called Queen Anne, with all the eccentricities and nonsensical features of the same entirely dispensed with, being free from all objectionable features and absurdities that have become so common in such styled houses the last two or three years. The exterior wood work is painted Indian red and bronze green, giving very happy contrasts with the buff and red brick, and they are probably the best colors that could be adopted.

The small perspective sketch on upper left corner of title page is a general view of design No. 3, plate No. 2.

The centre perspective on margin is a view of design No. 2, plate No. 2, and the lower one is a general perspective view of design No. 4, plate No. 2, to which the reader is referred for full particulars.

Palliser's New Cottage Homes

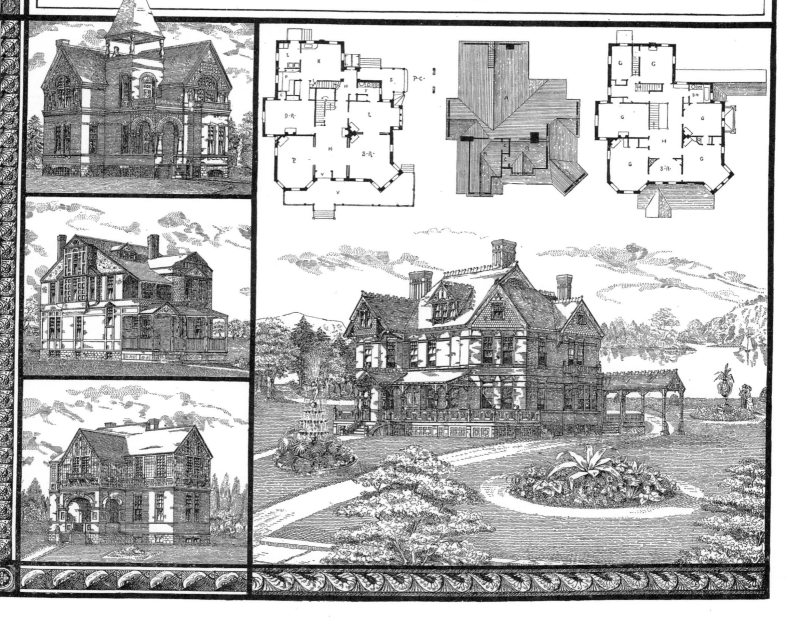

PALLISER'S NEW COTTAGE HOMES AND DETAILS.

PLATE 2.

Design 2 represents an attractive two-story cottage in wood, containing eight rooms and bath room, there being two very nice rooms on third or attic floor, where there is ample space for same; the front hall is large and roomy, answering nicely for a reception room, the seat by stairs and closet under stairs being very useful accessions; the back stairs are very handily arranged and the kitchen is nicely isolated from the main part of the house; the front porch and piazza are very spacious, giving ample room for two groups to gather without interfering with each other, and the second-floor balcony opening from the hall is a very nice feature, affording a cool and secluded nook in which to sit and read or sew. The style of this house, with first story clapboarded, second story shingled and gables finished in plaster with stencil work stamped into same and picked out in color, may be termed unique. Such a house painted on body of first story a green drab, shingles of second story old gold, the gable work buff, and general trimmings of sage green, with the mouldings, etc., picked out with Indian red, makes a very attractive appearance, very pleasing to the eye, and a bright spot in the landscape. Cost, $3,200.

Design 3 is a pleasant little brick cottage, suitable for a small family, and is one of those pleasant little buildings that are always agreeable to the eye in almost any position. The plan is a very compact and convenient one, and the design is suitable for a gate lodge to a brick mansion, which might be in harmony with the style here shown. The house, built with an even-colored, clean, common red brick, trimmed with pressed and moulded brick and terra cotta, all laid up in red mortar and oiled, the roofs tiled or slated with red or black slate, makes it very effective. The open balconies on second and third stories over hall

are nice features of the design which give a character to the whole not otherwise obtained. The sliding doors between parlor and dining room are a great help to sociability, and the fire places as arranged together in the corners of the rooms, come prettily into one chimney above the roof; the inside wood-work in natural white or Georgia pine filled and varnished. Range in the kitchen, brick set, and the whole house heated by a small furnace placed in the cellar at less cost than if heated by two stoves, and the latter could only heat about one-third of the house at best. Cost $3,800.

Design 4 is an example of brick, timber and tile, which makes an excellent combination when rightly handled. The first story is brick on a stone underpinning of irregular ashler in rock faced range. The front porch is particularly handsome and spacious. The first floor plan is conveniently arranged and well suited to the needs of a small family of refined tastes; the dining room has a recess for a sideboard, and the conservatory connecting with parlor and dining room is a nice feature and a source of enjoyment to the lover of nature in plant life; the second floor has four fine chambers with good closets, and there is space in attic to finish off servant's room. Cost, $4,100.

Design 5 is a neat frame cottage well adapted for a gardner's or a coachman's residence. Could be built with or without cellar, as circumstances require, and if placed in a proper location where it would be partially hid by foliage, would make a very necessary addition to a country seat, where the servant would always be within easy call and under the master's eye. Cost complete, $1,200.

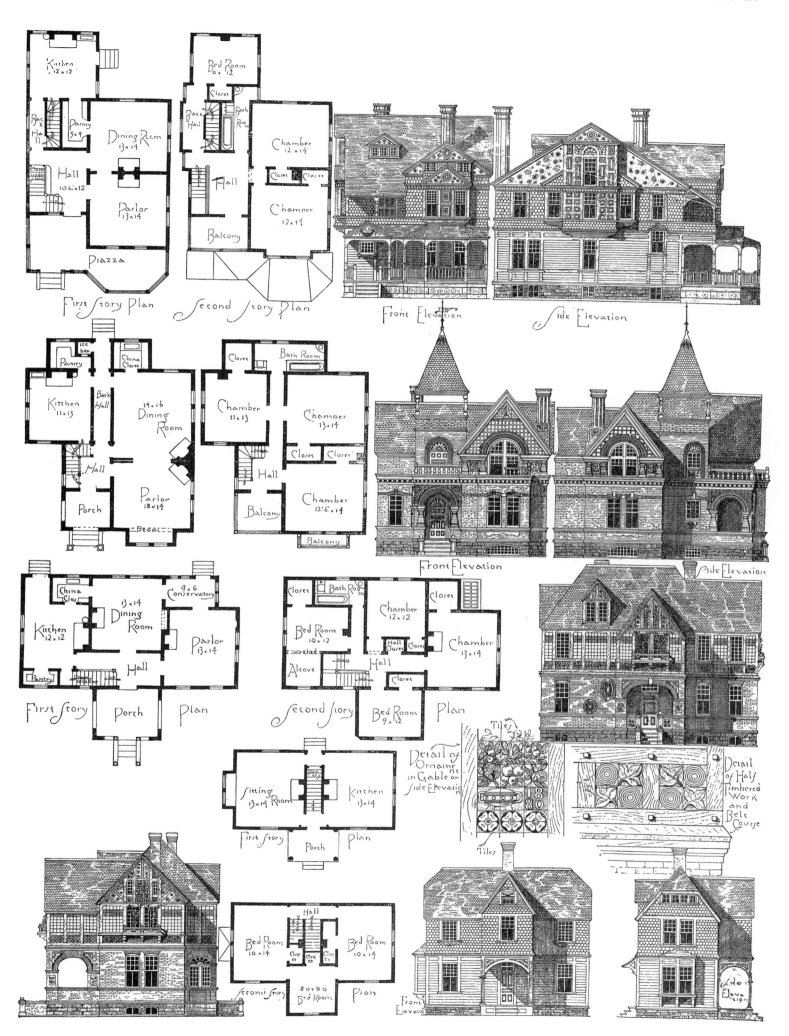

Design 6 comes somewhere near the requirements of the thrifty mechanic who, by dint of steady perseverance and self-denial, has saved enough money to buy a suburban lot where it is not too far out for him to walk to and from his daily toil. Such lots in the suburbs of a large city are nearly always laid out twenty-five feet wide and one hundred feet deep, and this design is adapted to a lot of this size and still leaves ample room to get all around it. By reference to plans it will be seen that it contains six good rooms, bath-room, front and back stairs and plenty of good closet room. A fireplace is provided in the parlor which would serve for ventilating the first floor. The front porch has seats on each side, thus providing a ready and convenient sitting-down place. The side-rear veranda is a nice, cozy spot to sit evenings and enjoy a quiet pipe and the daily paper. The sash door from the dining room renders it possible for anyone to pass out without disturbing the privacy of the kitchen. Such houses as this, neatly finished, painted in tints, with bath-room fixtures and cellar under whole house, cost about $2,000, and on a lot in value about $500 more would be a reasonable rent to live under.

Design 7 is another cottage suited to a narrow lot, and gives seven rooms on two floors. This house is very simple in plan and outline, and is, what is generally called, a one-and-a-half-story. There are no back stairs, no bath-room and no waste room. The only water fixture is a sink which can be supplied with water from cistern in rear, so arranged as to collect all the water from the roofs and supply it at kitchen sink through a pump. This would make a cozy home for quite a large family, and nicely built and finished, would make a home that no one need be ashamed of. The fireplaces on first floor can easily be left out if economy demanded it: though they would be better in, as they help to furnish the rooms, and are both useful and ornamental. Such a house as this is not so costly as No. 6 by some $300, and yet it gives as much available room.

Design 8 illustrates a small cottage of four large rooms, which can be placed on a lot 20 feet wide; the stairs start up from the living-room, and cellar is reached from hall; the general character of the design is pleasing, and would paint up very effectively in deep tones; there is room for one or more rooms in attic which would help out the accommodation; good closets are provided, porch-room ample, and with a cellar under the whole house gives sufficient room for an ordinary family at a small outlay, being simple and free from expensive features. Cost $1,600. In good localities where lumber and labor are plenty, the cost would be much less. This design is capable of several changes that would add or diminish the cost as parties might need.

Design 9 represents a very roomy and attractive house suited to an ordinary city lot, and would give ample accommodation for quite a large family, there being space enough in attic for two rooms, if needed; the entrance hall is large and makes a nice reception room and with a simple staircase of pine, with ash rails, newel and balusters, the hall windows stepping up with stairs and containing border lights of cathedral tinted glass, the effect would be very cheerful and enlivening to those entering. The space under stairs can be utilized for closets for hall and dining-room, and the three main rooms connecting as they do with front hall makes the first floor very desirable. A private back stair is arranged up and down from the kitchen and the back entry to kitchen and dining-room is a good arrangement. Four good chambers, each with large closet, are provided on second floor. A slate roof would be appropriate and add to the appearance more than the difference in cost over shingle. Cost, $2,800.

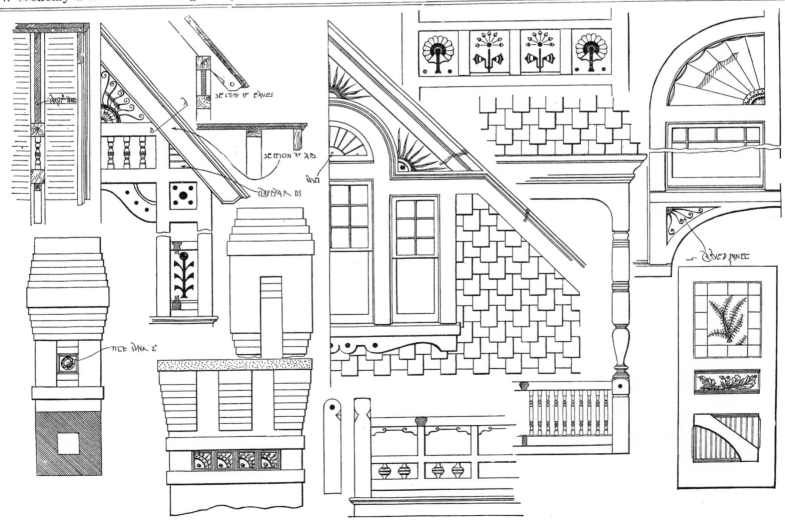

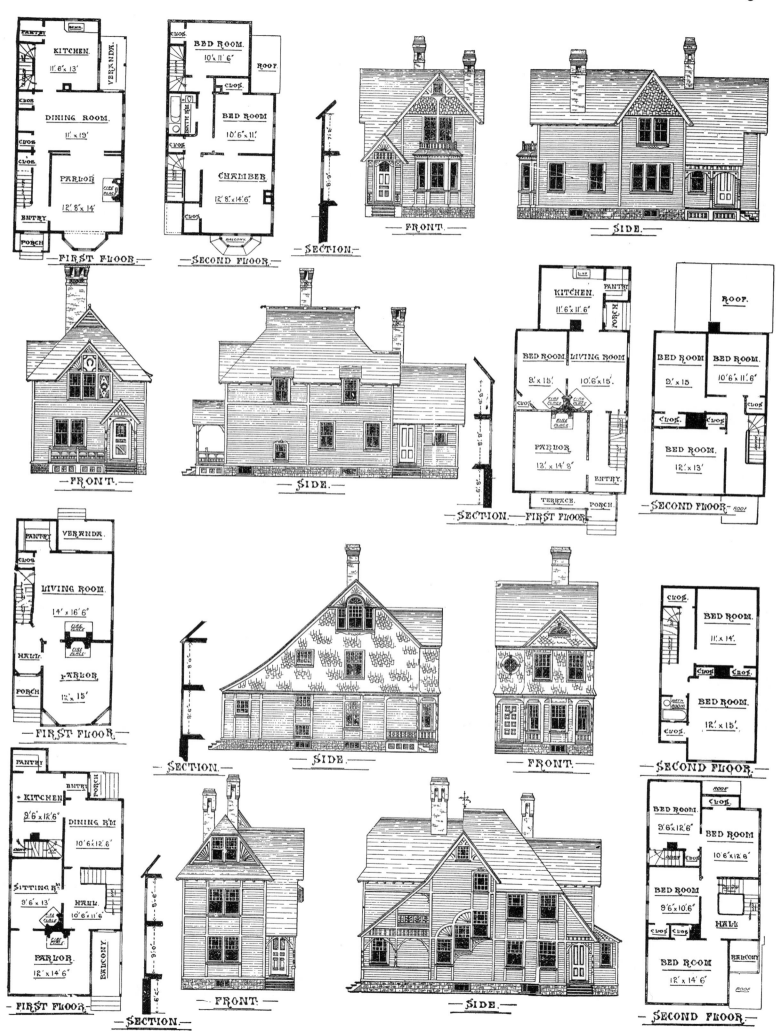

KITCHEN.
11' 6" x 13'

VERANDA.

PANTRY

CLOS.

DINING ROOM.
11' x 19'

CLOS.

CLOS.

PARLOR
12' 8" x 14'

FIRE PLACE

ENTRY

PORCH

FIRST FLOOR.

BED ROOM.
10' x 11' 6"

ROOF.

CLOS.

CLOS.

BED ROOM
10' 6" x 11'

CHAMBER
12' 8" x 14' 6"

CLOS.

BALCONY.

SECOND FLOOR.

SECTION.

FRONT.

SIDE.

FRONT.

SIDE.

KITCHEN.
11' 6" x 11' 6"

PANTRY

ROOF.

BED ROOM
8' x 15'

LIVING ROOM
10' 6" x 15'

PORCH

BED ROOM
9' x 15'

BED ROOM.
10' 6" x 11' 6"

FIRE PLACE

FIRE PLACE

CLOS.

CLOS.

FIRE PLACE

PARLOR
13' x 14' 8"

ENTRY

BED ROOM.
12' x 13'

TERRACE.

PORCH

SECTION. FIRST FLOOR.

SECOND FLOOR. ROOF

VERANDA.

PANTRY

CLOS.

LIVING ROOM
14' x 16' 6"

FIRE PLACE

FIRE PLACE

HALL.

PARLOR
12' x 15'

PORCH

FIRST FLOOR.

SECTION.

SIDE.

FRONT.

CLOS.

BED ROOM.
11' x 14'

CLOS.

CLOS.

BATH ROOM

BED ROOM.
12' x 15'

CLOS.

SECOND FLOOR.

PANTRY

ENTRY

PORCH

KITCHEN
9' 6" x 12' 6"

DINING R'M
10' 6" x 12' 6"

CLOS.

SITTING R.
9' 6" x 13'

HALL
10' 6" x 11' 6"

FIRE PLACE

FIRE PLACE

PARLOR.
12' x 14' 6"

BALCONY.

FIRST FLOOR.

SECTION.

FRONT.

SIDE.

BED ROOM.
9' 6" x 12' 6"

ROOF

CLOS.

BED ROOM
10' 6" x 12' 8"

BED ROOM
9' 6" x 10' 6"

HALL

BED ROOM
12' x 14' 6"

BALCONY

ROOF

SECOND FLOOR.

Design 10, a type of house that needs a special site, as a shallow lot with a good frontage, or a hillside lot where the rear would come well out of ground. The arrangement of rooms is good, and will suit a large number of people who want a very nice home of few rooms, and yet need the conveniences of a larger house. With the two rooms and front hall on first floor finished in hard wood, and other parts in pine, filled and polished, the effect would be very pleasing. The sideboard built in recess with a small art glass window through centre of same, with glass worked into an appropriate subject; the corner fireplace to have a neat mantel with shelves or overmantel above, on which to display a few pieces of china; the china closet forms the communication to kitchen, and is a convenient arrangement, as here the crockery can be stored handy to both rooms and a slide between pantry and china closet will save many steps around from one room to the other. The ice closet or refrigerator in back entry is so fixed that ice can be put into same from the back porch, the door from entry being used for access to same from inside. The bath room on second floor is convenient and well located, and if it were necessary to have more room on this floor it can be obtained by carrying up the part over pantries, and making two bed rooms over kitchen part where now only one is shown. Cost of erection, $2,500.

Design 11 is another type of house with some of the features similar to No. 10, and contains about the same amount of room and general conveniences, but with an entirely different exterior mold; the first story of this design is of brick on a stone underpinning or cellar wall, the whole having a decidedly classic feeling in the ornamentation of same; the main body of the second story over the brick work is covered with shingles, which can be of California redwood to very good advantage, finished natural with spar varnish, the other woodwork being bronze green, the roofs slated; a clothes shute is provided from bath room down through china closet to laundry under kitchen, which is a handy arrangement, as the dirty clothes can be dropped in at each floor, and they are always ready to the wash tubs when wanted. Cost to carry out as here shown, $2,800.

Design 12 represents another type of the six room house, giving a very nice entrance hall, containing stairs and fireplace and so connected to back hall as to shut off and isolate the kitchen nicely, and yet any part of the house can be reached from either entrance. This would make a very nice suburban home and a good servant's room can be provided in attic. The three chimneys are brought together in one large stack above the roof and thus reduces the expense and adds to the general appearance, as too much chimney is sometimes not desirable. The painting is—body color, a light sea green buff; trimmings of olive drab; outside blinds and shingle work, Venetian red, sash white. Cost, $2,700.

Design 13, another six room house with about the same room as the three preceding designs, is a very pleasant home and suitable for erection on a fifty feet front lot having a nice lawn and flower beds in front, to stand well back from the street line, say twenty-five feet, so as to make a proper appearance. It is often the case that attractive houses are spoiled by people locating them too near the street line; thus they cannot be seen to any advantage.

The angle bay window is a very nice feature, as are also the large piazza and balcony on front. Cost, complete with small furnace to heat whole house, $2,700.

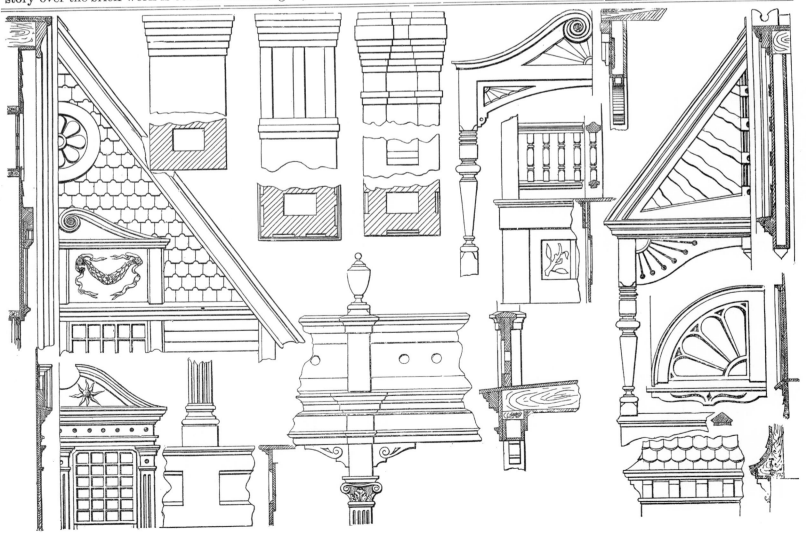

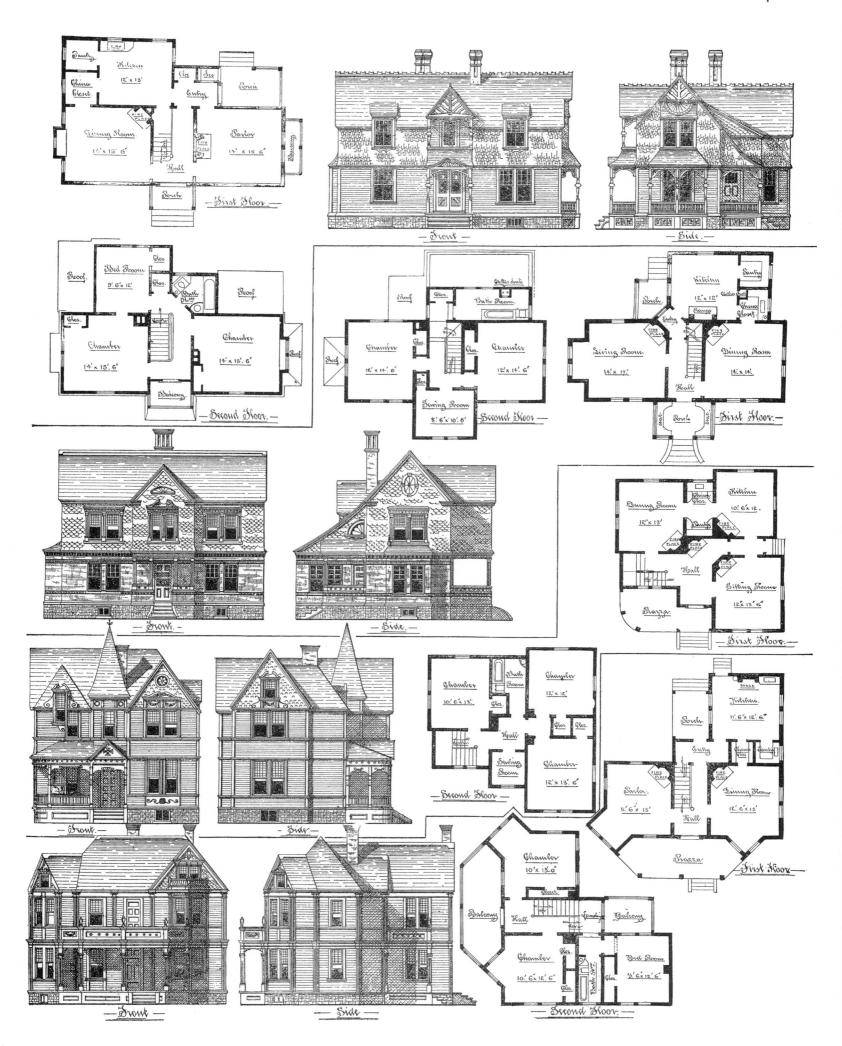

Design 14 represents an exellent plan for a country house, with good porch and veranda conveniences, the recessed front porch gives a secluded entrance and ample space for a good bed-room over. The stairs are well arranged, and are lighted by the large stained glass window ; there is a large closet in the front hall, and a wash-bowl in the junction between front hall and kitchen and cellar stairs. Library and parlor are thrown together by sliding doors. The fire-places are placed where the two come in one chimney, which is built to show on the outside, and is quite a feature of the design, the square panel containing sun dial is designed to be of terra cotta and the belt below with the inscription, "Tempus Fugit," is there to remind us of the flight of time and in the right position where it can be seen to good advantage. The general arrangement of this design will commend itself to those needing a plain, roomy home, and is one of those designs that will give as large amount of satisfaction for the money expended as it is possible to obtain, and the interior comforts are such that they can be enlarged upon or contracted to suit individual wants, The roofs are slated and have terra cotta ridge crest ; the cellar of stone with underpinning of irreg ular ashlar, rock faced work, laid with level beds and plumb joints, the chimneys built with good quality red brick laid in black mortar, clapboards painted Venetian red and vermillion, in equal parts, trimmings of bronze-green, shingles, old gold. The small panels between first and second story being of buff color, sash and chamfers, etc., in chrome yellow, all of which colors can be easily found in the many ready mixed paints now so popular in the market and which so greatly assist in the selection of combination of colors that will look best together and be in harmony with all the requirements. Cost, $4,000.

Design 15 is a plan well suited to many sites where the peculiar shape or circumstances dictate something radically differ-ent from the every-day plan so common to houses of this size. The arrangement is well adapted to quite a large family of taste, and would probably suit the ideas of more people needing eight or nine rooms, with the conveniences here shown than any other design of same size herein illustrated. The entrance hall is large, roomy and well lighted, the large window being susceptible to a fine heraldic effect in art glass of appropriate design. This hall communicates with the three principal rooms of first floor, and connecting, as it does, with parlor by sliding doors, it makes a very roomy and open arrangement, giving ample room and opportunity for hall furniture, which goes so far towards making a good impression on the visitor when entering. The staircase hall is well placed, being nicely isolated from main entrance and yet in close proximity and where it can be seen sufficiently to just give a charm to the general effect, the glimpse of stairs being far more desirable in entering a house than to see the whole stairs open before you ; and it is by far the nicest for the ladies of the house, as they are not compelled to walk down the whole flight of stairs in front of their visitor, which is too frequently the case. The toilet-room under stairs contains bowl and water-closet, and provides ample room for hanging wet or damp clothing, the stair hall giving ample room for the hat-rack and stand for general use of the household. The dining and sitting-room, connecting together as they do, make a desirable living part, the sitting-room having a corner cheffonier, built in opposite fire-place. The conservatory opening to dining-room by means of portiere is a very nice feature, and by means of door from same to terrace, an outside entrance to rear garden is obtained. The pantry, laundry and kitchen offices are excellent ; back stairs just right, and the general plan and conveniences on second floor unexcelled. The servants' rooms in attic are reached direct from back stairs, and the privacy of second floor is entirely preserved. Such a house, with all improvements and hard-wood finish on first floor, costs to build it about $4,800.

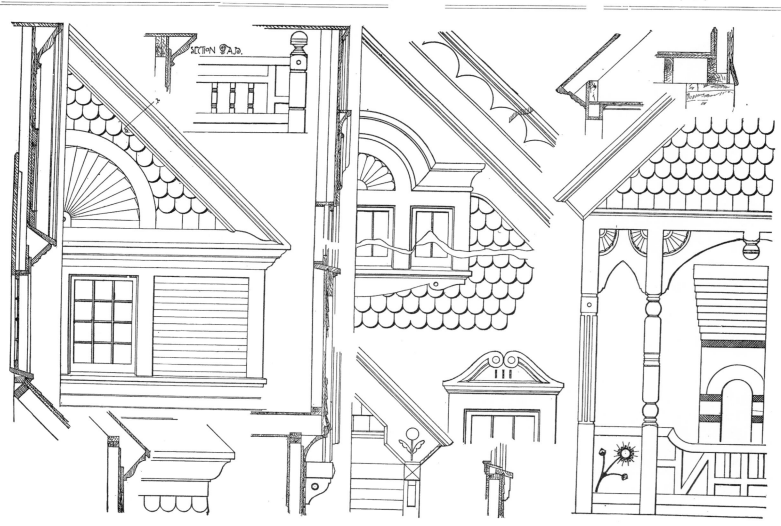

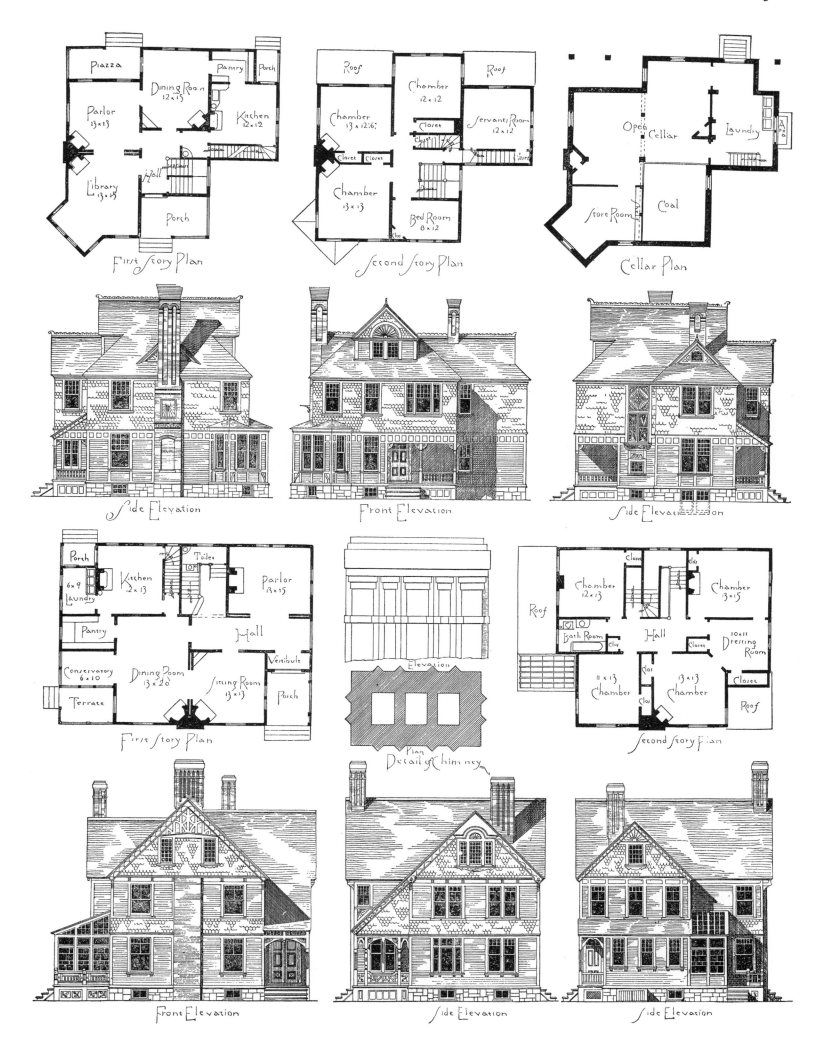

First Story Plan

Second Story Plan

Cellar Plan

Side Elevation

Front Elevation

Side Elevation

First Story Plan

Elevation

Plan
Detail of Chimney

Second Story Plan

Front Elevation

Side Elevation

Side Elevation

PLATE 6.

Design 16.—To the observing and studious this design will probably lend itself more, and help to indicate a national style, than the generality of designs here shown. In building of wood, as is largely the custom of our country, the great object is variety; and the difference in peoples' ideas and necessities of plan to suit them, creates an infinite variety of outline that in wood can be made very attractive, and when designed in good taste, with no desire other than to make a good, honest and artistic thing, with a proper clothing to cover the body, the exterior being simply the dress to cover the plan, the outcome cannot help but be a sensible consummation of the difficulties encountered. To the trained mind the plan is the first object of consideration, the exterior being subordinate to it. This design may very justly, we think, be called "Modern American Renaissance," the features being of a decided classic mould, adapted to the general style and construction of wood, the external effect when completed and painted in suitable tints of drabs, toned in together, cannot help but be pleasing and instructive; and as to the outlines of the building and the proportions of the different parts, the design speaks for itself, and we believe it will prove more than suggestive to many who are looking after models and designs, that they feel they can safely build after and make no mistake in so doing. The general plan of this house commends itself to a large majority of people who require a roomy house; and for a suburban residence, with good grounds and shrubbery, etc., it would make as pleasant and artistic a home as the most fastidious could desire, and the large number of houses we have planned of the size and general shape of this for erection in all parts of the country, convinces us that this will become a popular design and be universally liked by a large number of those who are looking for permanent homes. The entrance hall with a large fire-place, and the stairs well back from front, and sliding doors to both parlor and library, makes a fine reception-room, and a cheerful wood fire blazing on the hearth in the hall in the winter time, gives a welcome that only

needs to be seen to be appreciated. The fire-place in the hall is a feature that ought to be extended to every house, even when not near as large as this one. The main staircase is somewhat odd in plan, yet very sensible and easy of ascent, the large window over platform being filled with art glass, giving good light to the rear part of hall for first floor and also for hall of second floor. The back stairs are nicely located, and communicate with servants' room and attic, without interfering with the main house. A slight change converting the dressing-room on second floor into bath-room, and present bath-room into bed-room, would give another room on second floor, making five good chambers in place of four. The attic will give room for two or three good rooms and general storage room. The windows are intended to have lower sash glazed with clear plate, and the upper sash with plain glass in leaded frames, having a small square piece of cathedral tinted glass in the intersection of lights (see details); the windows to have inside blinds of cherry, or other suitable hardwood; the clapboards to show 3 inches wide, and be moulded on the bottom edge; shingles on side walls of California redwood, which could be oiled and stained; roof if of shingle, to be painted red, or red slate would be good, if not too expensive. Added cost of latter would be about $300. Chimneys built of good brick; fire-places of buff pressed brick, and showing the same open (see details.) The interior first floor ought to be finished in hardwoods—ash, oak, birch, cherry and maple all being suitable, and could all be used to good advantage; the kitchen part in Georgia pine and the second story in white pine, all filled and polished, so as to show up the natural grain of the wood. The cornices, centre-pieces and picture mouldings to be of wood, so as to match the general finish, mantel-pieces of wood with over-mantels and mirrors, side-board built into the recess in dining-room, the whole of the improvements adapted to such a house to be first-class and with laundry under kitchen. Cost, $7,500.

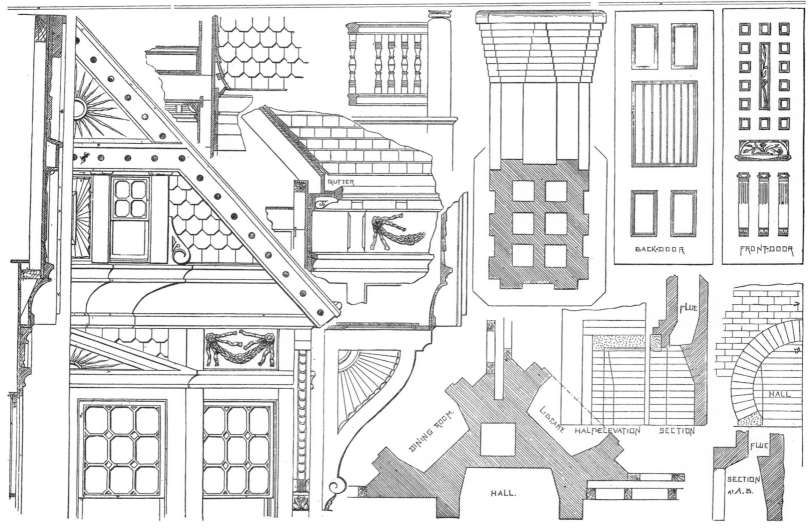

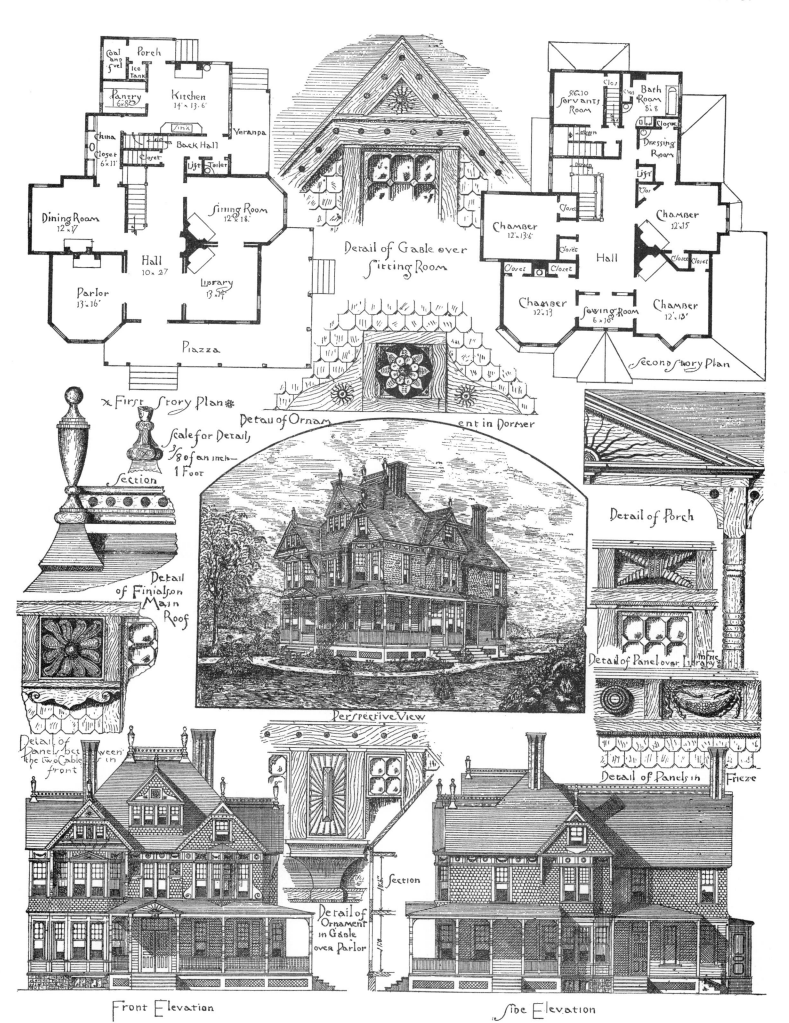

Coal and fuel Porch Ice Tank

Pantry 6x8 Kitchen 14'x13.6'

Veranda

China Closet 6'x11' Sink Back Hall Closet

Lift Toilet

Dining Room 12'x17'

Sitting Room 12'x18'

Hall 10x27

Parlor 13x16'

Library 13'x24'

Piazza

x First Story Plan ❋

Detail of Gable over Sitting Room

Detail of Ornament in Dormer

96x10 Servants Room Clos

Bath Room 8x8

down

Clos Closet

Dressing Room

Closet Lift Clos

Chamber 12'x13.6' Closet

Chamber 12'x15

Closet Closet Hall Closet Closet

Chamber 12'x13 Sewing Room 6x16' Chamber 12'x13'

Second Story Plan

Section

Scale for Detail, 3/8 of an inch = 1 Foot

Detail of Finials on Main Roof

Perspective View

Detail of Porch

Detail of Panel over Library

Detail of Panels between the two Gables in front

Detail of Ornament in Gable over Parlor

Section

Detail of Panels in Frieze

Front Elevation

Side Elevation

PLATE 7.

Design 17, shows floor plan, front and side elevation of a one-story cottage which might be termed the settler's cottage; this and the next design being very nicely adapted for that purpose. This cottage has three nice rooms, good pantry and closet and quite a spacious porch and is a capital plan for a small family of limited means. Such a house can be built on posts set in ground and tightly boarded up under sill to grade level and the interior can be finished by planing the timbers, the one thickness of sheeting forming both inside and outside covering (which often has to be done for economy's sake,) and the interior can be plastered at any time the owner might be able to do so; the roof is shingled and chimney built of brick. Such a house nicely built as above described, painted a lively red and trimmed with white would look well and cost in ordinary locations about $200. to build.

Design 18 represents floor plan, front and side of a two-room cottage built in a similar manner to No. 17 previously described, the side boarding being 8 feet high, making height of ceiling 7 ft. 8 in. as shown. The cost of such a house as this unplastered would be in the vicinity of $75 to $100.

Design 19 shows a small cottage of more pretensions, and containing two rooms down and three up stairs, the second floor being reached from back entry. The conveniences in this house are very ample and in external appearance it is all that is desirable for a house of this class. The exterior of first story is clapboarded, or might be covered with novelty siding, the second story and roof being shingled, the whole would paint up very nicely, always look attractive and homelike and make an excellent home for quite a large family or for a farmer having a small family of his own and a larger farm where he has to keep and house two or three men. Cost, $450.

Design 20 shows a four-room house with two rooms on each floor, and is a very attractive little cottage; the front entry gives access to both rooms. The back porch and door to kitchen keeps the front entrance more private; the stairs from kitchen communicate to second floor and are conveniently located for the best use of the room above. One of the advantages this house has over the three preceding designs is the front room which makes a best room and into which the visitors can be shown, although our observation has been that parlors are not of much use out in the west on farms where everything has to be turned to good account, and more especially in new homes. Cost, $400.

Design 21 is a type of house not at all uncommon in the New England States, built sixty to one hundred years ago, many of which are still in a good state of preservation, thanks to the honesty and good material used in their construction. The plan is square and gives a large amount of room and would meet the needs of quite a large family; with a good cellar under the whole house walls of which might be of stone in many cases picked up from the ground and could be built by the owner. Such a house can be built at a cost not to exceed $900, if rightly managed.

Design 22 illustrates a six-room cottage, the style and type of which is very popular. This would make a gate lodge or gardener's cottage and would be well adapted to any nice place requiring such a building. The rooms are well arranged, and for a design capable of being built economically, we can commend this plan. Cost, $850.

Design 23 has about the same room and conveniences as No. 22, with some slight changes in plan and a radical difference in external appearance. The gambril roof makes a low, roomy house, and utilizes the entire space almost up to the very ridge tree. The cost of this is about $40 to $50 less than the preceding design.

Design 24 gives a nice roomy cottage of six rooms, good conveniences and provides a small bath-room on second floor; a very desirable feature in many locations where water is conveniently had, and it is necessary to get the water-closet in-doors. This house would suit a small hillside lot and make a cosey home for a small family. Cost, $1,050.

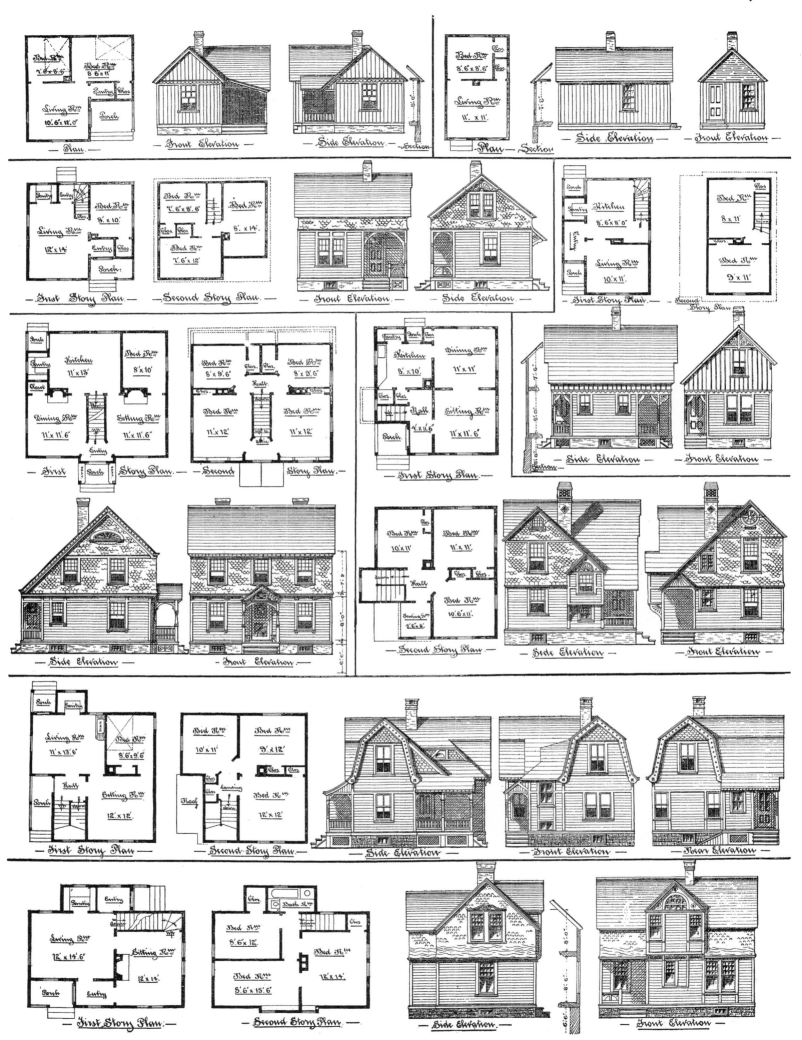

PALLISER'S NEW COTTAGE HOMES AND DETAILS.

PLATE 8.

Design No. 25 presents a plan of a very roomy and convenient house well adapted to the requirements of a large family, and would be equally a good house for the mountains or the sea shore. The large veranda on three sides gives ample room for a promenade and the balcony over front entrance makes a nice lookout from second floor. There is a cellar under the whole house, giving ample room for storage, heating apparatus, fuel; laundry under kitchen part containing stationary tubs, servants' water-closet, drying room and the general conveniences to be found in a first-class residence; the arrangement of first floor is well adapted to a summer residence where any of the family being old or infirm, can use the first floor chamber and have the use of the bath-room there provided, the small toilet room 'on first floor being convenient for use by the whole family from hall as well as forming the communication and private way from hall to chamber, which at times might be very desirable. The sliding doors between the sitting room, hall, parlor and dining room, make a very open house and one that would be well adapted to social events and parties. The dining room is a large room, an excellent shape for the purpose and the communication to kitchen through butler's pantry, having a sink in same, and thus placing two doors between the kitchen and dining room, makes it more private for both and keeps the fumes from back part of the house away from the main rooms. The kitchen is convenient in its appointments. The back hall is large and contains stairs to the second floor and to the cellar; the second story containing as it does five good chambers with good closets and dressing rooms, together with a large and commodious bath-room is all that can be desired; the stairs to attic are located from front hall, and in the attic there are three very nice rooms, finished in an inexpensive manner and still leaves a large open garret for general storage purposes; the fire-places come in the corners on the first floor, and the chimneys are brought into one stack under the roof so that they come out in the centre of main ridge; the roofs are covered with good shingles dipped in oil or shingle stain and finished a warm dull red; the side walls of frame sheathed diagonally on studs and covered with all wool sheathing felt before the exterior finish is put in place; this plan of protection against heat and cold is now accepted as preferable to the old method of filling in between the studding with brick, as the brick rots the timbers around the base quickly in many cases and when the timber shrinks it is apt to leave cracks between the brick and studding that the wind will blow through; while with the diagonal sheathing and the whole covered with paper, a wind-tight job is assured and the frame work is thoroughly protected and kept free from moisture of outside and will consequently last much longer. The siding on exterior is ordinary beveled and lapped and should in all cases be only the best of selected lumber perfectly clear and free from all imperfections whatever and with such properly fixed and secured it will last with good care in painting an indefinite length of time. A good treatment for the colours of this house would be a dark buff for body and bronze green for trimming colour, with roofs red as before named, sash white and outside blinds in maroon. A third colour of Indian red to be used on incised work, chamfers, etc., which would blend the whole together and make a very harmonious effect; the interior finishing can be mostly on the wood, pine or whitewood, if nicely stained, being very good and economical and could be made very effective and pleasing. Cost, $6,000.

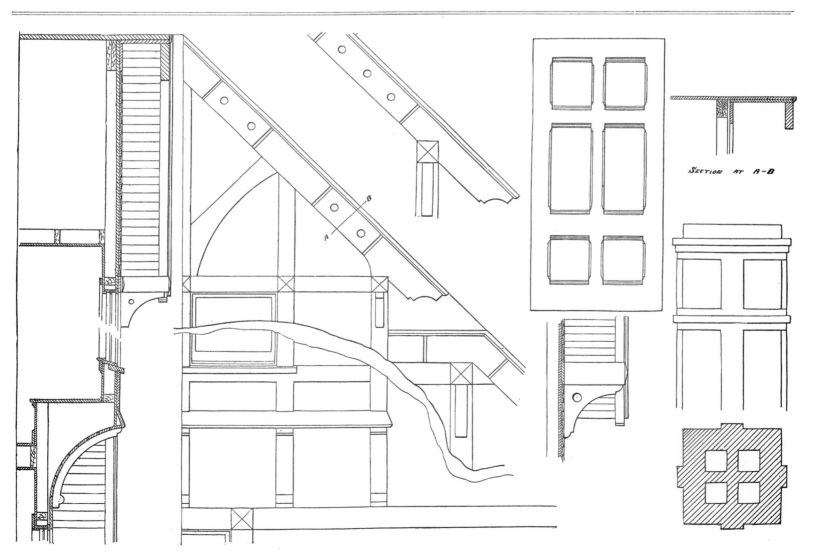

SECTION AT A-B

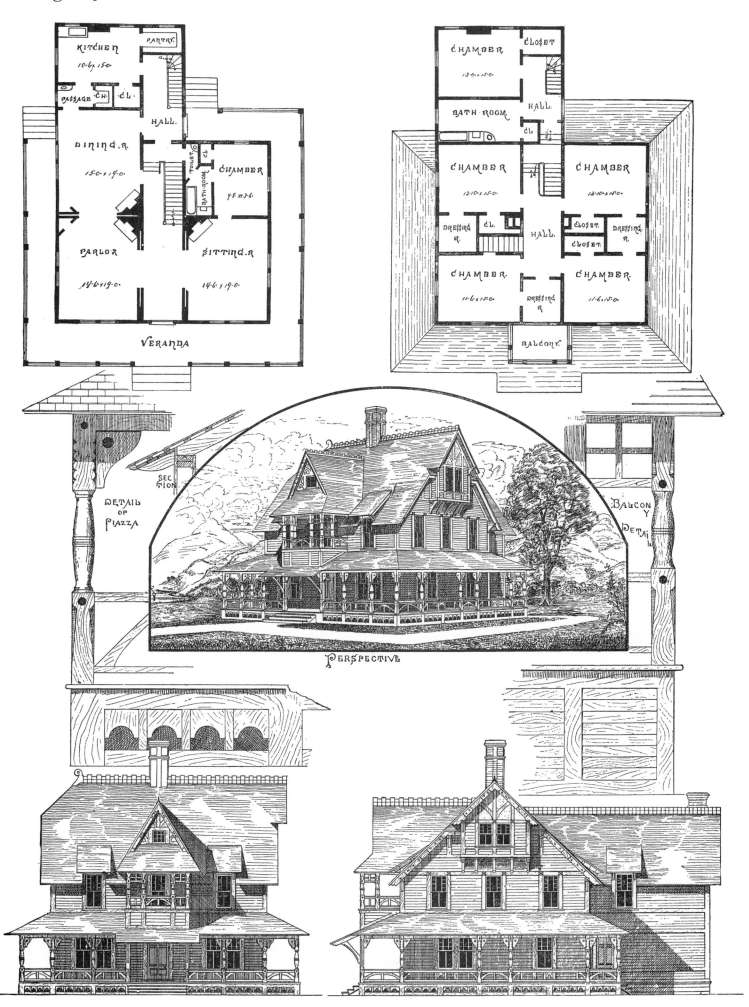

KITCHEN
10·6 x 15·0

PANTRY.

PASSAGE   CH   CL

HALL.

DINING.R.
15·0 x 19·0

BATH-ROOM   TOILET   CL

CHAMBER
9·6 x 13·6

PARLOR
14·6 x 19·0

SITTING.R
14·6 x 19·0

VERANDA

CHAMBER
13·0 x 15·0

CLOSET

BATH-ROOM

HALL.

CL

CHAMBER
12·0 x 15·0

CHAMBER
12·10 x 15·0

DRESSING R.   CL   HALL.   CLOSET   CLOSET   DRESSING R.

CHAMBER.
11·6 x 15·0

DRESSING R.

CHAMBER.
11·6 x 15·0

BALCONY.

DETAIL OF PIAZZA

SECTION

PERSPECTIVE

BALCONY DETAIL

FRONT ELEVATION.   SIDE ELEVATION.

Design 26 represents a type of the suburban or country home that will come near to the wants of a large class who need a good home, with such conveniences as are here shown. There are a very large class of business men who need such homes as this, and to take New York City as a guide, it might safely be said that there are not less than 5,000 people who need such a home as this and who could live in the country, within 25 miles of the city, in such a home at one-half the expense they are under in occupying a brick or brown-stone front and being hemmed in and crowded by their neighbors, very much to their discomfort generally. Such a house as this ought to have a lot about 100 ft. by 200. This would give ample room for a barn, garden and ground enough to keep the family in full supply, and, with the care of horse, etc., would just give one man all he could reasonably do to take care of the place and keep it looking as it should. Every man has his ideal and, at times, pictures and dreams of what his house must be when built. Some dream too long, others too large, and how many end in dreams, by trying and striving after that which is too far away from their reach, when by circumscribing their desires to the circumference of their means and ability to pay, they would be enabled to own their own homes, and avoid paying high rents for poor quarters in a crowded atmosphere. Another thing that few people think of is, it is certainly as cheap, and very generally a little more so, to own a place than to hire one, and that money is very plentiful, and in most of cases one-half to two-thirds of what a place would cost can be borrowed at a low rate of interest ; and to the man who pays his bills, where is the difference between paying rent and interest ? It is clearly every man's duty to himself and those dependent upon him to provide a home that will be permanent in the family, and to do this it is necessary to run into debt some ; and how many of the rich and successful men of to-day would have been as they are if they had never run into

debt at the outset of their business career. Such homes as this, built at an expense of $5,000, on plots worth about $2,000, would, no doubt, pay both to rent and to sell, if built in the right section, and to those who are seeking a home or investment we cheerfully recommend a careful study of this design. The general plan of first floor gives a spacious hall, communicating with and opening the parlor and sitting-room together by means of sliding doors. The front and back hall also connect together, so that it is possible to get to and from any part of the house without interfering with the privacy of any of the rooms. The dining-room is conveniently arranged ; is private and well isolated from front entrance, and is all that is desirable. As to kitchen connections and appointments the laundry being placed on the first floor, economizes fuel, and the expense of a stove for special laundry use is avoided, as the kitchen range answers both purposes. A toilet room is provided under stairs, and contains a water-closet and bowl. The second floor contains five good rooms, bath and sewing-room, together with good closets, and there is ample room on the third floor for four nice rooms, the attic stairs being placed over the back stairs, so that there is free access to attic from first floor, without troubling the main part of house. The store cellar, divided with brick walls from the main cellar, is a good feature, being placed where it is always cool and well lighted and being shelved makes a convenience very necessary in houses of any pretension. The shingled exterior and general character of exterior finish, gives a cosey and old-time appearance to the design, and takes away the general stiffness that goes with anything new. The main roofs could be of slate, veranda roofs being shingled same as the sides of house. The shingles on sides to be olive green, and other work painted red. Panels on front gable buff, and sash white. Whole house heated by furnace, and to have brick-set range in kitchen fire-place.

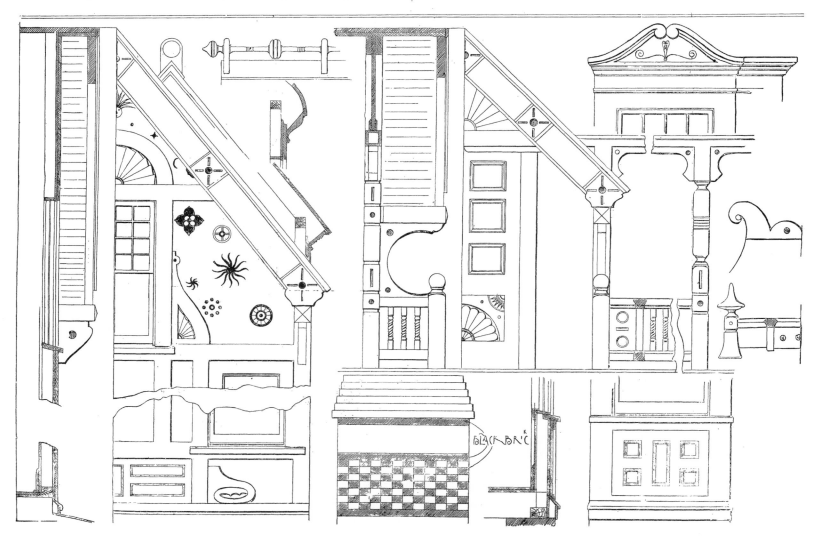

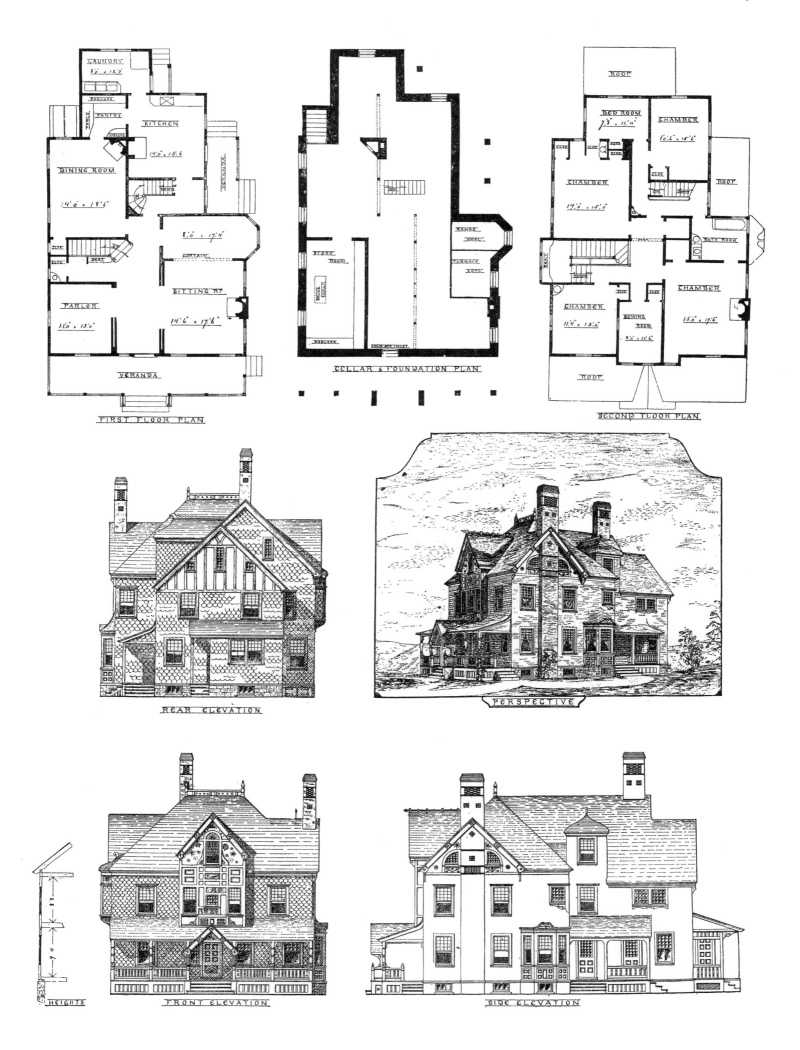

FIRST FLOOR PLAN

CELLAR & FOUNDATION PLAN

SECOND FLOOR PLAN

REAR ELEVATION

PERSPECTIVE

HEIGHTS   FRONT ELEVATION

SIDE ELEVATION

Design 27 illustrates a very nice four-room cottage, well suited as a gardener's cottage or gate lodge. The first story is built of brick on a stone underpinning and trimmed with bands of black brick. This cottage is very simple and plain, yet would present an excellent appearance if placed in just the right place and in harmony with the surroundings, the first story could be of frame, clapboarded if desired ; cost of such a house in favorable locality is $700 to $900, according to materials used in construction.

Design 28 shows a very pretty six-room house, with three rooms on each floor and a bath-room nicely located on second floor ; this is quite a roomy, small house, and one that would look well in almost any position where that amount of room is required. The general finish of this design, although in a similar vein to the preceding one, is more elaborate and has some very pretty features in general detail that cannot fail to commend itself to the lovers of architecture. The star and crescent in the side gable finish is quite a simple and effective feature and would look very well properly painted, with a good granite base wall, brown stone watertable, red croton brick, laid in red mortar and the black brick in black mortar, the woodwork properly painted in harmonious tints, this little cottage would make as artistic a home as the most fastidious would require and built well in a favorable locality, for $1,400. It is undoubtedly a good plan to study from and no doubt will serve a good purpose in assisting many to make up their ideas and ascertain what their wants are in the way of rooms and general conveniences, as one of the chief objects of this book is to help the inexperienced in putting their ideas into form ; the examples here illustrated being good guides more than otherwise as to what can or ought to be done for a given outlay.

Design 29 gives a very roomy and spacious house with modern conveniences ; first floor has three large rooms, the dining-room and parlor being thrown together with sliding doors ; the front hall and staircase are quite happy, the stairs being nicely placed out of the way and arranged to very good advantage from the front door so as to be seen just enough for a proper display of the detail of stairs and just enough out of the way to be pleasant for the ladies of the house when they are called down to meet a book agent who has succeeded in gaining entrance by his glib tongue well used on Biddy, whose business really is to keep such out rather than let them in. The kitchen is well placed, one chimney answering for both kitchen and dining-room fire-places ; the china closet is large and gives plenty of room for storage of all necessary crocks, the butlers sink in china closet being convenient and will save many steps ; the large store-room in rear of kitchen will be found handy for general work and answers for passage way to back door and is the mugby junction between the kitchen and outside rear porch ; as a play-room for the children and reception-room for the butcher, baker and candlestick maker, this room will play an important part and be found serviceable and just the thing in many ways ; the open balcony on second floor makes a quiet nook in which to sit and read or smoke. There is room for two good finished rooms on attic floor, which would make eight good rooms in all. The general appearance of this house is in a classic vein and works up well both for economy and good looks ; and costs to build, with heater and range nicely finished, $3,500.

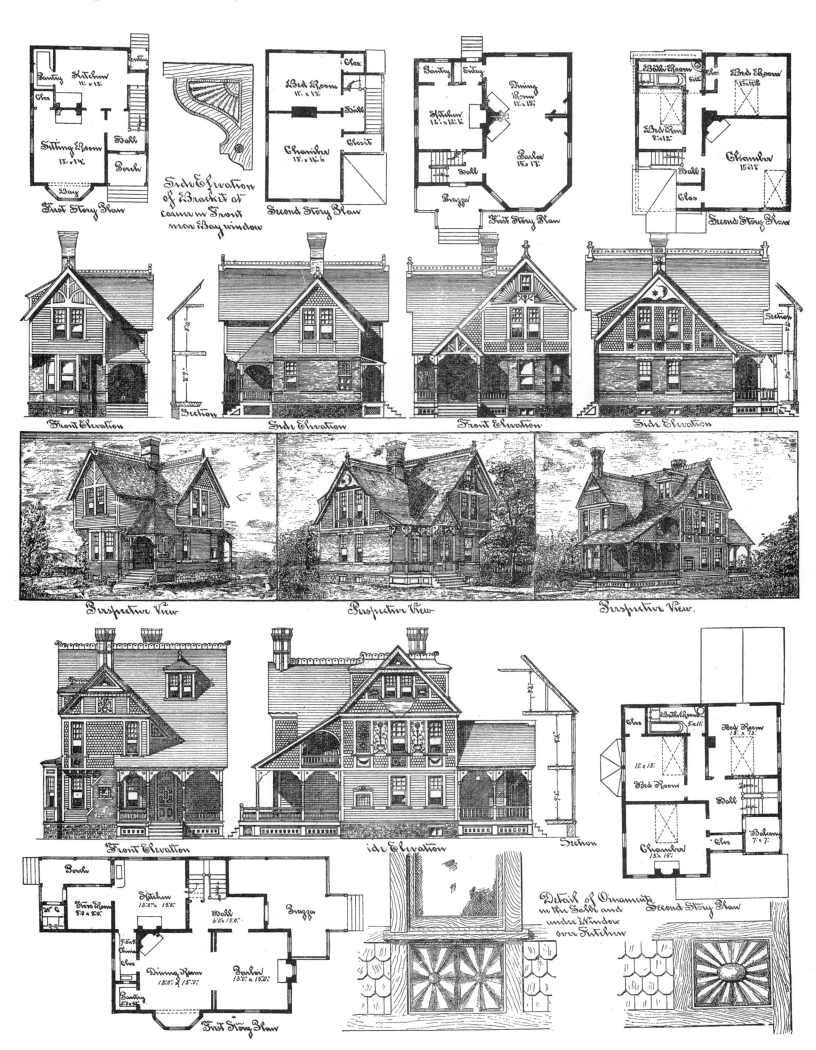

First Story Plan

Side Elevation of Bracket at corner in Front near Bay window

Second Story Plan

First Story Plan

Second Story Plan

Front Elevation

Section

Side Elevation

Front Elevation

Side Elevation

Section

Perspective View

Perspective View

Perspective View

Front Elevation

Side Elevation

Section

Second Story Plan

First Story Plan

Detail of Ornaments in the Gable and under Window over Kitchen

Design 30.—In this design we have three rooms besides a large reception hall, store-room, entry and china closet on the first floor, and three good chambers, servants' room and good closets on the second floor. This is what is termed usually a one-and-a-half-story house; is nearly square in plan and gives good rooms throughout. The first story walls are faced or veneered with brick, which is becoming quite a common way to procure a brick finish for one story, and still have the frame house inside; this is done by building the cellar walls larger than the frame by about 6 inches, the frame is then put up and sheathed in the ordinary manner, and the brick-facing built only 4 inches in thickness on the outside of frame and is anchored to same every two feet in height, by irons laid in and turned up at right angles against the sheathing and well secured to same with screws. We have had a number of houses carried out this way the last two or three years and they have been satisfactory in all cases. This method of construction commends itself to any one wanting a house of brick which can be built very economically and be warm, dry and strong, and requires very little material in the mason work to accomplish good results. This design would look well with a tile roof; the frame work of second story filled in with shingles of California redwood which, finished in red and the other portions of wood-work painted a bronze green trimmed with old gold would present a very handsome appearance, and certainly would be a great contrast to the ordinary style of houses of this size that are so common in the smaller towns and villages of the country, and it is to be hoped in the course of time, the ideas and suggestions contained in architectural works will be more followed by those building in such places than has been the case in the past, and that both the owners and those putting up the buildings will have more pride in their work and try and do something artistic as well as economical, and we think such books as this, and the general knowledge and information contained therein will greatly assist those who are willing to learn and study, and add to the features of the country largely by having more sightly buildings to look at, and give ones minds and eyes greater satisfaction as well as help to cultivate a love for the beautiful which inspires the soul to do more and more until we reach as great a degree of perfection as may be possible in the short stay allowed here, and after our departure leave such foot prints in the sands of time, as will be pleasing to and help educate those that follow, having to start where we leave off. Cost, $3,350.

Design 31 shows a very nice cottage, somewhat of an ordinary type as to general shape and plan; yet with some features that are far more suggestive than is usual in such plans. The large piazza is good for many locations and is susceptible of many changes to suit individual wants; the location of front stairs and the balcony from platform of same, is a very pretty feature. The general arrangement of main rooms on first floor could easily be changed and have sliding doors, so as to throw the three rooms and hall into one which would suit many people perhaps better than as here shown. The attic is roomy and there could be two rooms finished there to good advantage with furnace and range and improvements, and a nice finish in pine throughout, roofs slated; this house costs $4,000. There is, however, a vast difference in locations as to cost, sometimes a distance of fifteen or twenty miles, making a great change. As an instance; we have found the same work in New Haven, Conn., only seventeen miles from Bridgeport, to cost fully twenty per cent. more than in Bridgeport, a difference we could never explain, but which our experience has shown us existed.

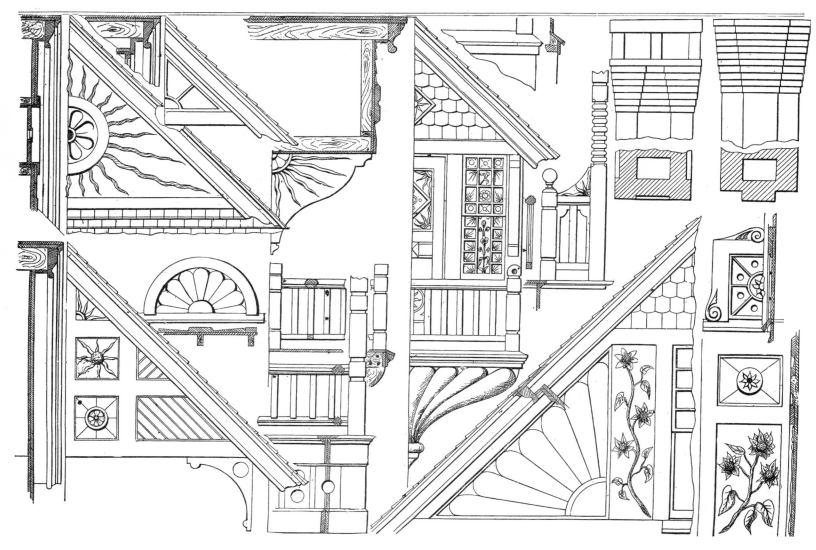

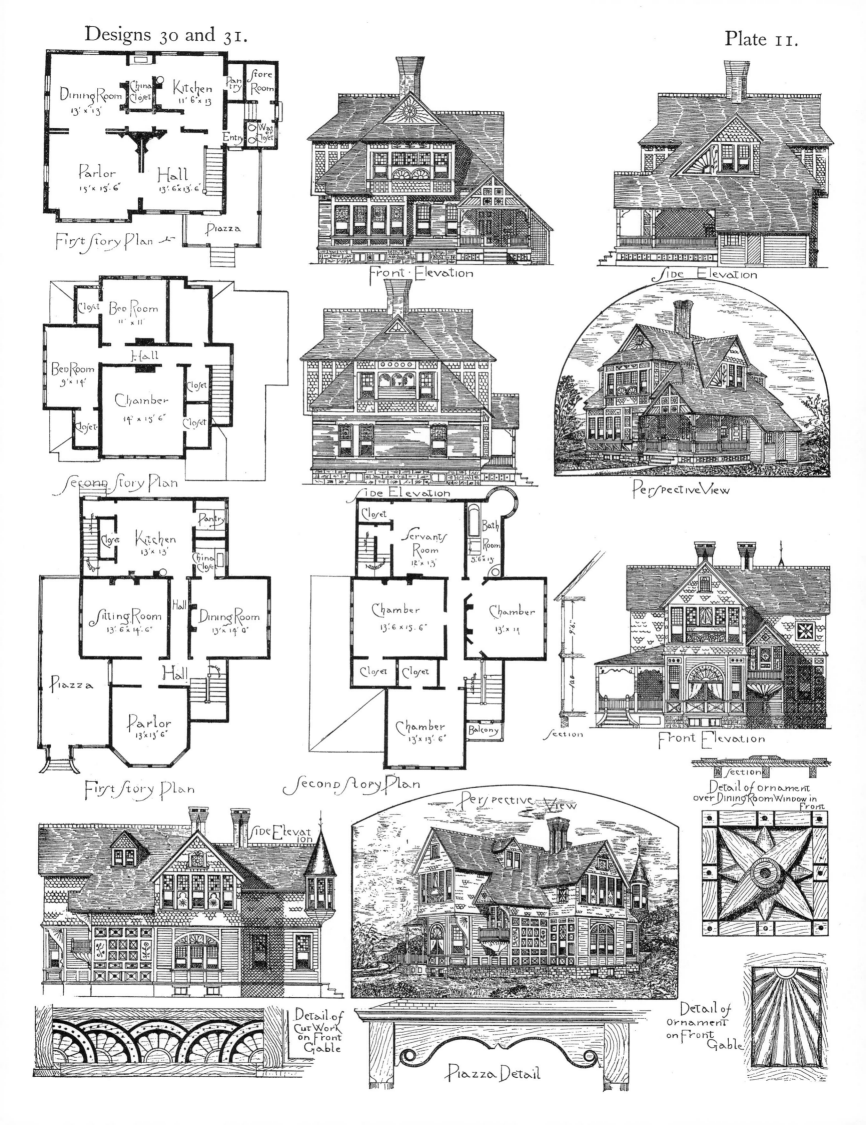

First story Plan

Dining Room
13' x 13'

China Closet

Kitchen
11' 6" x 13

Pantry

Store Room

Entry

Water Closet

Parlor
15' x 15' 6"

Hall
13' 6" x 13' 6"

Piazza

Front Elevation

Side Elevation

Second story Plan

Closet

Bed Room
11' x 11'

Bed Room
9' x 14'

Hall

Chamber
14' x 15' 6"

Closet

Closet

Closet

Side Elevation

Perspective View

First story Plan

Closet

Kitchen
13' x 13'

Pantry

China Closet

Sitting Room
13' 6" x 14' 6"

Hall

Dining Room
13' x 14' 0"

Piazza

Hall

Parlor
13' x 13' 6"

Second story Plan

Closet

Servants Room
12' x 13'

Bath Room
5' 6" x 13'

Chamber
13' 6" x 15' 6"

Chamber
13' x 11'

Closet

Closet

Chamber
13' x 13' 6"

Balcony

Section

Front Elevation

Section

Detail of ornament over Dining Room Window in Front

Perspective View

Side Elevation

Detail of Cut Work on Front Gable

Piazza Detail

Detail of Ornament on Front Gable

Design 32 illustrates a very happy little villa residence, showing a brick first story with tile or shingle covering overhanging above; the roofs are covered with red tile and ridges with terra-cotta. The first story, of red brick laid up in red mortar, would look best, the lower part of sash glazed with clear glass and the upper sash with cathedral glass in neutral tints set in small squares and leaded frame work. The stairs start up from back end of front hall, which gives a platform and landing over the front door; this leaves ample room for a nice alcove under same directly in front of door, which will be found very ample and convenient for hall stand. The second floor front balcony is large and roomy, and in some localities will be found very desirable. The rear part over kitchen by narrowing up the bath-room a little might be made into two bedrooms, which in some instances might be more desirable as it would then give an extra room for servants' use on the second floor in place of going up to attic for this purpose. The first and net cost of a furnace large enough to warm this house would be about $50, piping and registers about as much more. Net cost of a suitable brick-set range about $17, which with cartage and setting would cost inside $20; this includes the water-back and couplings for boiler connection; plumbing and heating work, including all fixtures for same, would cost about $350, painting $150, carpenter work $1,800, mason $1,250, tile work on roofs $280; to which add 2½ per cent. for plans amounting to about $100—makes the whole cost about $3,930. In some locations where brick, etc., are convenient and cheap it might be done for less, probably by $500, and would make a very satisfactory house at that price and one that would be a good improvement in any neighborhood even where large houses were the rule, as such houses as these are the ones that help so largely to educate the public taste to that in architecture that is better and will tend to sweep away much of that which is ugly and ill proportioned, and which can be seen on almost every hand. We have built several small houses of this stamp, and in all cases they have been very popular and pointed to as models that it would be safe to follow; and we could cite one house in particular of about this size that we have re-planned and changed over to suit individual wants more than twenty times.

Design 33 is a very handsome and roomy house similar in style as the preceding design. This house has kitchen and its conveniences in the basement, the back hall connecting with same and butler's pantry, with dumb-waiter from below nicely placed for use in connection with dining-room and back stairs. The general arrangement of this plan will no doubt commend itself to any large family of culture requiring a substantial and artistic home. The back staircase communicates with the attic, in which are provided servants' sleeping rooms, there being space for four good rooms if desired. The general interior wood finish in such a house should be of cabinet finish in hard woods on the first floor and pine elsewhere, all finished on the wood; to have cornices, picture mouldings and centre pieces of wood to match the finish; floors of hard wood filled and polished and with neat borders worked in same. The modern conveniences and comforts in the line of improvements incident and requisite to such a house, all of which would cost $6,000; and is a house that looks twice what its actual cost is when placed in the right position as to site, location, etc.

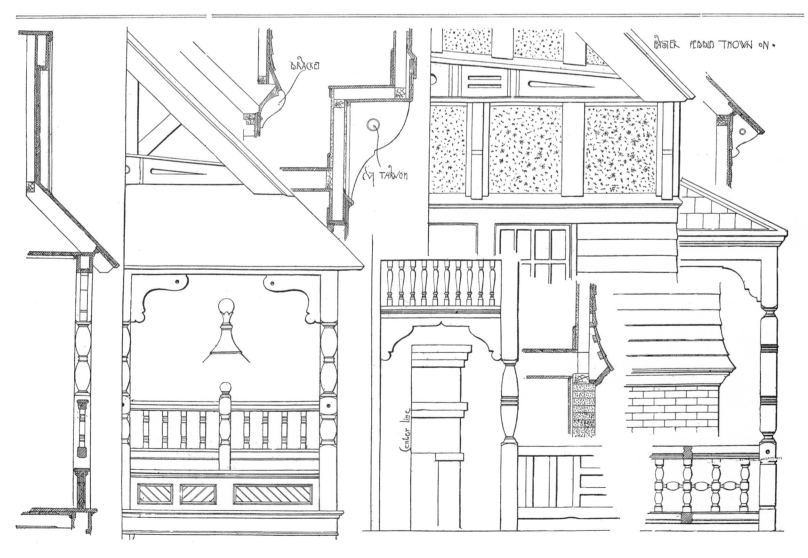

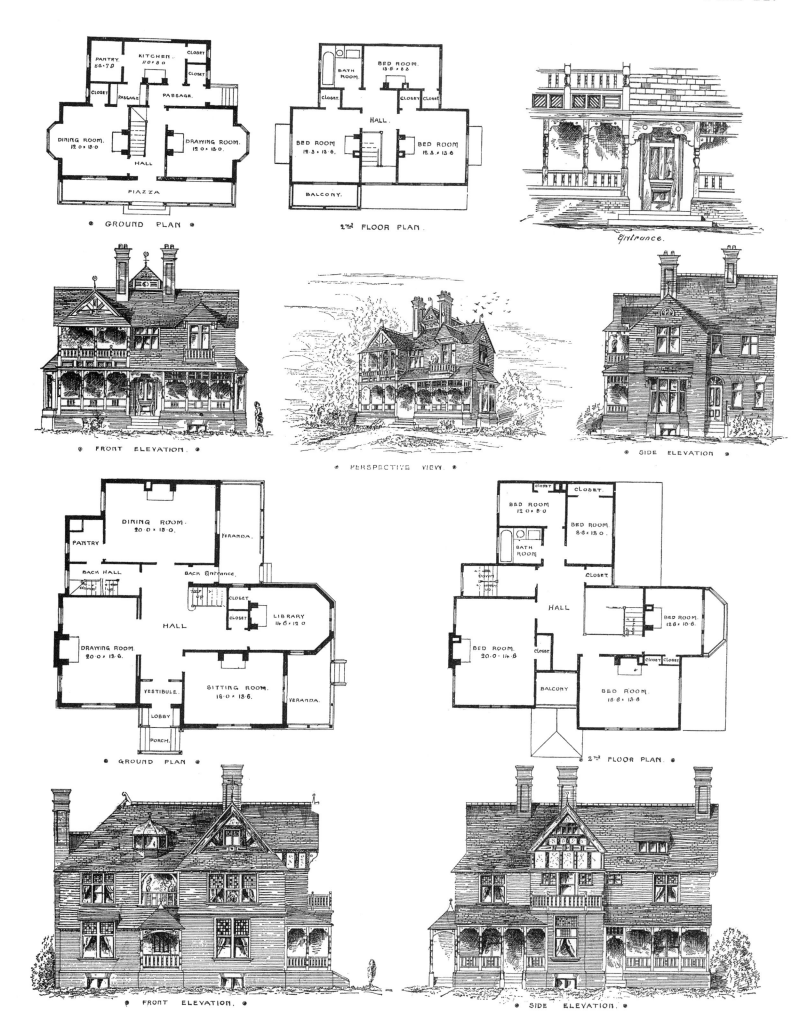

GROUND PLAN.

2ND FLOOR PLAN.

Entrance.

FRONT ELEVATION.

PERSPECTIVE VIEW.

SIDE ELEVATION.

GROUND PLAN.

2ND FLOOR PLAN.

FRONT ELEVATION.

SIDE ELEVATION.

Design 34 illustrates the first and second floor plan and front and side elevations of a type of house often built in the suburbs of cities where the rule of laying out the ground in regulation sized lots of 25x100 feet. In building on such sites it is generally the custom to place the house about one foot or so from the line on the least prominent side of the lot and build the house such width as will leave a suitable pass-way to the rear on the other side; hence houses from twenty to twenty-two feet in width by about forty to fifty deep are of the size required. This design gives four rooms on the first floor and four and a bath-room on the second, and provides room for two or three in the attic. Such houses as these are generally built on the same stereotyped plan, and any one who has lived in a city where such houses prevail cannot have helped but notice the monotonous appearance that the hundreds of gable ends facing the street, where the houses are all after one plan, presents. Such houses as this vary in cost from $2,800 to $3,500, according to location and improvements contained therein.

Design 35 shows the front and side elevation, first and second floor plans of another house suited to the narrow lot, the first floor being nicely laid out for a fair sized family. The porch and veranda both come under the second story, that part being run out and built over so as to increase the rooms above. The general plan, though somewhat odd, has some good features, and would make a good house for any one who does not care to keep a servant, as the rooms are all very nicely situated for the least labor in living therein. The stairs to attic are over the front or main stairs, and if necessary there could be two rooms finished on the third floor. To build this house would not require as large an outlay as the preceding design by about $400, calling the finish in them both about equal.

Design 36 gives us first floor plan, side elevation, front view and second floor plan of a very economical house for a narrow lot, and suited to the needs and requirements of two families. There are many young people who have saved a little money, perhaps just enough to buy them a building lot, and who are determined to own their own home, and who are known to be steady and industrious, hence can borrow enough money on mortgage to erect the house. To this class of readers this design is specially interesting for the following reasons:—First, the ground floor gives a good home for the owner himself to live in, the large living room being the kitchen and general dining-room, the front room or parlor making a nice room for the reception of visitors and for general best room. The two bedrooms are roomy and well placed; pantry large and convenient, and the front and back stairs accessible to both floors, and rear stairs to attic. One stove will in a general way warm the entire rooms, and the second reason is that the upper floor will rent at from $12 to $16 a month, paying the entire interest on amount borrowed, and thus enable the owner to live, as it were, rent free, in his own house, and enable him to save enough in time to pay off the entire indebtedness. It is well for many to consider this way of being their own landlords. Cost to build, $2,200.

Design 37 gives a small house, but only arranged for one family, and is a roomy, small house. The stairs go up from parlor, and to cellar from living room; a good pantry and china closet are provided, and the china closet answers as connecting link between the living room and kitchen. A house of this general design looks very well when built and costs about $2,000.

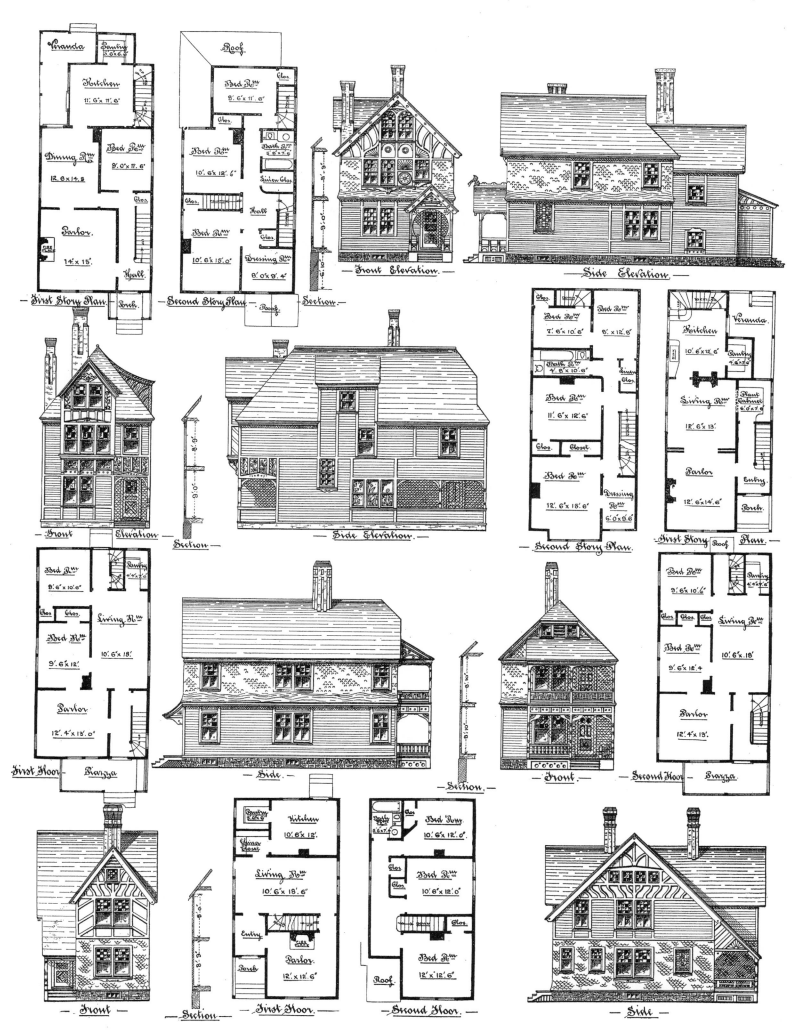

First Story Plan.

Veranda

Pantry
5. 6'x 6. 6'

Kitchen
11. 6'x 11. 6'

Dining Rm
12. 6'x14.8'

Bed Rm
9'. 0'x 11. 6'

Clos.

Parlor
14'x 15'.

FIRE PLACE

Hall.

Porch.

Second Story Plan.

Roof

Bed Rm
9. 6'x 11. 6'

Clos.

Bed Rm
10. 6'x 12. 6'

Bath Rm
6'. 6'x 7. 6'

Linen Clos.

Clos.

Hall

Bed Rm
10. 6'x 15'. 0'

Dressing Rm
9'. 0'x 9'. 4'

Section.

Roof.

Front Elevation.

Side Elevation.

Front Elevation.

Section.

Side Elevation.

Clos.

Stairs

Bed Rm
7'. 6'x 10'. 6'

Bed Rm
8'. x 12'. 6'

Bath Rm
4'. 8'x 10'. 6'

Linen Clos.

Bed Rm
11'. 6'x 12'. 6'

Clos.

Closet

Bed Rm
12'. 6'x 15'. 6'

Dressing Rm
6'. 0'x 9. 6'

Second Story Plan.

Kitchen
10'. 6'x 12'. 6'

Veranda

Pantry
4'. x 7.6'

Living Rm
12'. 6'x 13'.

Plant Cabinet
6'. 0'x 7'.

Parlor
12'. 6'x14'. 6'

Entry

Porch.

First Story Plan.

Roof

First Floor.

Bed Rm
9'. 6'x 10'. 6'

Clos.

Clos.

Pantry
4'. 4'x 6'

Living Rm
10'. 6'x 18'.

Bed Rm
9'. 6'x 12'.

Parlor
12'. 4'x 13'. 0'

Piazza.

Side.

Section.

Front.

Second Floor.

Bed Rm
9'. 6'x 10'. 6'

Clos.

Clos.

Pantry
4'. 4'x 6'

Living Rm
10'. 6'x 18'.

Bed Rm
9'. 6'x 12'. 4

Parlor
12'. 4'x 13'.

Piazza.

Front.

Section.

First Floor.

Pantry
5. 6'x 6'

Kitchen
10'. 6'x 12'.

China Closet

Living Rm
10'. 6'x 18'. 6'

Entry

Parlor
12'. x 12'. 6'

Porch.

Second Floor.

Bath
6'. 6'x 7

Clos.

Bed Rm
10'. 6'x 12'. 0'

Clos.

Clos.

Bed Rm
10'. 6'x 12'. 0'

Bed Rm
12'. x 12'. 6'

Roof.

Side.

Design 38 gives us a most excellent plan admirably adapted to a lot about fifty feet wide and is a good design for a suburban home. This plan is well adapted to a large class of house-owners who need a cosey and comfortable home for their own use, and who take a pride in seeing their families comfortably housed and provided for. Probably it would be a very hard matter to find such houses as this to rent as it is seldom they are built with that end in view, and such can only be rented in a general way when being vacated by owner for good reasons, and then they very seldom rent for enough to pay more than about five or six per cent. on the investment, having to be rented to compete with smaller plans of less cost and value, but which may give about the same amount of room. The arrangement of plan is clearly shown by the drawings, and it requires very little study to see and take in the good features illustrated. The hall and staircase are very nicely arranged, the fireplace being on opposite side of stairs, is well lighted, and the general perspective effect upon entering at the front doors could not fail but please the most exacting, for the first impressions obtained upon entering a house are always valuable and tend to help the mind of a visitor to a solution of what he may expect to find in the other part of the house, and also as giving some characteristics of the lives spent under the roof. A hall of this kind will generally be furnished and trimmed with as much skill and taste as most any part of the house. The toilet-room under stairs will be found a very useful arrangement both for toilet and general closet purposes and, although not quite so privately situated as is the case generally, it is only used by the family itself, who can appreciate the convenience thus afforded by its location enough to excuse any little unpleasantness arising from the same; and since the improvements that are now in use in water-closets, and the excellent system and means of ventilation they afford, there is no excuse for bad smells any more from bath-rooms and water-closets; but such places can be keep as sweet and as clean and free from anything objectionable as any other part of the house, and we know of bath-rooms that have had these vent-pipe arrangements applied where the room could be filled with smoke and it would all pass out through the water-closet in less than five minutes. It is needless to add that with such facilities for ventilation as this no smell can emanate from a water-closet at any time. The time has surely come when everybody having to put in water-closets and using them will make this their first care, and certainly it is the duty of all architects who have the welfare of their clients at heart to be diligent in their efforts to give them of the best appliances and to see that the same are properly set and put in place. The laundry, in some cases, could be placed under the kitchen, but in this instance it is well located and is very desirable as a saver of help as it enables the domestic to attend to all her duties in the kitchen on wash days, and saves a great deal of running up and down stairs; and there are locations where it is inconvenient and bad to place the laundry in a lower part of the house than here shown. The second floor contains five nice rooms and bath-room, and the back stairs continue up to the attic in which there is ample room for servants and storage rooms, etc. The veranda, porches and balconies are very generous and give opportunities for groups to sit and converse without hearing each other, and also to take advantage of the breeze and cool or shady places. To those requiring a home at a cost of from $5,000 to $6,000, this design will have special interest and will, we trust, assist many in making up their minds on a plan and serve as a guide to the practical solution of what, to many, is a very knotty problem—the planning of a home.

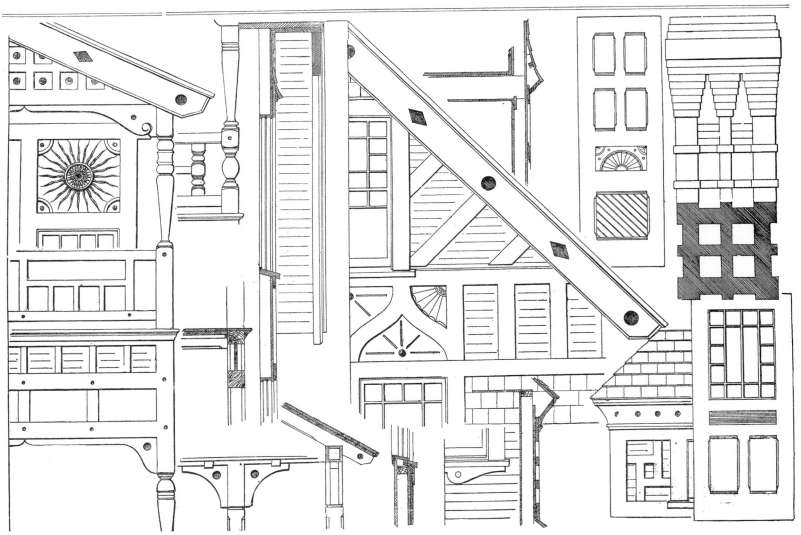

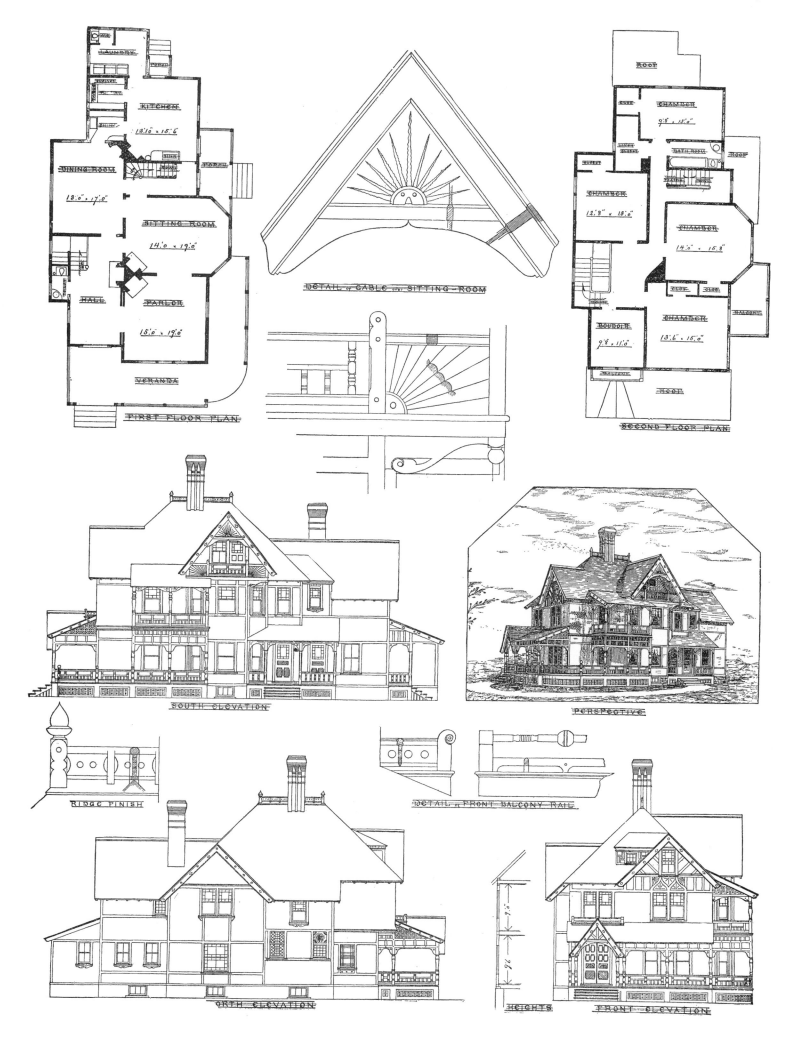

LAUNDRY

PORCH

KITCHEN
12'0" x 15'6"

DINING ROOM
13'0" x 17'0"

PORCH

SITTING ROOM
14'0" x 19'0"

HALL

PARLOR
15'0" x 19'0"

VERANDA

FIRST FLOOR PLAN

DETAIL of GABLE over SITTING-ROOM

ROOF

CHAMBER
9'8" x 15'0"

BATH ROOM

CHAMBER
12'8" x 18'0"

CHAMBER
14'0" x 15'8"

BOUDOIR
9'8" x 11'0"

CHAMBER
13'6" x 15'0"

BALCONY

ROOF

SECOND FLOOR PLAN

SOUTH ELEVATION

PERSPECTIVE

RIDGE FINISH

DETAIL of FRONT BALCONY RAIL

NORTH ELEVATION

HEIGHTS

FRONT ELEVATION

Design 39 gives us a neat design for a small cottage which would make a very comfortable home for a small family and give them largely of the comforts and conveniences of a larger house. The first story is designed for red brick, outer walls laid up one brick thick or eight inches, and furred inside for lathing and plastering which makes a warm and dry house; second story of frame and covered with shingle or tile covering, the shingle being cut to pattern as shown, secured to sheeting which should be placed horizontally across the framework well nailed and the sheeting covered with heavy rosin-sized felt paper before the shingles are nailed in place; roofs slated. The bath-room on second floor might be without the fixtures, and this room used as a bed-room, a water-closet being provided for in cellar or outside as circumstances required; such a house would look well in many situations and add largely to the harmony of the landscape, make a pleasant and cosey home, and cost from $1,200 to $1,400.

Design 40 gives us a design of a house built of brick, tile and terra cotta. This is really a plain, square house, with the exception of conservatory and pantry, which are one story high. The first floor plan is susceptible of some changes which would tend to improve it in some respects as to kitchen arrangements, which could be accomplished by the dining room and kitchen changing places. The second floor is good in its appointments and gives four very satisfactory rooms, with good closets and a bath-room well placed. There is probably no material used in the erection of buildings that will lend itself so freely to the hands of the designer as will brick and terra cotta, and the many buildings erected in these materials the last two or three years indicate that they have been taken advantage of and good results obtained in many instances. The use of terra cotta for ridge crests on a slate or tile roof is one of the best things in the world as when it is once on and properly set it is there for all time, and never needs repairs or painting as would almost everything else used for the purpose. This results in a saving in the first place many times, and avoids breakage of slate, not having to climb over same to paint or make repairs at the ridge, the quoins and brick work around openings would look well laid in buff brick and balance in red brick, the gable copings and chimney tops of terra cotta, window frames painted bronze green, and sash white. Cost of such a house, $4,500.

Design 41 illustrates a very attractive house which contains many excellent features in its composition. The chimneys are located in outer walls, and made very conspicuous, are nicely arranged for utility and effect, the date panels in terra cotta being very appropriate in their situation. The first story is of red brick, second story shingled or tiled, roofs tile or slate; painting would be similar to that described for No. 40. Interior wood work ought to be in natural woods; glass in upper part of windows in cathedral tints and other part plain glass. Such houses need no blinds, unless it be Venetian inside blinds to windows on such portions as may be subject to the glare of the sun in the middle of the day or afternoon. Almost any house will look much better and more cheerful when without blinds than with them, and far easier to keep clean and free from dirt and dust. Any one who doubts this only need to try it for a year without and they will never want them again. Cost about the same price to build it as No. 40.

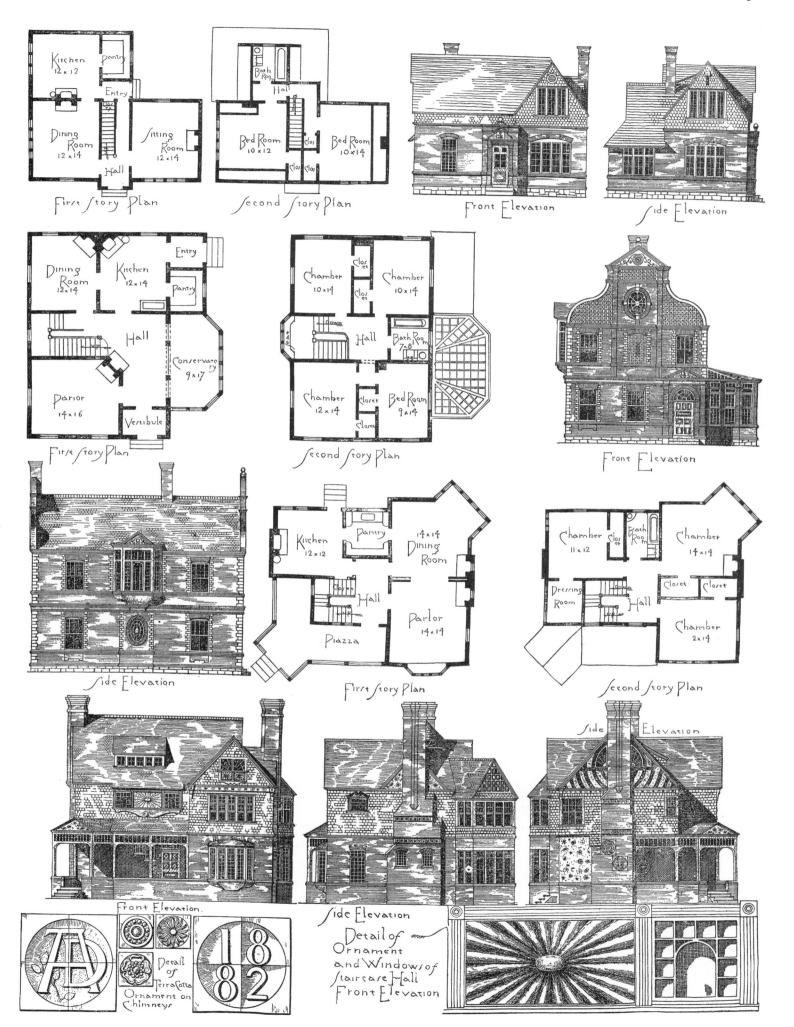

Kitchen 12 x 12
Pantry
Entry
Dining Room 12 x 14
Sitting Room 12 x 14
Hall

First Story Plan

Bath Room
Hall
Bed Room 10 x 12
Bed Room 10 x 14

Second Story Plan

Front Elevation

Side Elevation

Dining Room 12 x 14
Kitchen 12 x 14
Entry
Pantry
Hall
Conservatory 9 x 17
Parlor 14 x 16
Vestibule

First Story Plan

Chamber 10 x 14
Closet
Closet
Chamber 10 x 14
Down
Hall
Bath Room 7 x 8
Chamber 12 x 14
Closet
Bed Room 9 x 14
Closet

Second Story Plan

Front Elevation

Side Elevation

Kitchen 12 x 12
Pantry
14 x 14 Dining Room
Hall
Parlor 14 x 14
Piazza

First Story Plan

Chamber 11 x 12
Closet
Bath Room
Chamber 14 x 14
Dressing Room
Hall
Closet
Closet
Chamber 2 x 14

Second Story Plan

Side Elevation

Front Elevation.

Detail of Terra Cotta Ornament on Chimneys

18 82

Side Elevation

Detail of Ornament and Windows of Staircase Hall Front Elevation

Design 42 gives a nice little six-room cottage, one and a half story high, with good rooms and the conveniences suited to a small family of refinement. The front porch, or veranda, is of liberal size and front hall is very nice and convenient. The stairs are placed back from front and are well out of the way; connections to kitchen and cellar stairway are made under main stair platform, which shuts off the kitchen part from main hall. The dining-room is conveniently located, the pantry serving as the connecting junction between kitchen and it so the china, etc.; can be reached from either room as required. The parlor is a very nice room and well suited to such a house. The three chambers are large and roomy; bath-room well located for warmth and economy in piping and non-liability to freeze up in winter time. The flower shelf on dining-room windows makes a very pleasing feature, and with a southern exposure would be a very pleasing outlook from dining-room when the flowers, etc., were in bloom. The balcony on second story is also a very pretty feature and could be enclosed with sash in winter and used as a conservatory for plants, etc. Cost $2,600, which would vary fully $500 according to location and finish.

Design 43 illustrates a pair of semi-detached houses, the first and second floor plan of which are given, and front and side elevation of two styles, the first of which would be termed by some colonial and the other a free adaptation of Queen Anne; the first is about the general style and character of work which prevailed in this country seventy-five to eighty years ago, and we have seen some of these old houses which for execution and minuteness of detail were excellent models to copy and study from, and which, on account of their excellent materials and good workmanship together with the great care exer-

cised in their preservation by their owners, stand to-day as good examples of what honest work ought to be with proper care and attention in years to come. It is quite a common thing in some parts of our country, especially in the Eastern States, to build two houses together this way, and many times it is good economy to so build when it is known the people can agree and get along together, and especially when the two halves are owned by one party. This design would make very appropriate country homes and would need an elevated shady site well back from the road to look well. The plans present some features that would be very desirable for use as homes near a large hotel where the families could dine out or have their meals brought in, and as this is fast becoming a popular way of spending the summer months, we think the suggestion might be acted upon in some cases to good advantage. A pair of houses like this cost about $6,500 to build as here shown.

Design 44 shows a neat six-room cottage, which gives about the same amount of room and conveniences as No. 42, with the addition of attic room where two or three nice rooms might be added; cost to build $3,000, and makes a very successful house for that expenditure.

Design 45 gives a small five-room cottage, which contains some features in exterior design that may suit some on account of their oddity. The second story is built out over and is larger than the first. This is a feature often shown in modern work and is simply a repetition of many existing examples of work done from one to two hundred years ago in certain parts of Europe that is very familiar to the tourist and which is so much admired by the traveling public. Chester, England, presents some nice features of this kind that are worth study. Cost $2,300.

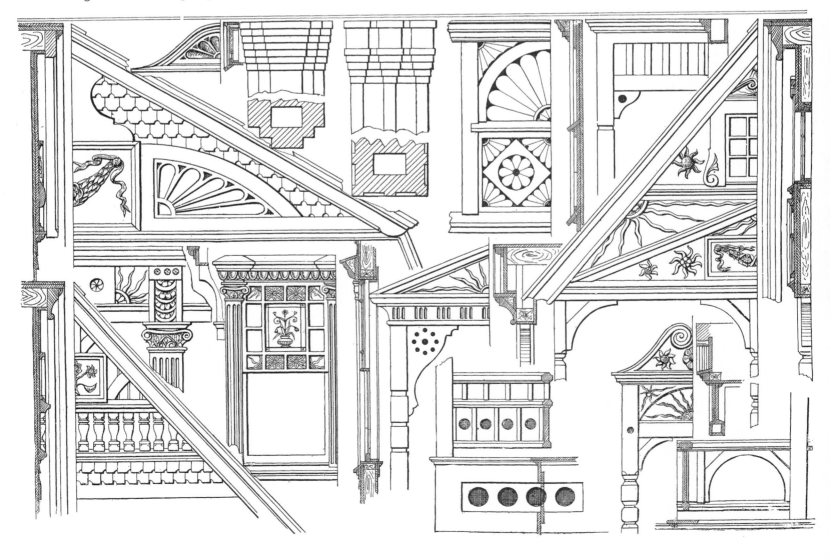

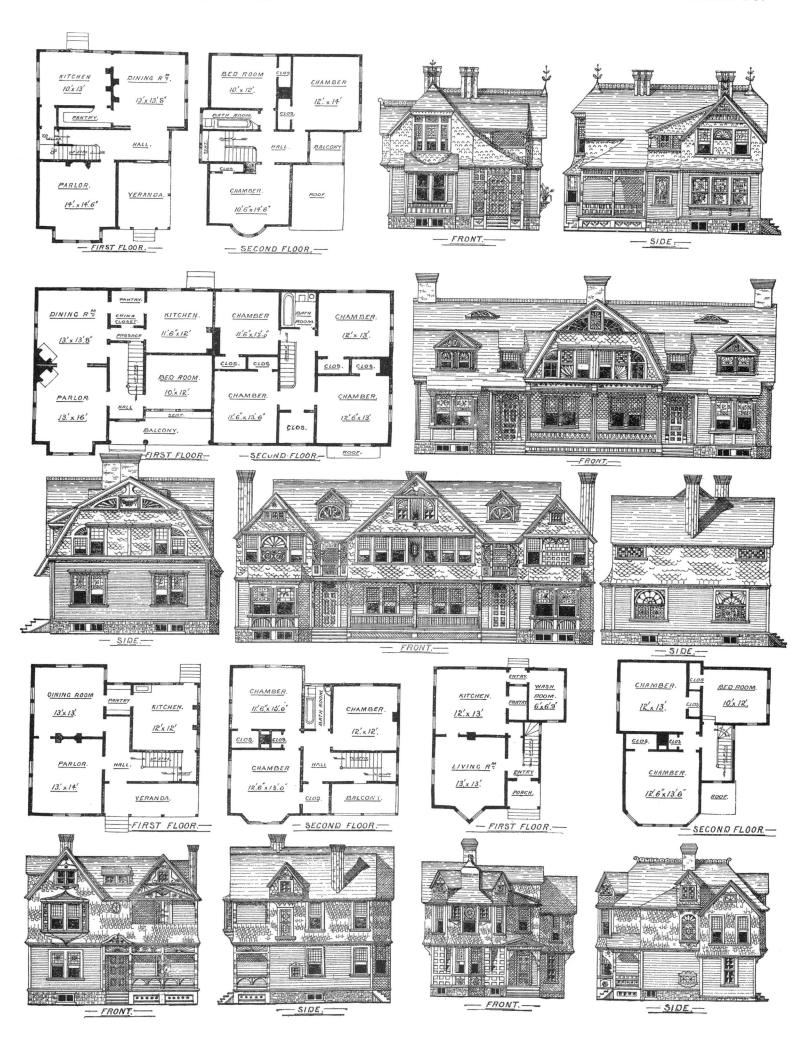

FIRST FLOOR.　　　—SECOND FLOOR.—　　　—FRONT.—　　　—SIDE.—

—FIRST FLOOR.—　　—SECOND FLOOR.—　　ROOF.　　—FRONT.—

—SIDE.—　　—FRONT.—　　—SIDE.—

—FIRST FLOOR.—　　—SECOND FLOOR.—　　—FIRST FLOOR.—　　—SECOND FLOOR.—

—FRONT.—　　—SIDE.—　　—FRONT.—　　—SIDE.—

Designs 46 to 56 illustrate eleven different front elevations for a twenty-two-foot front city house, adapted to the floor plan shown, with such changes in front as may be required to suit the individualities of the front chosen. In the erection of city houses it has always been a mystery to us why those building them should persist in making the fronts all alike; in many cases they are so for whole streets, and look like a lot of bakers' loaves set on end; there is no sky outline, no visible appearance of any artistic conception in the make-up and the general perspective effect is about as bad as it is possible to conceive. This is all wrong, and ought to be changed, and the only way to change it is by educating the people who buy and occupy such houses as these to that point where they can discriminate and know the good from the bad, and thus will insist upon getting the good, certainly as far as it is practicable to do so. Those who build such houses will try and cater to the public wants and demands by building in such improved ways as they think will enable them to sell or rent to the best advantage; and as soon as it is found that by going to a little trouble and expense and the pains to produce something more attractive and artistic, that will sell or rent more readily than the usual stereotyped styles, there will be no lack of energy put forth among builders, who are generally the most prominent men in such speculations, to vie with each other as to who shall take the lead and build the best and most artistic houses. And already in some portions of New York City this influence has been largely felt, and the improvement is becoming quite marked; while other parts, which are controlled by the worst and most greedy speculators, who are so parsimonious as to take nothing into account except how little of their own money and how small an amount of materials they can get along with and give a big show for an amount of money that will appear small to a purchaser, but still be enough to give about one-third profit to the seller. Just how many cases there have been that a buyer has bought such houses, and has found too late that his house was only half built, and the repairs would start with his ownership of the premises, it would be hard to say. The many improvements in building, both as to materials and workmanship, have played an important part in the erection of city homes, and architects have worked hard in shaping and forming their designs to conform to the improved possibilities of such materials, and have worked for good more than can be told or ever known by an unthinking public, who see only with their eyes, and care not to go beyond that point on account of the trouble and uninterestedness of the subject to them. These designs will, we trust, be suggestive in many cases and help mould the minds of those interested in what may be, and we think may tend to show it is a very easy task to build a block of houses similar in plan, but entirely different to outward appearances, and yet preserve a harmony throughout, and give to each house some individual characteristics not to be found in its neighbor. Variety of design and a unity of materials will accomplish this, if properly handled. The floor plans are such that they can be changed to suit any needs, made deeper or shorter, although the plan here shown is very good for ordinary places and purposes, and is such as can be carried out for from $6,000 to $7,000, according to location and style of finish, and we think is such that meets ordinary needs very generally.

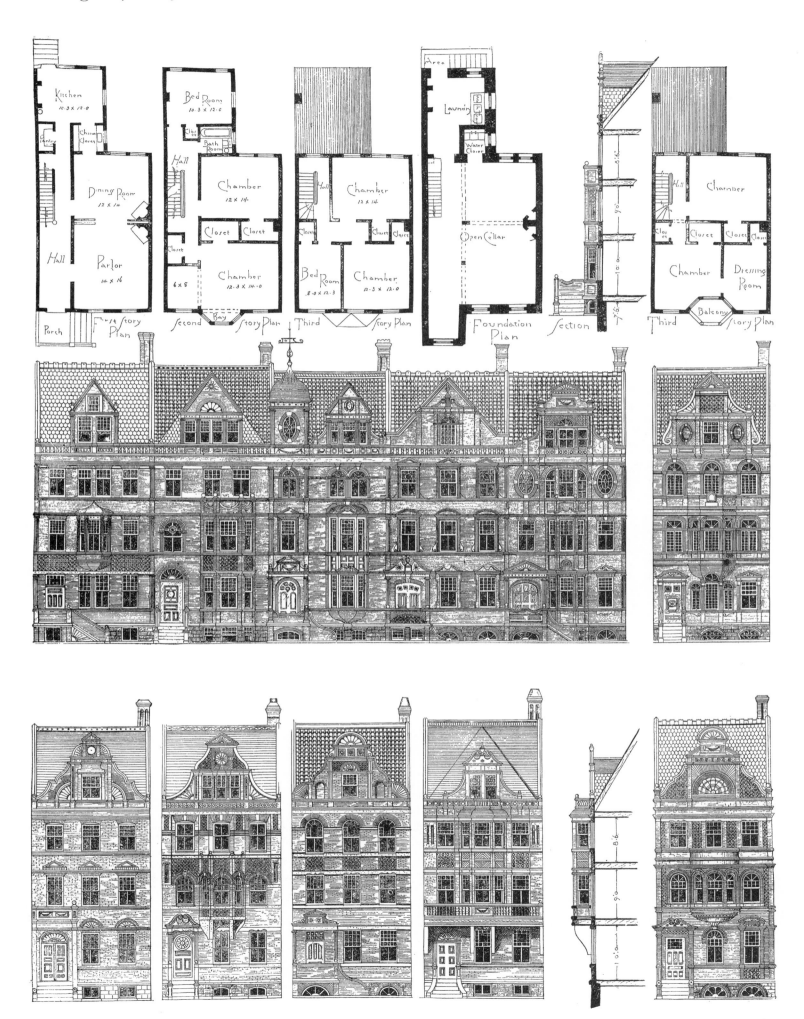

Kitchen
10.3 X 12.0

China Closet

Pantry

Dining Room
12 X 14

Hall

Parlor
14 X 16

Porch　First Story Plan

Bed Room
10.3 X 12.0

Closet

Bath Room

Hall

Chamber
12 X 14

Closet　Closet

Closet

6 X 8

Chamber
12.3 X 14.0

Second Story Plan　Bay

Hall

Chamber
12 X 14

Closet

Closet　Closet

Bed Room
8.0 X 12.3

Chamber
12.3 X 12.0

Third Story Plan

Area

Laundry

Water Closet

Open Cellar

Foundation Plan

Section

9.6　9.0　8.0　7.6

Hall

Chamber

Closet

Closet　Closet

Chamber

Dressing Room

Balcony

Third Story Plan

8.6　9.6　10.0

Design 57 illustrates a compact and roomy cottage which, although odd in plan, has some excellent features, and will make a good house to live in, being nicely planned to suit quite a large family who may be socially inclined, the parlor, library and hall being so connected by sliding doors that they can be thrown together and made one large room, as it were. The front entrance is somewhat oddly placed, yet is very convenient, and entering the large vestibule, from this opens the library and also the hall or toilet closet. The hall, with its large fire-place and settee built in with the stairs, makes an excellent living room; is finely lighted by the three large stained-glass windows over stairs, and, with a good fire blazing on the hearth, would be a welcome and pleasant room in which to usher a guest. Library and parlor are pleasant rooms, and the dining-room is well placed, both as to front hall communication, kitchen and pantry connections. The back porch from dining-room gives a garden entrance and saves the possibility of having to pass out to rear through the kitchen; and, if in the right location, this dining-room porch can, at a small expense, be arranged so as to be enclosed with glass, and made into a conservatory for winter time. This can be done and the sash, etc., removed in summer, and as it is desirable to have some place to winter the plants other than in the house, this would be convenient, as it can be easily warmed same as the room adjoining. The rooms on second floor are large and roomy, well closeted and very desirable; there is space in attic for two or three rooms, and stairs to same are directly over the front stairs. Such a house, with good cemented cellar, drains run and connected, water in, and all plumbing of good quality, and thoroughly ventilated traps and waste-pipes, furnace large enough to heat the whole, and a suitable brick-set range in kitchen fire-place; hall, parlor and library finished in ash or birch, and balance in white pine filled and polished, is worth about $4,300 to build it, and would make a good suburban home or a good house for the village street.

Design 58 gives us a very pretty cottage home, in which the large sitting-room hall, with its old-time fire-place containing seats, and the stairs with oriel bay on platform, constitutes the main features. It has become quite common to build even quite small houses with large reception-room and hall combined, and they have become popular, in many cases doing away entirely with the parlor and such rooms as are in so many houses little used and which are shut up and only opened on state occasions. In this case one chimney answers all purposes; it is designed to heat by furnace placed in cellar; there is space for two nice rooms in attic which would answer for storage or servants' use. This house is designed to be covered on exterior with shingles, and, if of red wood, in about four different patterns would look well, there being a great many different cuts that can be applied to the butts of shingles which bring out the pecular character of the detail and presents a very varied and harmonious appearance when completed; for the possibilities of what shingles will do and accomplish we think the general detail drawings of the designs here illustrated will tell a story that cannot help but be suggestive and agreeable if studied from the right stand-point. Cost of such a cottage as this, $2,600, with any good management.

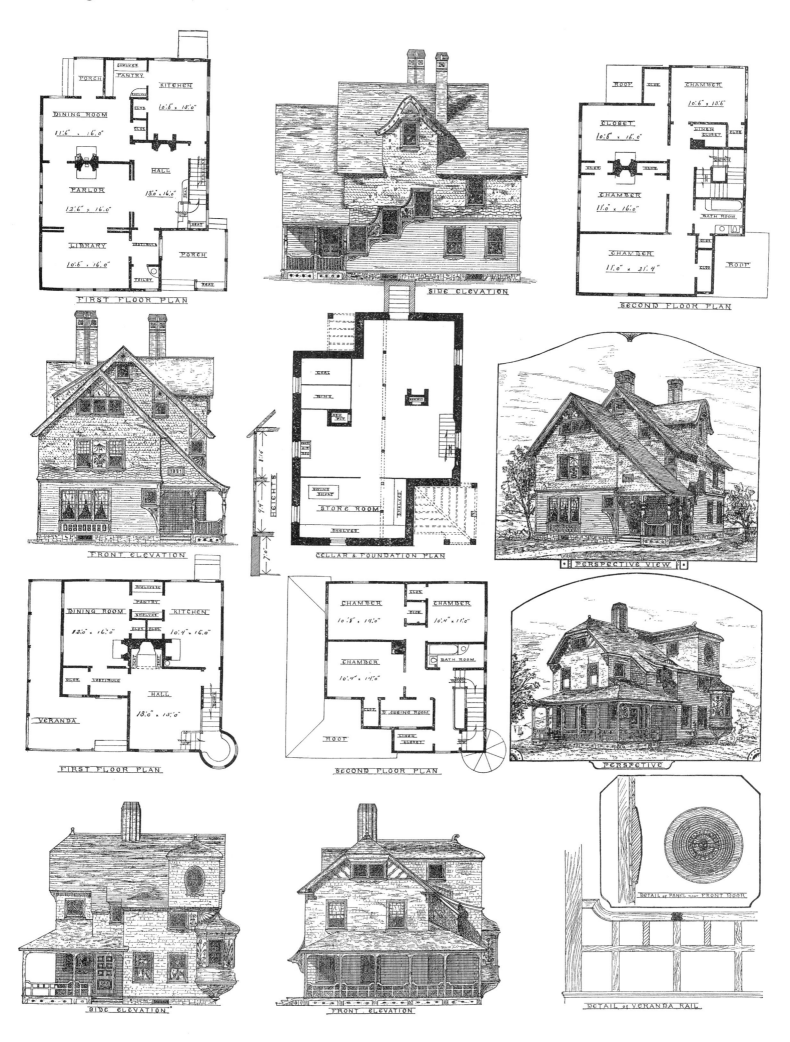

FIRST FLOOR PLAN

PORCH · PANTRY · SHELVES

KITCHEN
10:6" x 15:0"

DINING ROOM
11:6" x 16:0"

HALL
13:0" x 16:0"

PARLOR
12:6" x 16:0"

LIBRARY
10:6" x 16:0"

VESTIBULE

PORCH

TOILET

SIDE ELEVATION

SECOND FLOOR PLAN

ROOF

CHAMBER
10:6" x 13:6"

CLOSET
10:6" x 16:0"

LINEN CLOSET

CHAMBER
11:0" x 16:0"

BATH ROOM

CHAMBER
11:0" x 21:4"

ROOF

FRONT ELEVATION

HEIGHTS

CELLAR & FOUNDATION PLAN

COAL
STORE
ASH

SWING ROOM
STORE ROOM
SHELVES

PERSPECTIVE VIEW

FIRST FLOOR PLAN

DINING ROOM
12:0" x 16:0"

PANTRY · SHELVES

KITCHEN
10:4" x 16:0"

VESTIBULE

HALL
13:0" x 15:0"

VERANDA

SECOND FLOOR PLAN

CHAMBER
10:8" x 14:0"

CHAMBER
10:4" x 11:0"

CHAMBER
10:4" x 14:0"

BATH ROOM

DRESSING ROOM

LINEN CLOSET

ROOF

PERSPECTIVE

SIDE ELEVATION

FRONT ELEVATION

DETAIL of PANEL near FRONT DOOR

DETAIL of VERANDA RAIL

Design 59 gives us a good plan suited in its general lay-out and accommodations to a family of means, either as a permanent or as a summer home, space has been economized as far as possible in the internal arrangements, and the necessary conveniences placed where least outlay involved in their construction, and least liable to get out of order. The large and roomy veranda on four sides of the house gives a fine promenade as well as a choice of position and ample shade at any time from the sun's rays, a feature that is desirable in country houses, it being almost a necessity to have room enough on the exterior so as to move around and take advantage of the shady places. The Porte Cochere is a nice and convenient shelter for the occupants when stepping in and out of a carriage, and which has almost become an indispensible feature of all country houses of any pretension. The first floor is well laid out, the main rooms and hall being so connected by sliding doors that they can be thrown together and the whole house brought into one large room as it were. Entering the front door we find ourselves in a fine, roomy hall, twelve feet wide and thirty-two feet deep, the end of which terminates in a large, old fashioned alcove recessed fire-place, which, with its large, upholstered seats, wood mantel and stained glass windows, terminates the vista that meets the view upon entering; the stairs are placed in a side-hall, starting in the main or front hall and turning the corner by quarter-circle platform, continues up to large platform three steps below second floor level and from which opens a nice, cosey balcony, entered by a sash door in the centre of a stained glass window which lights the stairs; the back hall connects this side stair-case hall and gives through communication to any part of the house; the toilet-room is here provided and is in a very retired location and where the water works of the house are all placed. The dining-room is a fine one, having large fire-places at the end and a recessed sideboard on the side. The parlor and sitting-room are so arranged as to make one fine, large room, or yet be in two, the corner fire-place being nicely placed for effect and utility. The kitchen offices, laundry, pantries, etc., are well arranged for the best and easiest doing of the work for a large family, and as arranged we consider this floor plan a model that can be safely followed by those needing such room and conveniences. The second floor has seven good rooms, bath-room and halls, good closets, and the balconies give pleasant outlooks of the surrounding country and make the rooms more desirable for summer use. The back stairs continue on up to attic, in which there is space for five or six nice rooms, which will accommodate servants and part of the family if desired. A house of this kind should have painted shingle roofs, and be painted in about four tints, nicely trimmed and shaded to blend together; the interior to be finished throughout in white pine, which can be stained to give variety to the finish; the mantels, sideboard, cornices, etc., being of same woods as general finish and floor of birch, yellow or norway pine and such woods as will avoid the necessity of using any carpet; such a home as this would be very suitable for and fill the wants of a large class of people who are looking for country homes and it will no doubt be suggestive to many as to what they ought to do for a given amount of room at a certain cost, which is $7,500 in a favorable location.

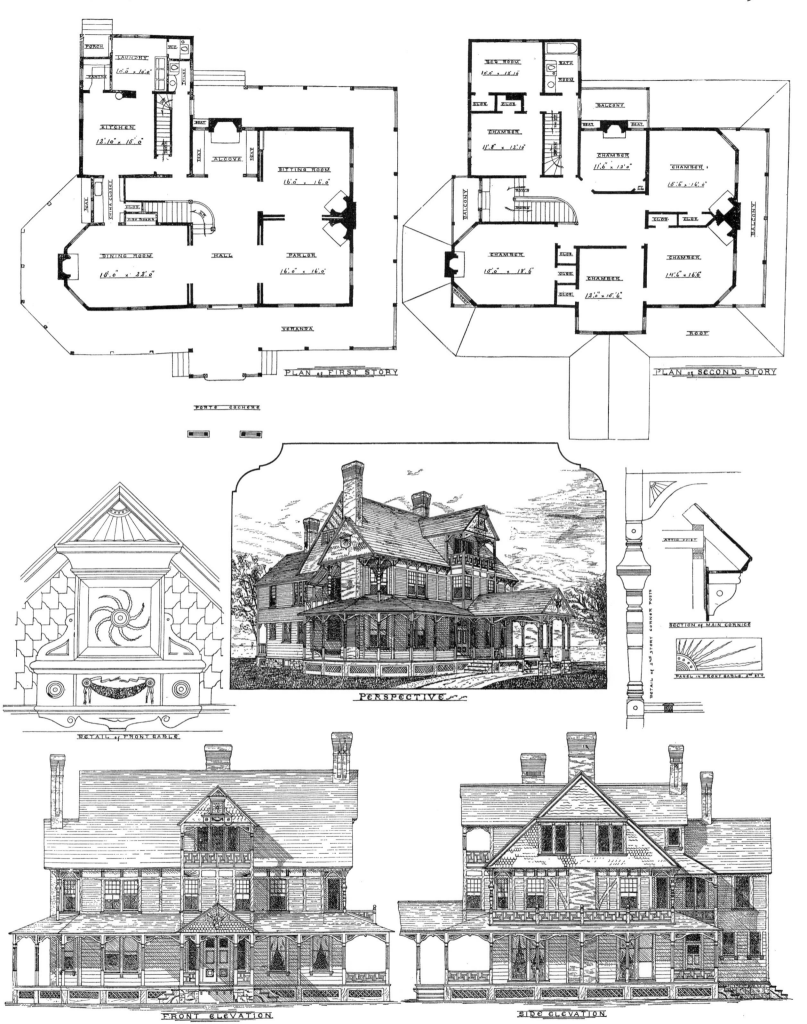

PLAN of FIRST STORY

PLAN of SECOND STORY

PERSPECTIVE

DETAIL of FRONT GABLE

SECTION of MAIN CORNICE

FRONT ELEVATION

SIDE ELEVATION

Design 60 gives a narrow house suited to a twenty-five foot lot and arranged for one family only. It gives four rooms on each floor, and is so fixed that one chimney answers all purposes.

The front and side verandas are roomy, and the small balcony over front door would be a nice feature. The front and back and also attic stairs come in very handy when only to be used by the family occupying the house. Such a house built in a neat, solid and substantial form, using good materials and having the work well and faithfully done, could not help but be satisfactory if done at the lowest possible cost, which could be defined either by contracting it out to one of four responsible men, any of whom the owner would be glad to have build it, and who in their estimating figure honestly as low as they dare with a hope of getting the work. By this way of figuring, a bottom price is generally reached at once, and when the bottom is once touched it is folly to try to get it at less than cost, or below the market value. Or better than this would be the plan of engaging a good man at a certain rate per diem for his services, and let him have the entire control of the work ; to make all bargains and contracts, buy materials, and take such measures as may seem best in the premises to get the work done in the best manner at the least possible outlay. We have had several jobs done this way, and with a right man to manage, we have found a saving of from twenty to thirty per cent. and better work as the result, and we always prefer this plan of operations when practical, and we can name work executed this way at prices that, to the ordinary practical builder, would be laughed at and doubted as to its truthfulness ; but still we cannot change the facts, and would not wish to if we could. Such a house as Design 60 is worth about $2,200 to build it.

Design 61 gives a house which is laid out to accommodate two families, one on the first and one on the second floor, giving to each five rooms with the neccessary conveniences. These floors are fixed on the flat system, and are very nicely laid out for the purpose intended. One flue answers for the entire house, the kitchen stove and one which could be placed in the living-room being ample to warm the whole floor. This class of house is very popular in many suburbs, both to own and to rent, and is generally a good investment that pays handsome dividends. Cost $2,700, which, with lot at $800 and other incidentals inside $200, would make $3,700 in all, and would rent for $18 to $20 per month for each floor.

Design 62 gives another plan, a little larger than the preceding one, having one more bedroom and two chimneys. There is also a side veranda on second floor, thus giving to each floor equal conveniences in this line. This house would be worth about $300 more than the last design, and to some people needing the added room this would be cheap. The back stairs go up to the attic, in which might be finished two neat rooms, which could be used for servants' use if so required and still leave ample room in the attic for general storage purposes and clothes drying in winter time. The details of this plate present some excellent features which are well worth the study of the practical mechanic.

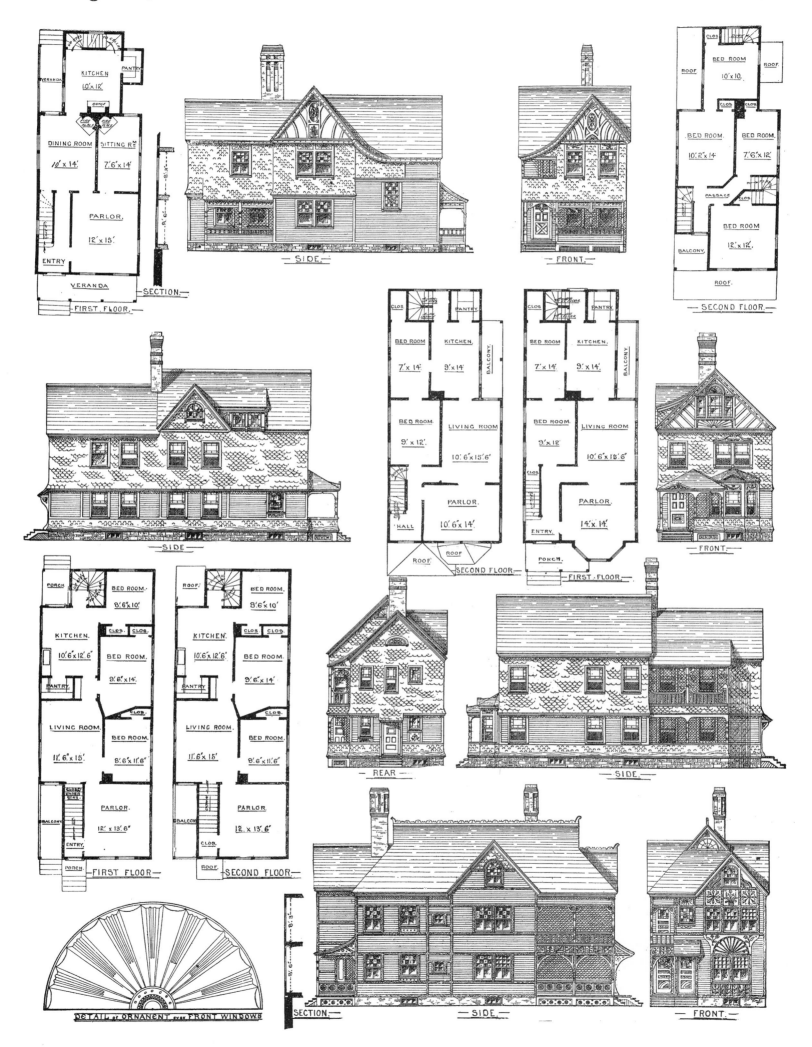

KITCHEN
10'x12'

PANTRY

VERANDA

DINING ROOM
10'x14'

SITTING R.M
7'6"x14'

PARLOR.
12'x15'

ENTRY

VERANDA

FIRST FLOOR.

SECTION.

— SIDE —

— FRONT —

BED ROOM
10'x10.

ROOF

ROOF

CLOS.

CLOS.

BED ROOM
10'2"x14'

BED ROOM
7'6"x12'

PASSAGE

BED ROOM
12'x12'

BALCONY

ROOF.

— SECOND FLOOR —

— SIDE —

CLOS.

PANTRY.

BED ROOM
7'x14'

KITCHEN
9'x14'

BALCONY

BED ROOM
9'x12'

LIVING ROOM
10'6"x15'6"

PARLOR.
10'6"x14'

HALL

ROOF

ROOF

SECOND FLOOR

CLOS.

PANTRY.

BED ROOM
7'x14'

KITCHEN
9'x14'

BALCONY

BED ROOM
9'x12'

LIVING ROOM
10'6"x15'6"

PARLOR.
14'x14'

ENTRY.

PORCH.

— FIRST FLOOR —

— FRONT —

PORCH

KITCHEN
10'6"x12'6"

PANTRY

LIVING ROOM
11'6"x15'

BALCONY

ENTRY.

PORCH

BED ROOM.
8'6"x10'

CLOS. CLOS.

BED ROOM.
9'6"x14'

CLOS.

BED ROOM
8'6"x11'6"

PARLOR.
12'x13'6"

FIRST FLOOR

ROOF

KITCHEN
10'6"x12'6"

PANTRY

LIVING ROOM
11'6"x15'

BALCONY

CLOS.

BED ROOM.
8'6"x10'

CLOS. CLOS.

BED ROOM.
9'6"x14'

CLOS.

BED ROOM
8'6"x11'6"

PARLOR.
12'x13'6"

CLOS.

ROOF

SECOND FLOOR

— REAR —

— SIDE —

DETAIL OF ORNAMENT OVER FRONT WINDOWS

— SECTION —

— SIDE —

— FRONT —

Design 63.—In such a varied lot of designs as are presented in this volume it would seem as if those who are looking for ideas and plans of something near their wants, would be able to come closely to being suited, yet our large experience in planning and designing houses for erection in all parts of the country, many of whom had our books and worked up their ideas therefrom, we have invariably found there were always changes desired, and it is a very difficult matter to find one house that is suited to two families, and this is especially the case when locations differ. We have thus re-planned some houses illustrated in our publications many times over to suit different locations, wants, and individual ideas, and we suppose it will continue to be the case that individual wants and tastes will differ, and thus give added employment to architects and those interested in building that will stimulate them to strive for something new and fresh, as each problem is solved, and thus lead eventually to the highest degree of perfection possible in the art, and it is needless to add that if the same progress is made in the future as in the past ten years the present generation will live to enjoy much of the good felt, and future posterity will only wonder at that which has passed. In small houses, where the outlay is of limited amount, the improvements will be of great benefit, as anything tending to help the rich always has a like effect on the poor, and works for the common good.

The Design 63 tells its own story, and is a nice, roomy cottage, giving six good rooms and the necessary conveniences, which cost not to exceed $1,400.

Design 64 shows a small double or semi-detached cottage which gives four good rooms on each side, and for which one chimney is made to answer. The entrances are placed as far apart as can be, and are thus private from each other. To build such houses as these requires for the two an outlay of $2,250, and would be cheap homes for the price, and give good accommodations for a gardner and coachman on a large place as well as add to the value and appearance of the same.

Design 65 shows a six-room cottage which in plan is somewhat ordinary in arrangement, yet presents a very attractive and picturesque exterior, and one that by proper treatment would be very agreeable to the eye and form a pleasing feature in the landscape ; such homes as these are sadly in need for use of working people who desire to give play to their good sense and good taste, and who would rather live in a pretty house than a poor-looking one ; such homes are generally occupied and are always appreciated. Cost about $1,650.

Design 66 gives a very simple double cottage which would not be expensive to build, such a home being plain and with few corners and little detail. Erected for $1,600.

Design 67 gives a picturesque cottage which contains some nice features, and will also give rooms in attic in addition to the six on first and second floor. This plan gives front and back stairs, and might be used by two families did occasion require, as it is often the case that small families need but three rooms or so and for some people this design may present a peculiar interest on this account Such a cottage costs $1,900.

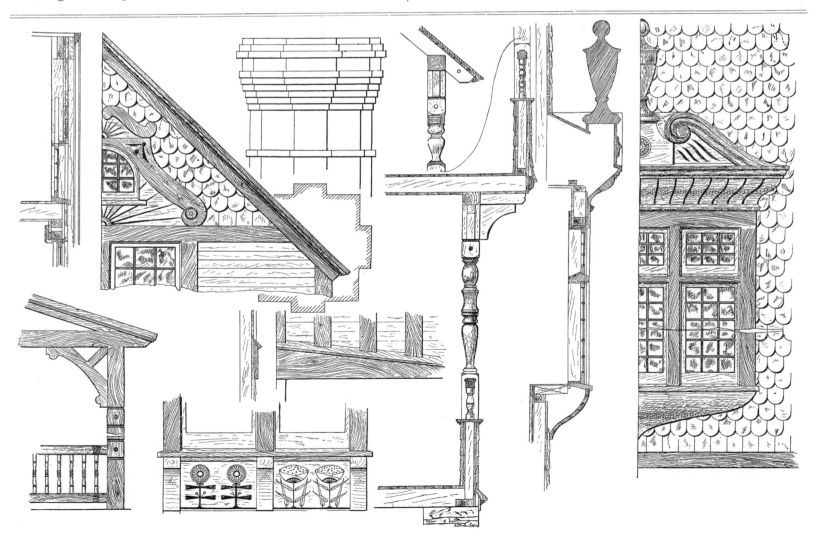

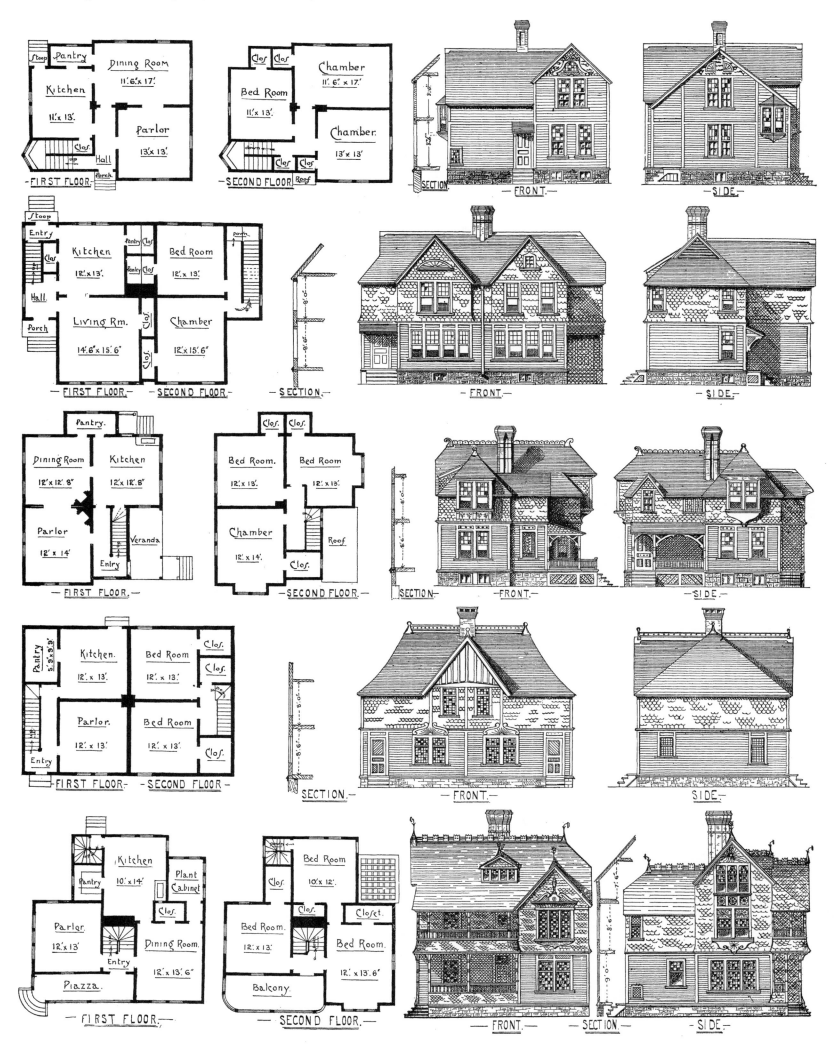

Design 63

FIRST FLOOR.
Stoop
Pantry
Kitchen 11'x 13'.
Dining Room 11'.6'x 17'.
Clos.
up Hall
Parlor 13'x 13'.
Porch

SECOND FLOOR.
Clos. Clos.
Bed Room 11'x 13'.
Chamber 11'. 6'. x 17'.
Chamber 13'x 13'
Clos. Clos.
Roof

SECTION. FRONT. SIDE.

Design 64

FIRST FLOOR.
Stoop
Entry
Clos.
Hall.
Porch
Kitchen 12'x13'.
Pantry Clos.
Pantry Clos.
Living Rm. 14'.6'x 15'.6'
Clos.
Bed Room 12'x 13'.
Down
Chamber 12'x 15'.6'

SECOND FLOOR.

SECTION. FRONT. SIDE.

Design 65

FIRST FLOOR.
Pantry.
Dining Room 12'x 12'.8'
Kitchen 12'x 12'.8'
Parlor 12'x 14'
Veranda
Entry

SECOND FLOOR.
Clos. Clos.
Bed Room. 12'x 13'.
Bed Room 12'x 13'.
Chamber 12'x 14'.
Roof
Clos.

SECTION. FRONT. SIDE.

Design 66

FIRST FLOOR.
Pantry 5'.3'x 9'.9'
Kitchen. 12'. x 13'.
Bed Room 12'. x 13'.
Clos.
Clos.
Parlor. 12'. x 13'.
Bed Room 12'. x 13'.
Clos.
Entry

SECOND FLOOR.

SECTION. FRONT. SIDE.

Design 67

FIRST FLOOR.
Pantry
Kitchen 10'x 14'
Plant Cabinet
Clos.
Parlor 12'x 13'
Dining Room. 12'x 13'.6'
Entry
Piazza.

SECOND FLOOR.
Bed Room 10'x 12'.
Clos.
Clos.
Closet
Bed Room. 12'x 13'.
Bed Room. 12'. x 13'.6'
Balcony.

FRONT. SECTION. SIDE.

Design 68 shows a neat five-room cottage which would give nice accommodations for a workingman and his family, and which by its plan is well adapted to the needs of a large class who are generally house owners to the extent of their own homes; the first floor being planned with only two rooms, and closets, pantry and entries, etc., as shown, may strike some as wanting the third room. In this case, however, the large kitchen is intended to cover the needs of a dining-room and kitchen, and to be used as a general living room; the front room being used as a sitting-room, the back entry is large and contains a water-closet, or this might be an earth-closet, if the house is built where there are no water conveniences other than cistern, as is frequently the case where such houses as this are built; with proper care and attention the earth-closet is a very desirable convenience, and can safely be placed in connection with the house and under the same roof in a lean-to or shed, and when proper fixtures are put in and a system of ventilation arranged for, which can be done in connection with chimney flue, they are preferable to any outside fixture, and in many cases to the ordinary water-closet, as there is in the earth-closet, no complicated plumbing work to get out of order or freeze up in winter and no bills to pay for use of water, etc. The second floor gives three good rooms. Cost, $1,050.

Design 69 illustrates a nice plan for a cottage that is well adapted for a mountain home, and which would give good room and suitable conveniences for quite a large family; the hall running as it does through the house gives a good draught of air through, and placing the stairs on one side they are more private and it gives nice room for china closet under platform. The rear

porch for kitchen use is shut off from main part by a screen of lattice work; the second floor gives four good chambers and closet room; each chamber opens out upon the balcony or veranda over first floor veranda; this is also a good plan for a Southern house, and well adapted to Florida for a winter home, our experience being that the house well suited to a summer mountain home in the Adirondacks, is also good for winter in Florida. Cost $2,500, with right management and in a good locality for obtaining materials.

Design 70 illustrates another popular plan for a mountain or Southern cottage, giving good rooms and conveniences and plenty of veranda room; there is room for three bed-rooms on second floor, and leave the hall open to the veranda over front entrance, this house is in finish, etc., about same as the preceding design. Cost, about $1,700; this does not include any foundation other than the necessary posts set firmly in the ground to support all work above, and the necessary foundations for chimneys.

Design 71 gives a style of house suitable for summer use, the living hall being the main room, and communicating as it does with the two chambers on second floor, it is very desirable; the dining-room is retired and very well arranged for privacy, the portiere between it and the hall being all that is necessary to close it during meal times or when needed. The cottage-like appearance of this house makes it appropriate for many places, and the cost of erection at $1,400 makes it a desirable plan generally.

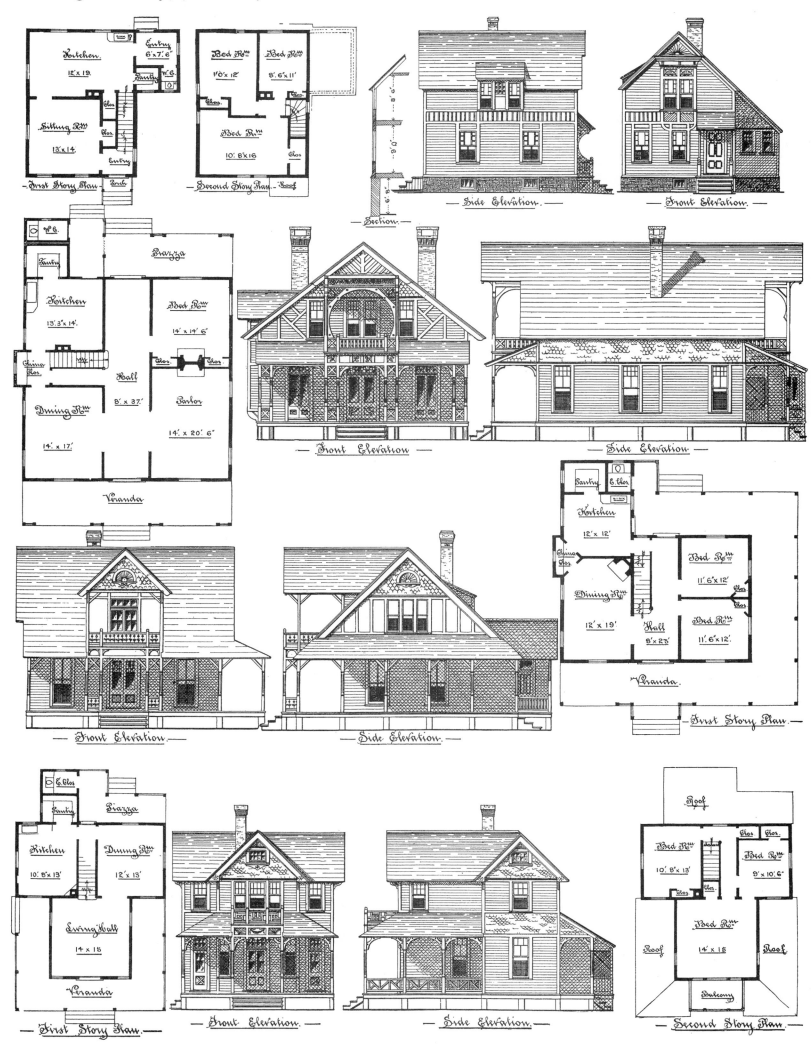

— First Story Plan —

Kitchen
12' x 19.

Entry
6' x 7'.6"

Pantry

W.C.

Clos.

Sitting R.m.
13' x 14.

Clos.

Entry

Porch

— Second Story Plan —

Bed Ro.m.
10' 0 x 12'

Bed Ro.m.
8'.6 x 11'

Clos.

Bed R.m.
10' 8 x 16'

Clos.

Roof

— Section —

— Side Elevation. —

— Front Elevation. —

W.C.

Pantry

Piazza

Kitchen
13'.3 x 14'.

China Clos.

Dining R.m.
14'. x 17'.

Hall
8'. x 37'.

Clos.   Clos.

Bed R.m.
14' x 14'. 6"

Parlor
14'. x 20'. 6"

— Veranda —

— Front Elevation —

— Side Elevation —

— Front Elevation. —

— Side Elevation. —

Pantry   E. Clos.

Kitchen
12' x 12'

China Clos.

Dining R.m.
12'. x 19'

Hall
8' x 23'

Bed R.m.
11'. 6' x 12'

Bed R.m.
11'. 6' x 12'

Clos.

Clos.

— Veranda. —

— First Story Plan. —

E. Clos.

Pantry

Piazza

Kitchen
10'. 8 x 13'

Dining R.m.
12' x 13'

Clos.

Living Hall
14 x 18

Veranda

— First Story Plan. —

— Front Elevation. —

— Side Elevation. —

Roof

Bed R.m.
10'. 8 x 13'

Clos.   Clos.

Bed R.m.
9' x 10'. 6'

Clos.

Bed R.m.
14' x 18

Roof   Roof

Balcony

— Second Story Plan. —

PALLISER'S NEW COTTAGE HOMES AND DETAILS.

PLATE 23.

Design 72 gives us an illustration of a semi-detatched pair of cottages, giving four rooms on the first floor and three on the second. The first-story walls are designed to be faced with brick, and the second of frame, shingled, with the exception of part of the sides, which is of frame and finished with a paneled face, the panels being formed with plaster and painted, which has become a popular way of doing some pieces of work, and which gives a good contrast with the adjoining work when properly treated. This is a repetition of old methods of construction, specimens of which are very plentiful in England, many of which are two hundred years old, the frame-work there being mostly of oak, filled in with brick and plastered between, showing the face of the timbers, the common method of treatment being to whitewash the plaster and paint the woodwork black, which is very effective and looks well from a distance. Still the combination of black and white is not what we would advise for such work, preferring buff and bronze-green or buff and red, or several other combinations which would be acceptable, in good taste, and in harmony with the general design. Unless where the immediate surroundings are such that it is necessary to build in this way, it is rarely the case that a semi-detached house would be built of materials other than wood; still it is policy to build well and good in all cases, and at times to gratify even a little pride and strive for something a little better than usual and different from that of the neighbors. Such pride means progress and improvement at all turns, and results in the cultivation of public taste which cannot help but be felt in the long run. Cost $4,500.

Design 73 gives us a delightful and convenient cottage in stone for first story and timber and plaster for second story, with tile or shingle-hanging for gables. The stone walls are intended to be laid up with rock-face stone in irregular Ashlar work, the joints being tucked in with colored mortar to match the stone or give a suitable contrast with same. The roofs would look best if of red tile ; they might be of red slate, or even good shingle painted or stained red ; interior wood-work in natural woods. Such houses always look well built on grounds appropriately laid out, and with suitable background and trees surrounding same would be a very agreeable home to live in, and is a good house for a young couple to start houskeeping in, and one that it would not be expensive to furnish. Cost $3,600.

Design 74 illustrates a very nice brick and wood cottage, the principal feature of which is "ye hall" on first floor, which makes a general living-room, it being parlor, library, sitting-room and hall combined ; the large fire-place by the stairs, with seat built in, makes a cosy nook ; the sliding doors between hall and dining-room gives a fine lengthy room, and opens up the whole house to good advantage. The back stairs are well located and convenient from either kitchen or dining-room, and the cellar is reached by stairs under same by either of two last rooms mentioned. Second floor has three good rooms, bath-room and two good balconies, the front one of which could be enclosed and another bed-room obtained. Such a house as this costs $3,500.

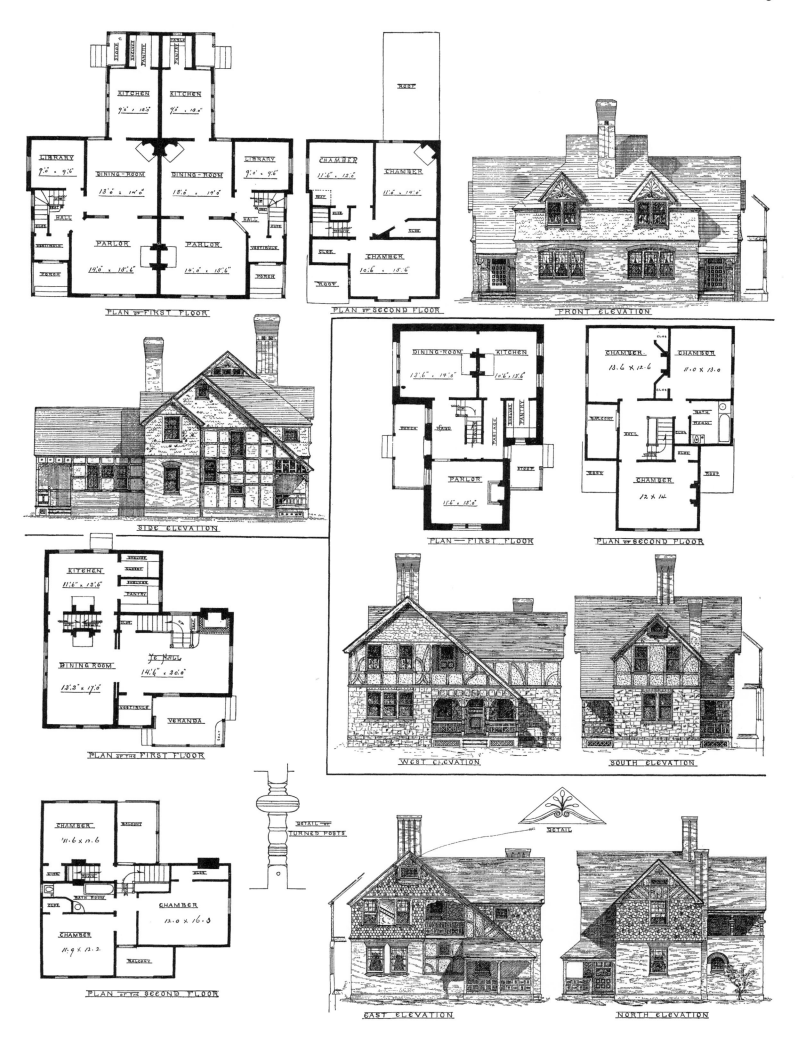

PLAN OF FIRST FLOOR

KITCHEN 9'0 x 13'0
KITCHEN 9'0 x 13'0
LIBRARY 9'0 x 9'6
DINING-ROOM 13'0 x 14'0
DINING-ROOM 13'6 x 14'0
LIBRARY 9'0 x 9'6
HALL
HALL
PARLOR 14'0 x 15'6
PARLOR 14'0 x 15'6

PLAN OF SECOND FLOOR

CHAMBER 11'6 x 12'6
CHAMBER 11'6 x 14'0
CHAMBER 10'6 x 15'6

FRONT ELEVATION

SIDE ELEVATION

PLAN — FIRST FLOOR

DINING-ROOM 13'6 x 14'0
KITCHEN 10'6 x 13'6
PARLOR
PANTRY
PARLOR 11'6 x 13'0

PLAN OF SECOND FLOOR

CHAMBER 13.6 x 12.6
CHAMBER 11.0 x 13.0
BATH
HALL
CHAMBER 12 x 14

PLAN OF THE FIRST FLOOR

KITCHEN 11'6 x 12'6
PANTRY
DINING ROOM 13'3 x 17'0
YE HALL 14'6 x 20'0
VESTIBULE
VERANDA

WEST ELEVATION

SOUTH ELEVATION

DETAIL OF TURNED POSTS

PLAN OF THE SECOND FLOOR

CHAMBER 11.6 x 13.6
BATH ROOM
CHAMBER 12.0 x 16.3
CHAMBER 11.9 x 13.2
BALCONY

DETAIL

EAST ELEVATION

NORTH ELEVATION

Design 75 is decidedly a house for some one of good taste, and will suit the requirements of a hill-side lot where the rear part of the house would give ample room for kitchen and dining-room offices on the basement floor, which, although not at all times desirable under certain circumstances, owing to the peculiarities of site it is almost necessary to utilize the basement in this way. In this plan the basement is reached from the floor above by the back hall, which contains the back-stairs and connects to all parts of the house. The kitchen contains the sink and wash-tubs. The range is intended for brick set, the jambs and fire-place being built to suit the same. The dining-room is a generous room, with good connections to the kitchen through passage-way in which is placed two good closets for general use in connection therewith. There is also a separate door from the hall to this room which is a great convenience, as the two doors to the room can be used without interfering with each other, as might happen if but one door were used. The other parts of the basement give ample room for fuel, furnace and general storage. The first-floor hall is entered from the front porch, and is a large room well lighted, and contains the main stairs and a fire-place, and communicates with the three rooms and back hall on this floor. The two main rooms are large, and when thrown together make very desirable parlors. A toilet room is placed in the back hall and contains closet and bowl, and the bed-room on this floor, connecting as it does with both halls, makes a desirable room for use as a library, or other uses than as marked. The second floor has three large rooms, and there is room in the attic for two or three more, which would answer for servants' use, the attic being reached from back stairs. The first story is designed for brick construction, and would look best in good red pressed brick with stone sills, etc. The upper part is of frame with plaster panels.

The entire design is treated vigorously, and is strong in good points and features that will wear well. And in the general style and make-up of this design we trust many of our readers may find something that will please them, and if it happens to please as a whole, or even with slight alterations, we hope it may be strictly carried out, as when it is, it will be a credit to all concerned when built right. This is what may be called a good example of modern work without any of the nonsensical features and gew-gaws so often met with in the so-called houses of Queen Anne style, many of which are as foreign to their pretensions of style as it is possible for them to be. And as it has been the custom lately for some architects to call everything Queen Anne, for want of a better name, we must excuse many mistakes that have been made, as it really would be impossible to give any name to a large number of the designs made unless they were honestly called, what they are in reality, "American Vernacular," as they come nearer to what might be termed an American style than anything else, being the results of the needs of each case and the materials at hand with which to combine and form the construction as well as the cost or amount to be expended, which has to be largely taken into account and has had great effect upon the formation of a style for general use. Cost about $5,500.

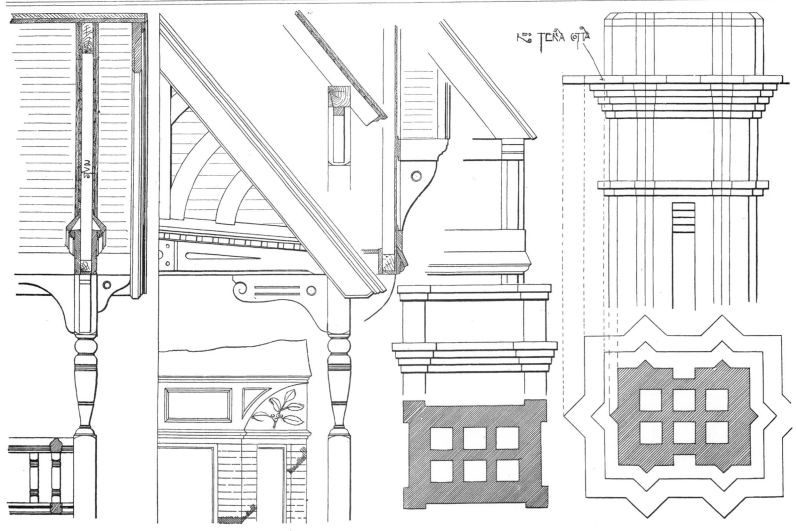

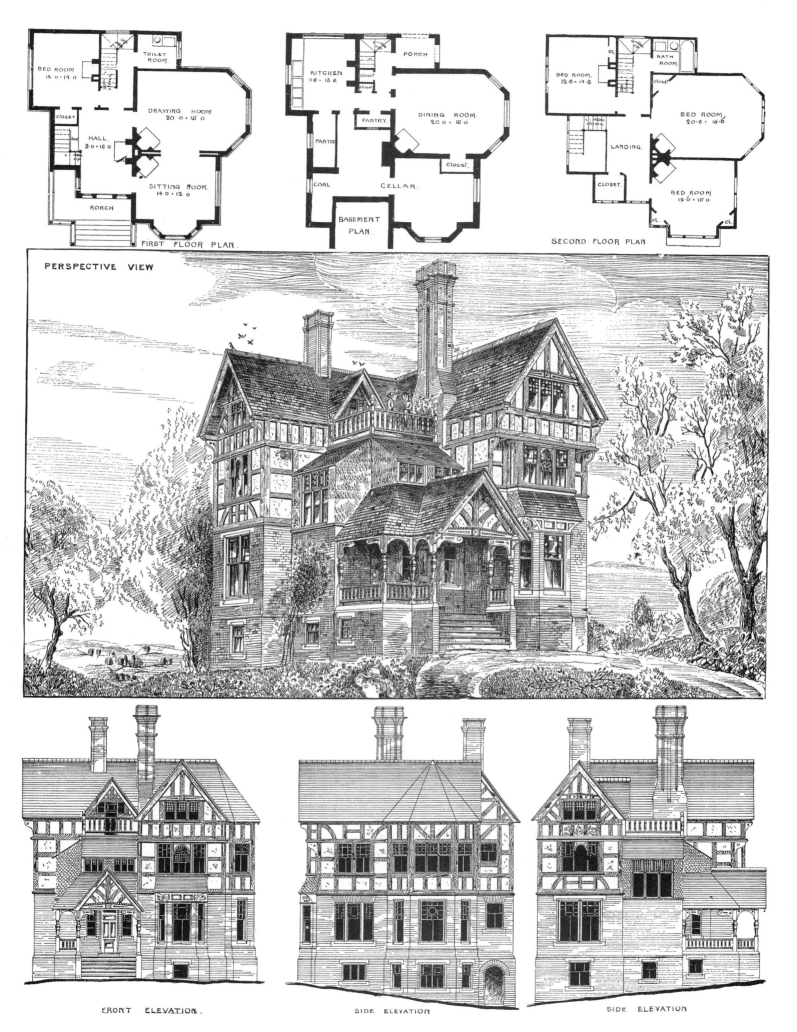

BED ROOM
12·0·14·0

TOILET
ROOM.

closet

DRAWING ROOM
20·0·15·0

HALL
9·0·16·0

SITTING ROOM
14·0·12·0

PORCH

FIRST FLOOR PLAN.

KITCHEN
11·6·13·6.

PORCH

closet

PANTRY

DINING ROOM
20·0·15·0

PANTRY

closet

COAL

CELLAR.

BASEMENT
PLAN.

BED ROOM
12·6·14·6

CL

BATH
ROOM

closet

BED ROOM
20·6·15·6

DOWN

LANDING.

CLOSET.

BED ROOM
12·6·15·0

CL

CL

SECOND FLOOR PLAN

PERSPECTIVE VIEW

FRONT ELEVATION.

SIDE ELEVATION

SIDE ELEVATION

Design 76.—Invariably the house that in plan gives the broadest front view and most number of rooms looking to the street will present a better appearance than if of the same number of rooms so planned as to give only one room and front door to the street; hence a broad house is preferable to a deep one when the size of the site will allow of same, and it is generally the case that a broad house will work up in nicer shape and proportion than a narrow one, and look much larger than it really is; and for country homes we like to get the main entrance on the broad side when possible on the above account; also another feature, which is no small one to be considered in the erection of a small house, is the advantages to be derived from its general shape and adaptability to increased needs and enlargement in the future when the purse or family is increased in accordance with same. We have met with a great many cases where, having planned and built houses just to suit present needs and funds, not taking into account the fact that any more room would ever be needed, it has, in such cases, been a hard study to know just how and where to build on, to do it in any way for convenience in internal arrangement and external appearance, and this especially on a narrow house, while on a wide house additions can be made that will always harmonize with the general design and with less outlay by reason of the advantages derived from the shape and ease of adding thereto, and it is well in most cases to look a little to the future in building homes, especially when building to suit young people. The design here shown is a good house for a small family, and is capable of being added to at some future time so as to make quite a large house. The first story is of brick, second story shingled or tiled, roofs slated or tiled; erected in a nice manner with all conveniences at a cost of $3,350.

Design 77 gives us a very nice plan of a cottage with about same room and cost as the last one, and which is nicely adapted to the needs of a small family with a view to future enlargement. The conservatory is a very pretty feature, and being large and roomy, gives as it were almost another room on the first floor. This house is only one and a half story high, yet is very well proportioned and looks very well when executed. One of the principal parts of a building, and which have much to do with the successful appearance thereof are the chimneys, and there is certainly a great deal of character given to a house by the chimneys. Many good designs are spoilt by their being too low, small, or not in proportion to the general size and shape of the whole mass, it being too often the case that chimneys are simply treated as necessary evils, and anything that answers to carry away and get rid of smoke is considered ample, and no further thought given to the matter. Again, many who are planning houses have one peculiar style of chimney; and we know of cases where a certain style chimney has been made to answer for a $25,000 mansion, a school house, stable, cottage, and several buildings, all totally different from each other in use, style and cost, that common sense would say needed chimneys as different as possible from each other, and which it was the duty of the designer to study and obtain, had a plain duty been done.

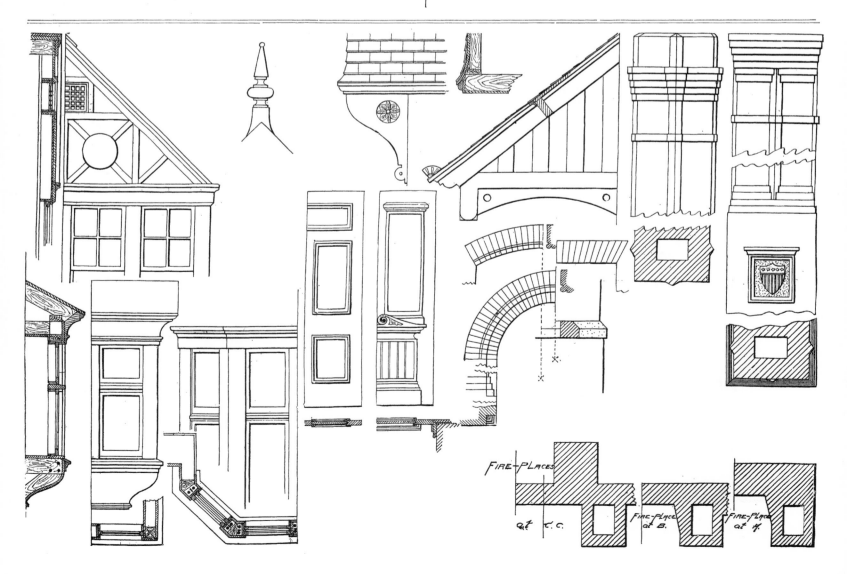

FIRE-PLACES

at C. C.   FIRE-PLACE at B.   FIRE-PLACE at A.

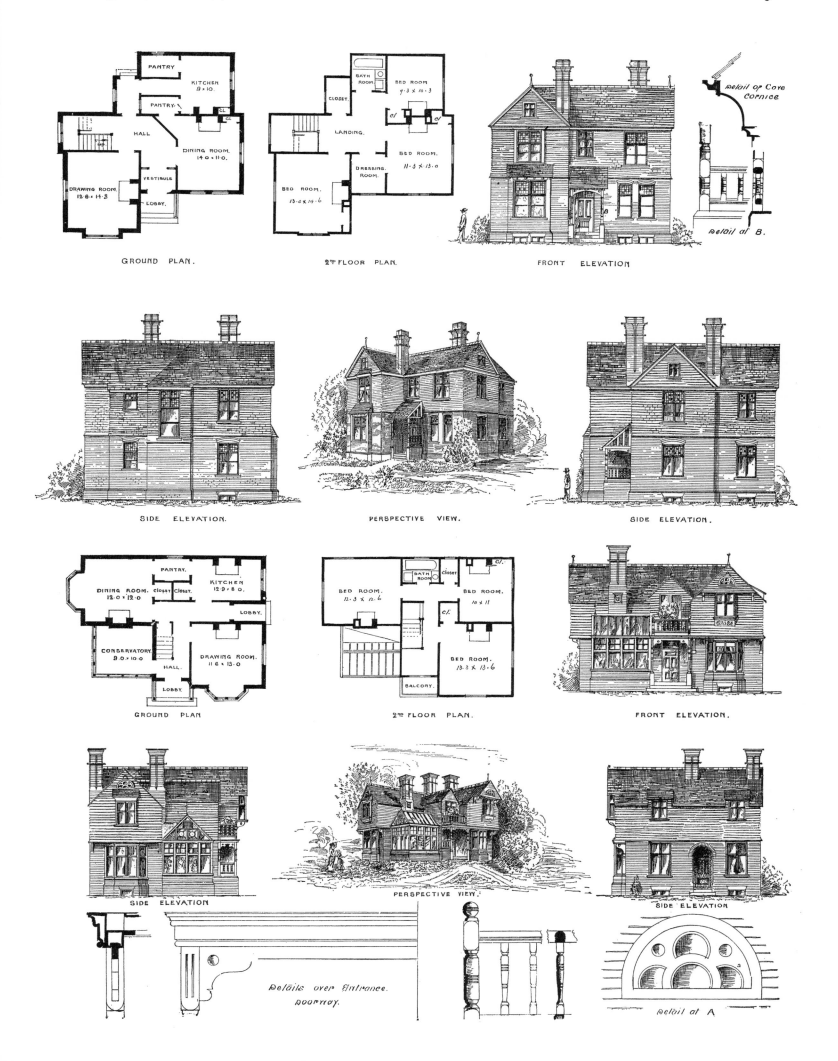

GROUND PLAN.

2ᴺᴰ FLOOR PLAN.

FRONT ELEVATION

Detail of Cove Cornice.

Detail at B.

SIDE ELEVATION.

PERSPECTIVE VIEW.

SIDE ELEVATION.

GROUND PLAN

2ᴺᴰ FLOOR PLAN.

FRONT ELEVATION.

SIDE ELEVATION

PERSPECTIVE VIEW.

SIDE ELEVATION

Details over Entrance Doorway.

Detail at A

Design 78 gives a roomy plan for a very economical and good house, suited to many locations, and which, with such slight changes as might be necessary to suit individual wants, would fill the requirements of many who are longing for homes, some of which perhaps will never come. This house is all frame, the first story being clapboarded and the second story shingled. The details are very simple and expressive, and when painted properly give character to the general design, which would always be interesting to study, there being constantly something new or overlooked before that is of interest every time the building is passed. And it is simply astonishing how interesting a nice building is to the studious public, and how they will stop, talk, look and become intensely bent on the features contained thereon almost every time they pass by. To appreciate this it is only necessary to live in such a house for awhile, as the writer has done, and watch from the windows inside the different expressions of the passers-by, as they would see the house for the first time or find new things to wonder at. Such houses as these are also always marketable and will sell readily, where a common-place design will hardly be noticed ; and it is certainly policy to build something that will be likely to please others as well as be suitable for the wants and necessities of the party building, even though necessary to go a little outside the strict requirements of the case. 'Tis an old saying, that fools build houses and wise men live in them. This may apply in some few cases, but in a general way it is wrong, as the wise man will invariably build his own house, and live in it too, it being far more interesting to live in a house that has been planned and built after the owner's ideas and that has grown from castles in the air to a castle in reality than in other people's cast-off ideas or failures, as is often the case when the fool builds the house for the wise man to live in ; the wise man in the latter case being he who buys for probably half its real value that which some one else has built and on account of various reasons, many of which might have often been avoided, has failed to carry out that which was planned for his own comfort and enjoyment, and hence it is sacrificed and sold, and the wise man (so-called) gets the benefit of the other man's loss. It is few who cannot recall such cases as this ; and in planning a new house, it may be sometimes a good thing to have the fable of the foolish and wise men in mind to help keep within your means and to help you profit by the failures of others. This design costs somewhere about $4,400 and makes a very pleasant country home.

Design 79 illustrates a simple cottage, one and a half story high, with front and back stairs, and four rooms on each floor and bath-room, and is a very neat suburban house, well suited to a fifty-foot lot, and can be built at a cost of $2,500, or it may be made to cost $3,000, according to finish, it being a very easy matter to vary the cost of a building, by a variation in the general character of the detail and quality of materials used, by fully twenty per cent., and in some cases the management will vary as much more. So it can safely be said in many cases that in some hands prices may vary as much as forty per cent. from what could actually be done if taken hold of right, and the bottom price reached and adhered to.

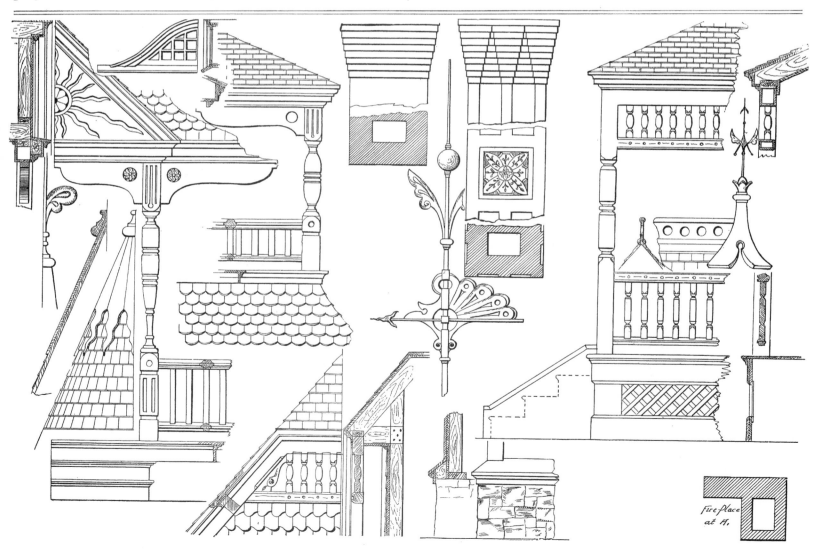

fire place at H.

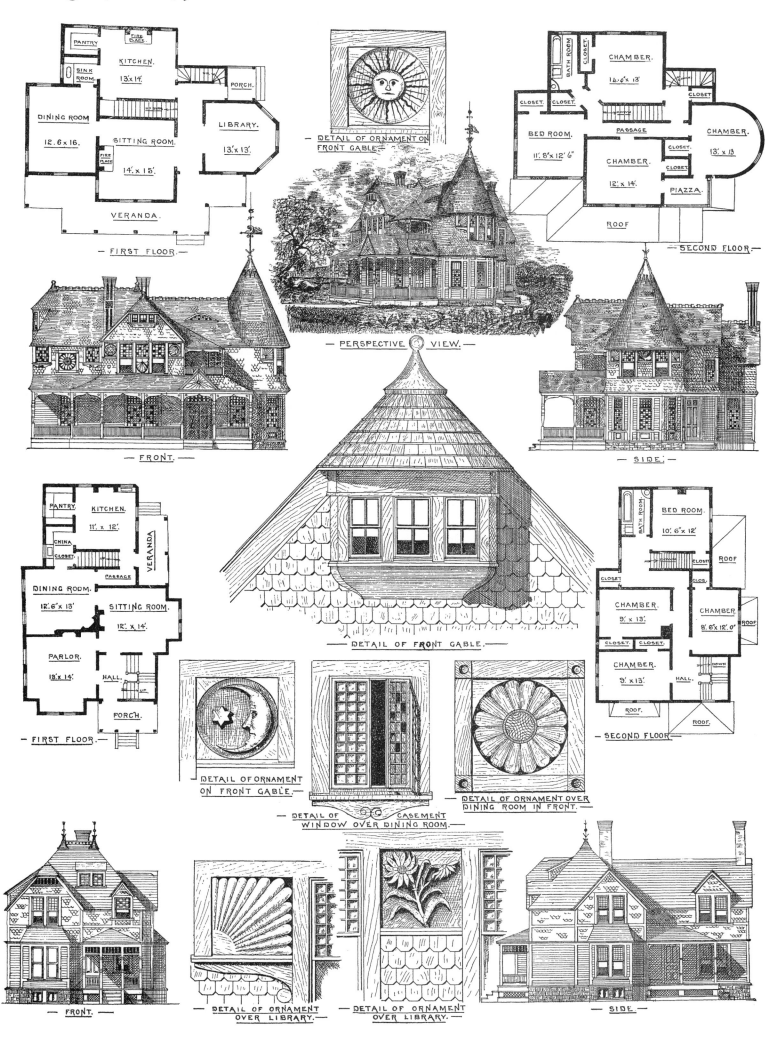

PANTRY
FIRE PLACE
KITCHEN.
13'x 14'
SINK ROOM.
PORCH.
DINING ROOM
12.6 x 16.
SITTING ROOM.
14'. x 15'.
FIRE PLACE
LIBRARY.
13'. x 13'.
UP ROOM.
VERANDA.
— FIRST FLOOR. —

— DETAIL OF ORNAMENT ON FRONT GABLE. —

BATH ROOM
CLOSET
CHAMBER.
14'-0"x 13'
CLOSET.
CLOSET.
CLOSET
BED ROOM
11'. 8'x 12' 6"
PASSAGE
CHAMBER.
13'. x 13
CHAMBER.
12'. x 14'.
CLOSET.
CLOSET
PIAZZA.
ROOF
— SECOND FLOOR. —

— PERSPECTIVE VIEW. —

— FRONT. —

— DETAIL OF FRONT GABLE. —

— SIDE. —

PANTRY.
KITCHEN.
11'. x 12'.
CHINA CLOSET.
VERANDA.
PASSAGE
DINING ROOM.
12.6"x 13'.
SITTING ROOM.
12'. x 14'.
PARLOR.
18'x 14'.
HALL.
UP.
PORCH.
— FIRST FLOOR. —

BATH ROOM.
BED ROOM.
10'. 6"x 12'
ROOF
CLOSET
CLOS.
CHAMBER.
9'. x 13'.
CHAMBER.
8'. 6"x 12'. 0'
ROOF
CLOSET.
CLOSET.
CHAMBER.
9'. x 13'.
HALL.
DOWN
ROOF.
ROOF.
— SECOND FLOOR. —

— DETAIL OF ORNAMENT ON FRONT GABLE. —

— DETAIL OF CASEMENT WINDOW OVER DINING ROOM. —

— DETAIL OF ORNAMENT OVER DINING ROOM IN FRONT. —

— FRONT. —

— DETAIL OF ORNAMENT OVER LIBRARY. —

— DETAIL OF ORNAMENT OVER LIBRARY. —

— SIDE. —

PALLISER'S NEW COTTAGE HOMES AND DETAILS.

PLATE 27.

Design 80 gives us a two story frame house, with good rooms and the necessary conveniences in connection therewith, and which gives some good points and features that may be studied with profit. The first floor is nicely arranged, having the two largest rooms connected by sliding doors. The absence of any large veranda on front is marked, the porch being arranged to give the necessary covering and shelter to the entrance, and the large vestibule, with its hard-wood or tile floor, with an ample mat at the front door, would presage a comfort and welcome within; while the glass partition and door to conservatory on left and the art glass on each side of the inner door between main hall and vestibule will lend a charm in which nature and art combine to vie with each other in giving a welcome and render the vestibule light, cheerful and mellow with the grace and freedom of nature, the conservatory being really a part of the vestibule. The main hall is large and roomy, and so arranged that it communicates to all parts of the house. The stairs ascend by easy stages to the floor above and are lighted by a large stained-glass window, which does duty for both first and second-floor halls and gives a desirable light; and the many-tinted hues of the cathedral glass in this window impart a tone that pervades the whole and shows that good taste is as much within the reach of modest as of those of more liberal incomes, it being possible to obtain the effect in glass by a proper combination of colors at very little expense. A hard-wood floor in the main hall and two principal rooms, with a nice, plain finish of oak, ash or cherry, would be the appropriate thing, and with nice rugs and a border worked in around the floors of cherry and oak would be a fine contrast and make a finish to the wall sides where the rugs do not cover. Even a plain floor is preferable to the ordinary carpet covering of the whole floor. The room on first floor marked bed-room will do for library or office-room as well as for sleeping-room, and makes a nice one for many purposes. Back hall and stairs are well located, and the back stairs can be carried up into the attic floor, where the necessary rooms can be finished for servants' use. This is an ordinary frame-house, with diagonal sheathing placed on frame and covered with rosin-sized sheathing-felt under clap-boards and all exterior finish. The greatest of care ought at all times to be exercised in the putting on of this paper, so as to be sure and have it cover all parts, and especially to come under the joints of all work, so as to insure tightness at the most important places. We have seen many houses built where they made out to paper it, but failed to put any strips under the casings, corner-boards or other constructive parts; hence the paper, being only put on under clap-boards, did not lap at corners, and when the wood shrinks, as it very often does, there is a crack up the full length of the casing, where the wind and rain can find entrance through and between the joints of sheathing, and the result is cold drafts and a cold house generally, and the most critical parts of a house are left exposed; this may be termed one of the reasons why in driving storms so many leaks occur around the edges of window-frames and such places. The simplicity of this design commends itself, and to those needing a house of this size we trust it may be more than suggestive, and that it may meet with the approval of many who are looking for a home. Such a house, nicely carried out, costs in the vicinity of $4,800, which includes furnace, range, laundry under the kitchen, and all necessary improvements.

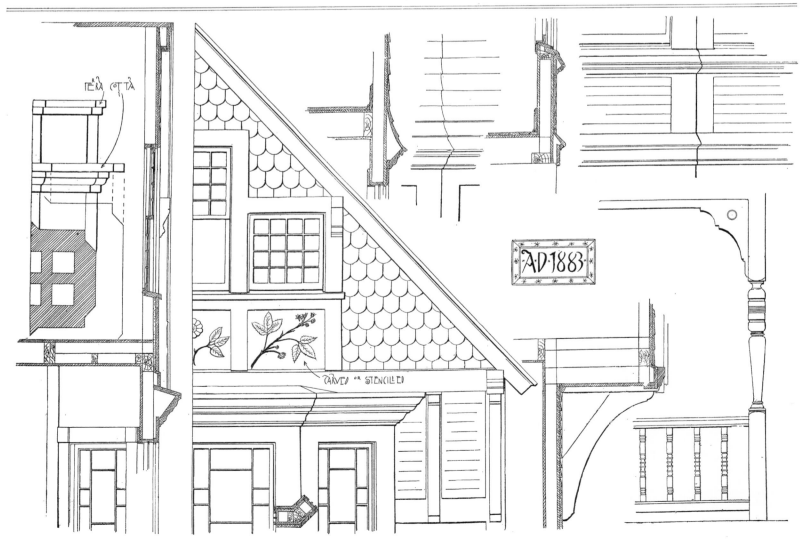

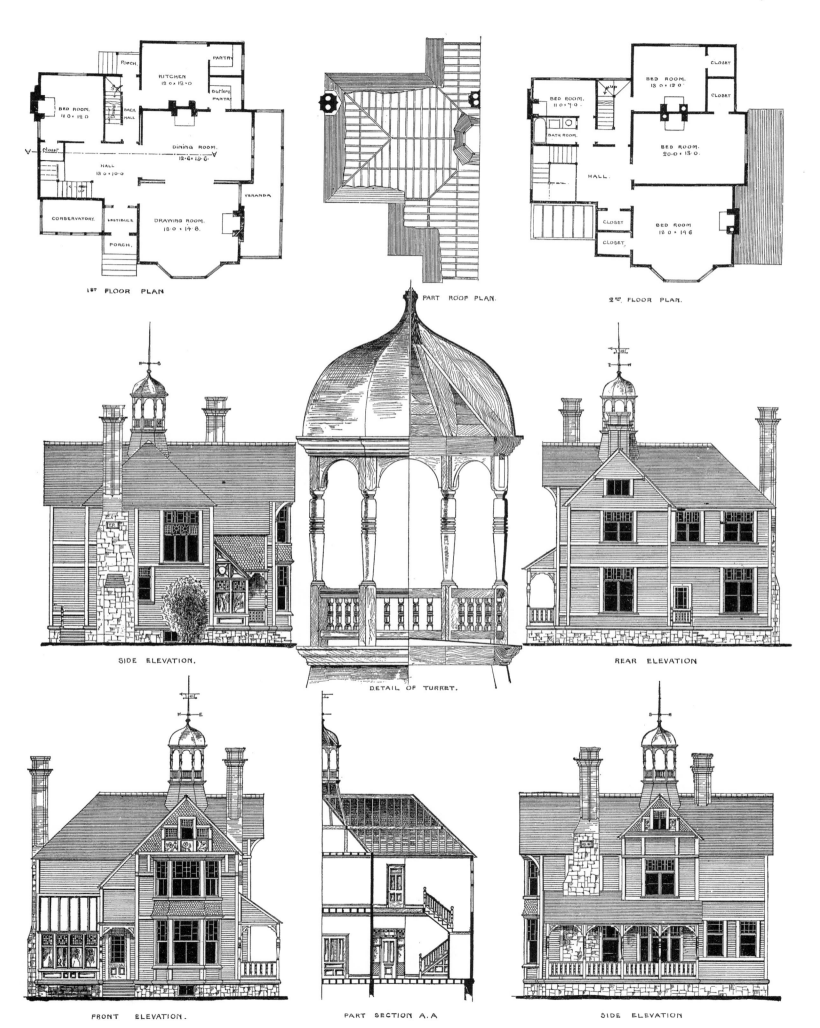

1ST FLOOR PLAN.   PART ROOF PLAN.   2ND FLOOR PLAN.

SIDE ELEVATION.   DETAIL OF TURRET.   REAR ELEVATION

FRONT ELEVATION.   PART SECTION A.A   SIDE ELEVATION

Design 81.—Among the general wants of those owning and occupying houses there is a large class whose first need is room, and all other requirements have to be made subordinate to this great need, to accomplish which the question of halls and large open staircases have in a great measure to be dispensed with, and the maximum of room obtained with the minimum of outlay in construction ; and as it is desirable at all times to make the best possible appearance and to work in such features as will enhance the value and architectural beauty of a design, care and judgment has to be used in putting the parts together to secure the most satisfactory results as above. Such a design as this is well adapted to the country and would not be a bad plan for a farm house; there being good room below for general storage purposes, milk room, etc., the cellar being reached very conveniently from either the kitchen or dining-room under the main stairs. The parlor and dining-room being connected together makes these two rooms very desirable, as either of them can be entered from the front entry ; the latter being large and roomy and well lighted, and the front porch coming, as it does, within the main building and the roof of the same covering the whole, makes a picturesque finish and simplified the construction, leaving the roofs less liable to leakage than would be the case did one roof come in below the other, as is usually the way. The room over the porch can also be floored over and is useful for storage, there being no attic room above the second story. The stairs going up from the dining-room are convenient, this being the living room of the house and will be the most used of any. The four good bed-rooms and closets on the second floor give good accommodations for a large family. This design, with a shingle roof and the work faithfully and honestly executed, costs about $2,000 ; in some locations a little less.

Design 82 illustrates a six-room cottage, which is nicely adapted for use as a gate lodge or gardener's residence, and would be an ornament to any well kept place. One chimney answers for all rooms, and it consisting of but one flue, the expense is light and the greatest degree of economy possible in mason work practised. Many people think that a chimney consisting of one flue 8x8 in size will only do for one stove connection ; this is a mistaken idea, as we have known cases where as many as six stoves, all connected with their pipes into a flue of this size, and all worked well. In building such flues provision ought always to be made at the bottom for cleaning out the dust and dirt, else it may stop up in time by filling up solid above the lowest connection and make trouble. Usually too little care is taken in arranging the cleaning-out holes at the base of tight flues, such matters being generally left to guess work and the mason building the chimneys. Such a house as this costs $1,475.

Design 83 represents a nice little cottage, only one story high sensible and simple in plan and in outline, easy to construct, and would fit many locations where the amount of room here shown is needed and the house must be kept down low. Such houses as these are needed on almost every place of two or three acres where the accommodations provided in the stable for the use of coachman are not sufficient for the gardener's use as well. This design would be good to build in any out-of-the-way corner, would never be noticeable, and when it was seen would always suggest comfort and happiness by its general shape and surroundings. Cost of this cottage is $900.

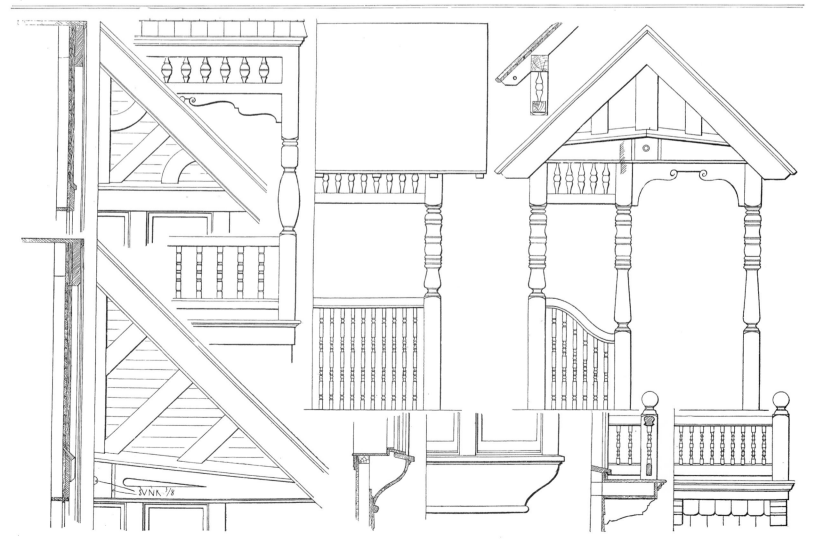

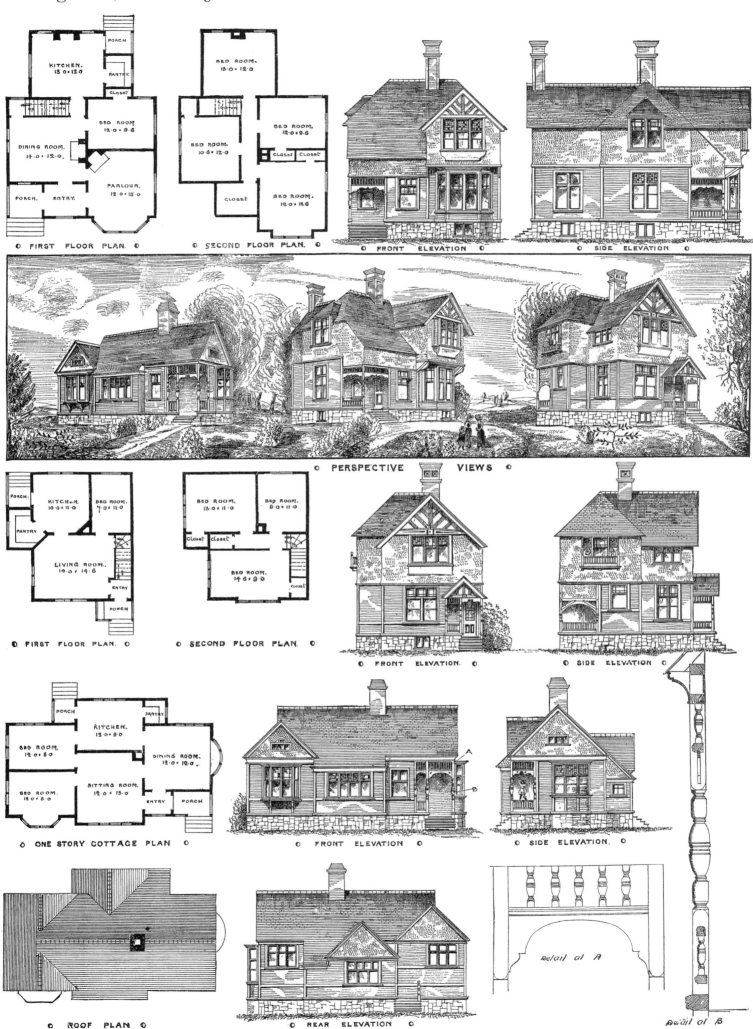

KITCHEN.
13·0 × 12·0

PORCH

PANTRY

CLOSET

BED ROOM
12·0 × 9·6

DINING ROOM.
14·0 × 12·0

PORCH. ENTRY

PARLOUR.
12·0 × 15·0

○ FIRST FLOOR PLAN. ○

BED ROOM.
13·0 × 12·0

BED ROOM.
10·6 × 12·0

BED ROOM.
12·0 × 9·6

CLOSET   CLOSET

BED ROOM.
12·0 × 12·6

CLOSET

○ SECOND FLOOR PLAN. ○

○ FRONT ELEVATION ○

○ SIDE ELEVATION ○

○ PERSPECTIVE   VIEWS ○

PORCH

KITCHEN.
10·0 × 11·0

BED ROOM.
9·0 × 11·0

PANTRY

LIVING ROOM.
19·0 × 14·6

ENTRY

PORCH

○ FIRST FLOOR PLAN. ○

BED ROOM.
13·0 × 11·0

BED ROOM.
9·0 × 11·0

CLOSET   CLOSET

BED ROOM.
14·6 × 9·0

CLOSET

○ SECOND FLOOR PLAN. ○

○ FRONT ELEVATION. ○

○ SIDE ELEVATION ○

PORCH

KITCHEN.
12·0 × 9·0

PANTRY

BED ROOM.
12·0 × 8·0

DINING ROOM.
12·0 × 12·0

BED ROOM.
12·0 × 8·0

SITTING ROOM.
12·0 × 13·0

ENTRY

PORCH

○ ONE STORY COTTAGE PLAN ○

○ FRONT ELEVATION ○

A

B

○ SIDE ELEVATION. ○

○ ROOF PLAN ○

○ REAR ELEVATION ○

Detail at A

Detail at B

PALLISER'S NEW COTTAGE HOMES AND DETAILS.

PLATE 29

Design 84 gives an excellent plan for a country house with good rooms and plenty of attic room. The style is after that of 100 years ago, and is very simple in arrangement and detail. This has become a very popular style in the last few years, and is capable of the most economical construction, giving good solid results for the least outlay possible. The first story is clap-boarded, and the walls of upper part are shingled, the finish being placed on sheathing boards which are put on diagonally on frame and with felt paper between these and exterior finish, thus, making a warm and wind proof house in every respect. Such houses as this, with the front door in the centre, give a better appearance than a plan with the same amount of room, having the entrance on one corner, or to side of front, and are better adapted to general country use than narrow houses which are more for city and suburban use on narrow lots where the ground is more valuable. Such houses as this require plenty of room, and should not be crowded together into small spaces, but have large plots and stand about the centre of the grounds. This then allows for nice drives, walks, and the proper planting of trees, which latter should never be so close to the house as to throw a shadow on the same before 2 P. M. Many fine places are spoilt just by this, and we have known of instances where property has been sold cheap, and at a loss, on account of the dampness and gloominess of the situation, which has been entirely cured by the new owner having sense enough to just cut down the trees and bushes too near the house, and let in the genial sunshine. There is space for three or four nice bedrooms in the attic, which can be finished in an inexpensive manner, making a good ten-room house, which, with a suitable furnace, to heat two floors, plumbing, painting, and other requirements to make a complete and first class job. Costs $4,300 to $4,500.

Design 85 gives a nice, roomy, country house, in style of architecture, somewhat similar to the preceding one. The plan is very well arranged and adapted to the requirements of a life in the country, and would be a home for the city business man who appreciates country life enough to give his family the full benefit thereof, and take whatever comfort he can from it himself, after hours of business. With the rapid growth of such cities as New York, and the enormous rents charged for as much room as herein shown, whether it be in the high-toned flat, or the poorer house in a block there cannot help but be a change tending toward an appreciation of the suburbs, as it is cheaper to live twenty-five miles from the city, pay about $100 a year commutation fares to and from business, keep a man, a horse and carriage, and have ground enough to keep the man's time employed in raising fruit, vegetables, etc., for the family use, and the time is certainly coming when the careful business man will avail himself of the benefits that can be had from having a permanent home in the country. Such homes as this will help play an important part in settling the question, and no doubt there are many convenient locations within easy distance of the city where a number of such houses would rent readily and for fully 10 per cent. on the investment. A careful inspection of the plan is all that is needed to explain the good points. The attic will supply about four good sleeping rooms, making a good 12-room house, the appearance of which no one desiring a quiet dignified and pleasant home need be ashamed to live in. Such a house ought to be painted a warm chocolate color for body, trimmed with bronze green, sash white, blinds red, roofs painted red, the chimneys being laid up with red brick. Such a house finished inside in white pine, natural wood, nice mantels, stairs, etc., of ash, good hot air furnace well plumbed and water supply, will cost about $5,000 under good management and in an economical neighborhood.

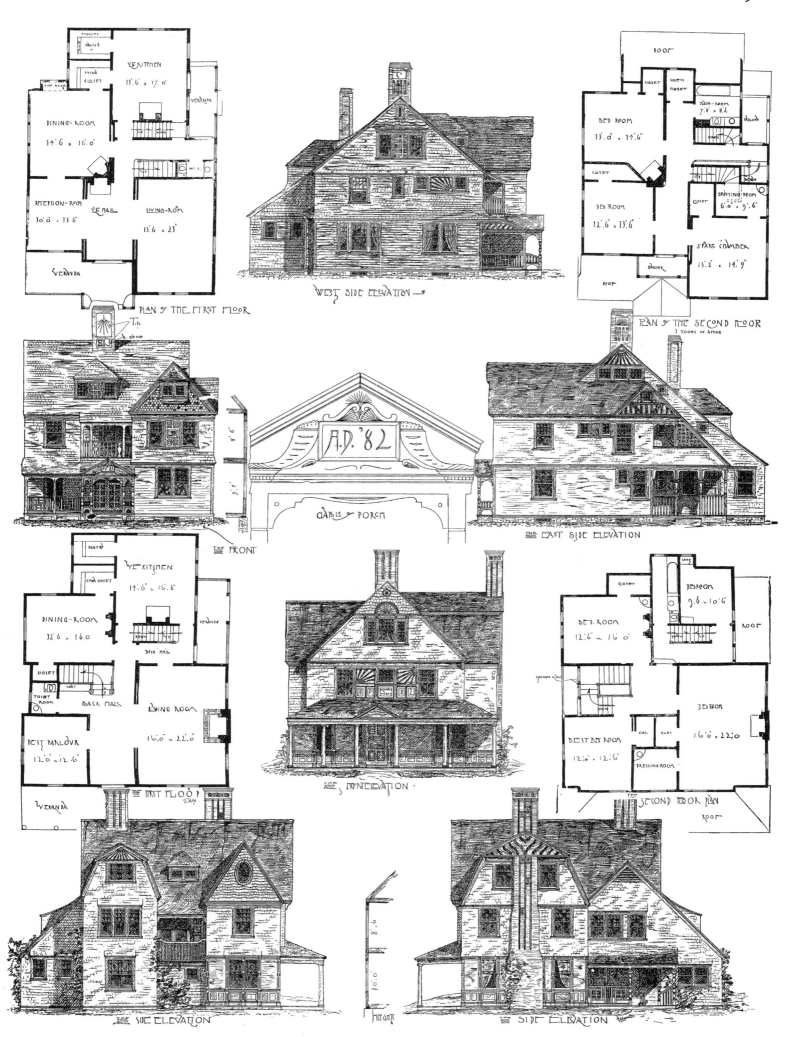

PLAN OF THE FIRST FLOOR

WEST SIDE ELEVATION

PLAN OF THE SECOND FLOOR
3 ROOMS IN ATTIC

YE KITCHEN
13.6 x 17.0

DINING-ROOM
14.6 x 16.0

RECEPTION-ROOM
10.0 x 13.6

YE HALL

LIVING-ROOM
13.6 x 23

VERANDA

BED ROOM
13.0 x 14.6

BED ROOM
12.6 x 13.6

SPARE CHAMBER
13.2 x 14.9

THE FRONT

GABLE & PORCH

A.D. '82

THE EAST SIDE ELEVATION

YE KITCHEN
14.6 x 16.6

DINING-ROOM
12.6 x 16.0

BEST PARLOUR
12.0 x 12.6

LIVING ROOM
16.0 x 22.0

BACK HALL

VERANDA

BED ROOM
12.6 x 16.0

BEST BED ROOM
12.0 x 12.6

BED ROOM
9.6 x 10.6

BED ROOM
16.0 x 22.0

DRESSING-ROOM

FIRST FLOOR PLAN

FRONT ELEVATION

THE SECOND FLOOR PLAN

SIDE ELEVATION

FRONT

SIDE ELEVATION

PLATE 30.

Design 86 illustrates a very cosey cottage, designed to be built of stone. The basement, first and second floors are shown, together with front and rear elevations. This house is for a hill-side location, the rear being one story more out of ground than the front. The kitchen is therefore placed in the basement, and service to dining-room is obtained with dumb-waiter placed in the corner of kitchen, and opens into closet on first floor, which is well lighted and provides ample room for china, etc. The one chimney is so located that it answers for the entire house, giving two fire-places on the first floor and ample facilities for stove connections at other points. The second floor gives four nice bedrooms and good closets, and the attic provides room for two or three more rooms, which would be very desirable at times. The general appearance of this design when executed is very effective, and adds to the beauty of the landscape. For heating such a house as this a Jackson grate, a Fire on the Hearth heater, or Boynton fire-place heater, set in either the dining-room or parlor fire-place would be the thing. This would heat the rooms above and the first floor very nicely, and an abundance of pure warm air be insured. The plumbing consists of one sink and pump to draw the water from a cistern which is supplied from the roof gutters and leaders. The first floor to be finished in ash, with neat mantels; the balance in pine, plainly painted. Such a house costs, in a neighborhood where stone can be had cheaply and where the same does not require too much labor in working, about $2,800.

Design 87 illustrates a convenient six room cottage, nicely adapted for a variety of situations, and suited to the wants of a mechanic of limited means. Such a home as this a poor man would be proud of, and it is certainly as desirable to have the poor build in good taste as the rich; and it in nowise goes as a rule—that to be in good taste is to be expensive, but it requires a proper amount of judgment and good management (that many ladies know how to apply in making up a neat and stylish dress at little expense) to lead to the most practical result and obtain the best combination of art with economy, and in all ways observe the proper fitness of things. Such a design as this ought to be executed at about $2,200.

Design 88 gives a small cottage, well adapted for use as a gardener's cottage or gate lodge. The plan is well arranged, and is roomy, though small, and in every way desirable for a large variety of locations. The one chimney answers for all; pantry and sink-room are convenient. Down to the cellar from kitchen, to attic over the main stairs, the sink and pump with cistern constitute that part of the service. A cellar is under the whole house, the cellar being 6 feet 6 inches, first story 8 feet and second story 7 feet 6 inches, all in the clear. The first story (body color) painted a bright red; second story, old gold, trimmed with bronze green. Paint the sash white, blinds maroon, roofs medium brown; and this combination produces a very happy effect, and gives a harmonious and artistic appearance that would be lost if not properly painted, as color is the life of all design and must not be lost sight of. This cottage cost $1,200.

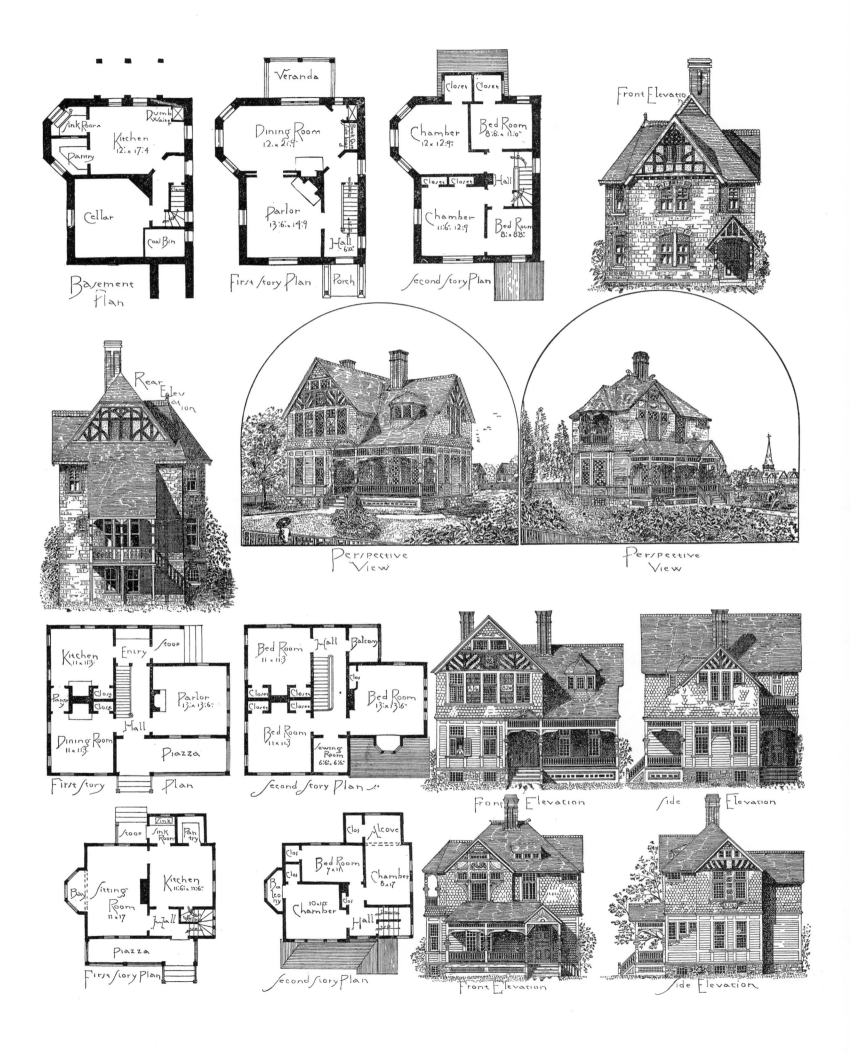

Kitchen
12 x 17:4

Sink Room

Pantry

Dumb Waiter

Cellar

Coal Bin

Basement Plan

Veranda

Dining Room
12 x 21:9

Parlor
13:6 x 14:9

Hall
6:0.

First Story Plan

Porch

Closet Closet

Chamber
12 x 12:9

Bed Room
8:6 x 11:0"

Closet Closet

Hall

Chamber
11:6: x 12:9

Bed Room
8: x 8:8:

Second Story Plan

Front Elevation

Rear Elevation

Perspective View

Perspective View

Kitchen
11 x 11:3

Entry

Stoop

Pantry

Clos
Clos

Parlor
13: x 13:6:

Dining Room
11 x 11:3

Hall

Piazza

First Story Plan

Bed Room
11 x 11:3

Hall

Balcony

Closets

Clos
Clos

Clos

Bed Room
13: x 13:6"

Bed Room
11 x 11:3

Sewing Room
6:6: x 6:6:

Second Story Plan

Front Elevation

Side Elevation

Sink

Stoop

Sink Room

Pantry

Bay

Sitting Room
11 x 17

Kitchen
11:6: x 11:6:

Hall

Piazza

First Story Plan

Clos

Alcove

Clos
Clos

Bed Room
7 x 11

Chamber
8 x 17

Balcony

Chamber
10 x 10:

Clos

Hall

Second Story Plan

Front Elevation

Side Elevation

PALLISER'S NEW COTTAGE HOMES AND DETAILS.

PLATE 31 AND 32.

American business men and others possessing considerable wealth have been in the habit of making the city house the home; but during the past ten or twelve years the tide has again turned to the country, and it is now the proper thing to make the country house the home, and for the family to occupy it, if not all the year round—from Spring until Christmas, and for three or four months of the indoor season to live in an apartment or hotel in the city.

Designs 89 and 90 give the floor plans, elevations, perspective views, together with the details of the exterior points of interest, of a pair of semi-detached country houses, having a driveway built in common; practically these are two distinct houses, and each contain the features of a single house.

To build two such houses together as are here shown, a location peculiarly adapted would be necessary to insure success. A level plateau overlooking a valley, or the ocean, and commanding a good view of the surrounding country, would be the best. These are houses that would suit many people for summer use, and would be very desirable homes for many families who might well afford to own their own summer homes, and could keep house at less cost than they could live in a hotel. There is ample space in attics to finish six or eight rooms, in each, which would give plenty of servant's rooms, trunk or spare rooms. The large halls answer for general living-rooms, and communicating as they do with the other rooms of first floors, make a good arrangement for social gatherings. The verandas are also large, and supply room enough to live out-doors as much as may be needed—a very desirable feature in houses for summer use. These houses are not by any means what can be called cheap houses, and to carry out the design as here shown, in a good and first-class manner, would involve an outlay of not less than $15,000.

A careful study of the plans with the details for the outside work, as shown, will, no doubt, give a great many ideas which can be used to good advantage, sometimes on smaller houses. The terraces in front of the verandas are a nice and novel feature, built up on boulders in the wall, and with the rail containing seat on one side and the flower shelf on the other, an excellent effect is obtained, which ever way it is seen. Sometimes the building of a country house in an artistic manner proves to be quite an undertaking. One case we have in mind where a party having bought a piece of shore property on which he started out to build a house and barn by days work, under a noted City Architect, expecting to spend about $6,000 on former, and $600 on the latter, which resulted in changes and alterations that brought the final cost of the house up to $30,000, just five times the cost originally intended, while the barn followed suit, and the $600 wound up with an outlay of $10,000. This result certainly shows that it is policy to have a well-developed plan before the job is started; many useless expenditures would then be avoided, and in the end a more satisfactory solution of the question be arrived at. Many people start to build when the fit takes them, never taking time to study their wants or find out what a given amount will do or how much of a house can be had for a stipulated sum. The most satisfactory ending of building operations is that which is conducted and carried out without any changes or alterations, as at the final wind-up there are no fights about extras and overcharges for doing this and that, and which, in many cases, do not fairly compensate the builder for what he has done. When changes are made in contract work, the price should always be agreed upon on the spot, and paid for as soon as it is done, so as not to interfere and get mixed in with other work. If people who are building would adopt this plan, about one-half the changes usually made would be dispensed with. Another source of changes often arises from the desire of those who are having the work done to change simply because they do not like this or that when the work is in an unfinished condition, and we have often known changes made at this stage of the work which have resulted in great additional expense, and when done, the work has neither looked as well or been as good as first designed. Such houses as these should be finished in hard wood on first floors and pine for other parts, the whole being filled and finished in natural woods, the mantel-pieces, stairs and general finish designed with a special fitness for their places. The general detail of the exterior work on an enlarged scale gives a good idea of the finish on the different parts of the building, and a study of the same and comparison with the design cannot but prove interesting to those who are engaged in building or thinking of doing so. The general appearance of these houses give an impression of solid, every-day comfort and an abundance of the good things required to make life pass pleasantly. When we look back and see what has been accomplished the last fifteen years in this line and anticipate by contrast what the future will bring forth, we are obliged to give up the problem and leave it for the future to decide when and how these things shall come about, and leave the future to take care of itself, busying ourselves with the present and struggling to do whatever we can towards elevating our art to the highest plain attainable with the times and means at hand, so that when future races run they may see our footprints on the sands of time.

In selecting a spot for the erection of a country house great care should be exercised to avoid plague spots or their making; as a careless step, or one of inattention, may lead to the most disastrous results.

Early last spring the elegant mansion of one of New York's wealthiest capitalists, situated on a beautiful hill in New Jersey, was turned into a house of mourning. It had been constructed on the most approved sanitary and scientific principles. Thousands of dollars had been expended in the drainage, plumbing and ventilation. The surroundings were healthful, the air was pure, and yet an epidemic of diphtheria swept away a family of young and beautiful children. It was the theory of the physicians that the house was filled with malaria, which always invites diphtheria, and, skeptical as the father was, he instituted a rigid examination. Every closet, pipe and drain, was found to be perfect, and they were about to give up, baffled, when by accident they examined the furnace fresh-air box, and a few feet from its opening, in a neighbor's lot, they discovered a mass of putrifying garbage! The mystery was explained. The malaria had found an entrance through the "fresh" air flue, and three loved ones perished because "somebody had blundered!" The same result was seen at Princeton College, seven students losing their lives by the faulty drainage of the college grounds. These occurrences were not "dispensations of Providence," they were the result of plain carelessness.

Life is a constant struggle for existence, and as the fittest always survives, it is the duty of every man to acquaint himself with the methods of prevention and cure of influences which would hurry him to the grave. There is much doubt nowadays as to what, for instance, causes malaria, but there is no doubt that it is the basis of the most obstinate chronic disorders.

Eratta on First Story Plan.

On the right-hand side, first-floor plan, the dining-room should have been marked parlor, and the room marked parlor should be dining-room.

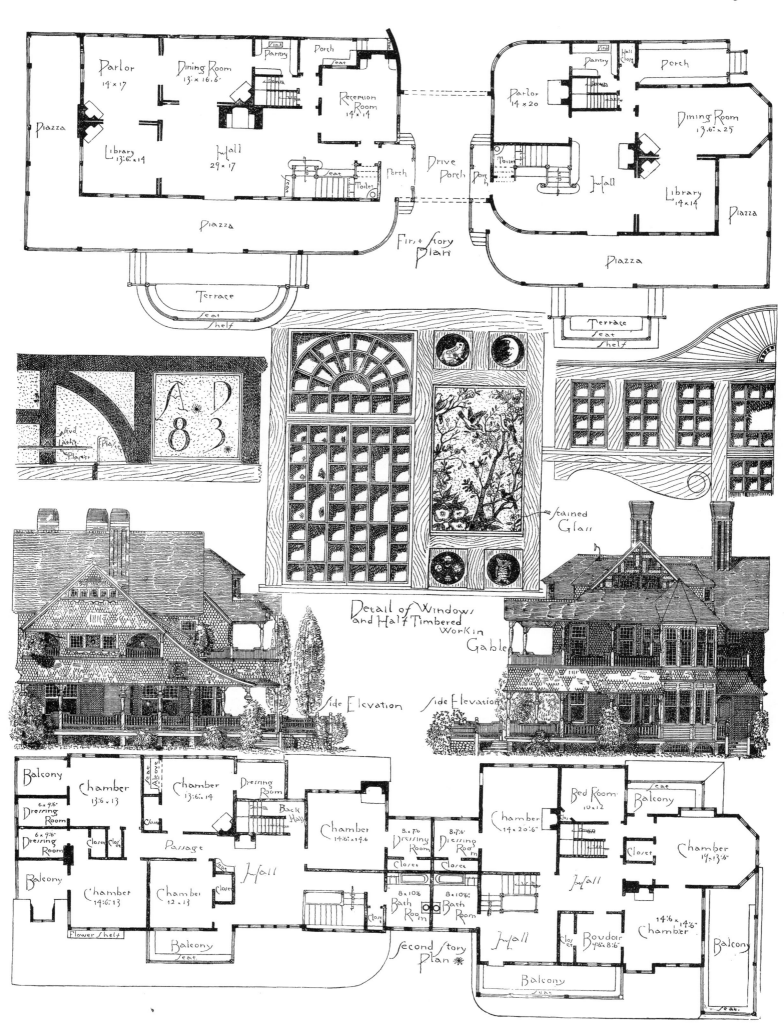

First Story Plan

Parlor 14 × 17

Dining Room 13 × 16.6

Pantry

Porch

Seat

Reception Room 14 × 14

Piazza

Library 13:6 × 14

Hall 29 × 17

Seat

Porch

Toilet

Piazza

Parlor 14 × 20

Pantry

Hall closet

Porch

Stairs

Toilet

Dining Room 13:6 × 25

Hall

Library 14 × 14

Piazza

Drive Porch

Piazza

Terrace

Seat Shelf

Terrace

Seat Shelf

A.D. 83

Stud Lath Plaster

Detail of Windows and Half Timbered Work in Gable

Stained Glass

Side Elevation

Side Elevation

Second Story Plan

Balcony

Chamber 13:6 × 13

Dressing Room 6 × 9:6

Dressing Room 6 × 9:6

Alcove

Closet

Chamber 13:6 × 14

Dressing Room

Back Hall

Balcony

Closet Closet

Passage

Chamber 14:6 × 14:6

Dressing Room 8 × 7:6

Dressing Room 8 × 7:6

Bed Room 10 × 12

Seat Balcony

Chamber 14 × 20:6

Balcony

Chamber 14:6 × 13

Seat

Chamber 12 × 13

Closet

Seat

Hall

Closet

Bath Room 8 × 10:6

Bath Room 8 × 10:6

Hall

Hall

Closet

Chamber 14 × 13:6

Flower Shelf

Balcony Seat

Hall

Boudoir 4:6 × 8:6

Chamber 14:6 × 14:6

Balcony

Balcony

Seat

Plate 32.

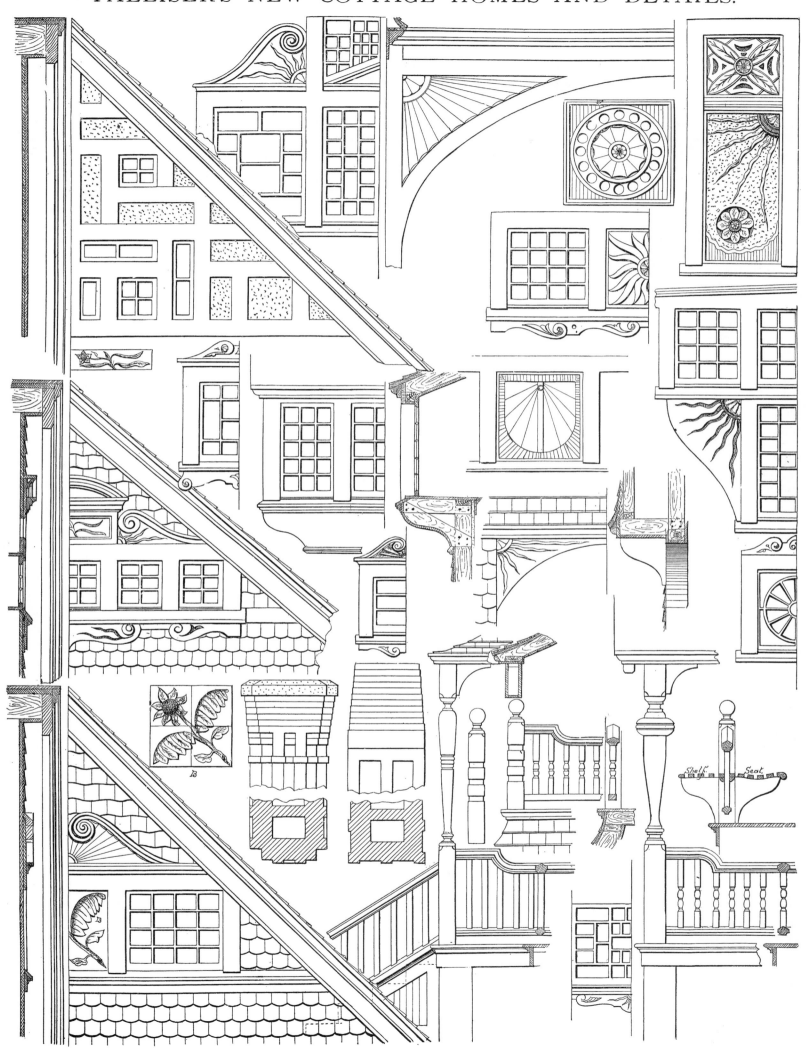

Shelf. Seat.

Design 91 represents a two-family cottage suited to the requirements of two small families, one on each floor, each family using the same front door, and the rear side doors also being fixed that both can use the back stairs up to the attic. There will be room there to finish two nice rooms, thus giving to each family an extra room on third story with an abundance of attic room for general storage purposes. Such houses as these are needed in the outskirts of large towns and cities as homes for the working people, and would rent for about $16 a floor, in the New England cities. This house would require a lot not less than 35 to 40 feet front, roofs to be shingled, cellar divided into two parts. Such a house with drainage properly applied and the water run in and connected to two sinks, and the work finished in a good, plain way, and painted throughout ought to be built at a cost of $2,200. This, with land, ought to come within an expenditure of $3,000, thus making a good investment, paying about ten per cent. on the outlay.

Design 92 shows a more simple and less expensive two-family cottage, giving four rooms on each floor with ample room for two finished ones in attic. The cost of this cottage is estimated at $1,900, and ought to be built in a very complete and substantial manner for that sum.

Design 93 shows a more elaborate plan which gives ample accommodation for quite a large family on each floor and which, if built near the city of New York, would be called a French flat in preference to the more unpretentious name, "a tenement." That it might not be quite so high-toned to live in a house of this kind in a quite refined rural neighborhood con- venient of access to the city where the full benefits and enjoy- ments of plenty of room, pure air, genial surroundings and a few pleasant neighbors who would always be on visiting terms, as it would be to be crowded into one of the so-called apart- ment-houses in New York where from ten to one hundred families are housed, and for which they pay enormous rents for miserable, dark, unventilated and in many cases unlighted rooms, looking down upon squalid back yards and rears of tenement blocks. We know of some of these high-toned tene- ment houses in the heart of New York City that house nearly one hundred families under one roof running up ten, eleven or twelve stories high, giving groups of rooms in suites of from three to eight each, some of which do not have more than three exterior windows, and nearly all contain more or less dark rooms that rent from $800 to $3,000 a year. That this class of people are paying enormously for the privilege of living in what they no doubt think a fashionable house in a location close to their business cannot be denied, and no doubt the same people if offered double the room and conveniences in a suburban location at one-third the rent would think they were being robbed to pay such. Still, for fashion sake, they will do much, pay cheerfully and get along with all kinds of inconveniences and murmur not. We predict for these lofty tenements a large fall in rents and shall find them given up to an entire different class than at the present in a few years time, while the present incum- bents will have taken up a suburban residence and will be appreciating a house by themselves. Such a design as 93 should be carried out for about $2,550 and would rent for about $20 per month for each floor, a good return on the investment.

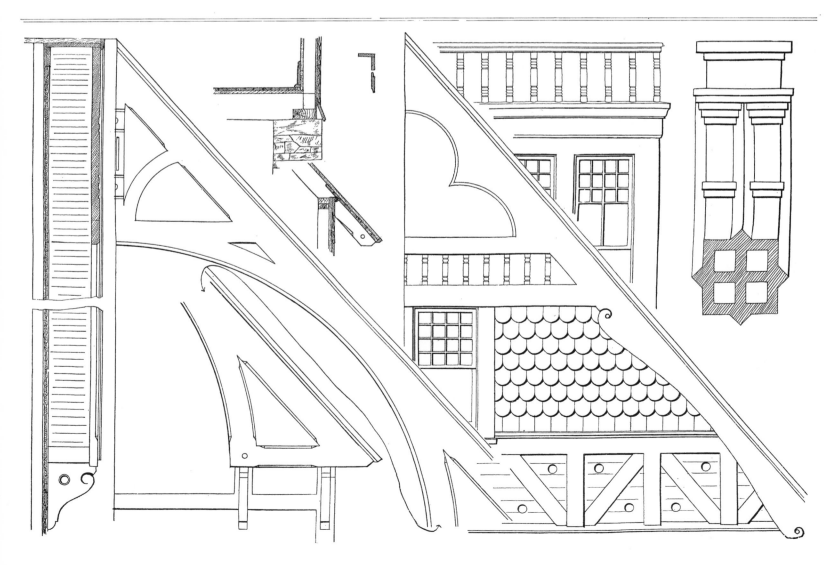

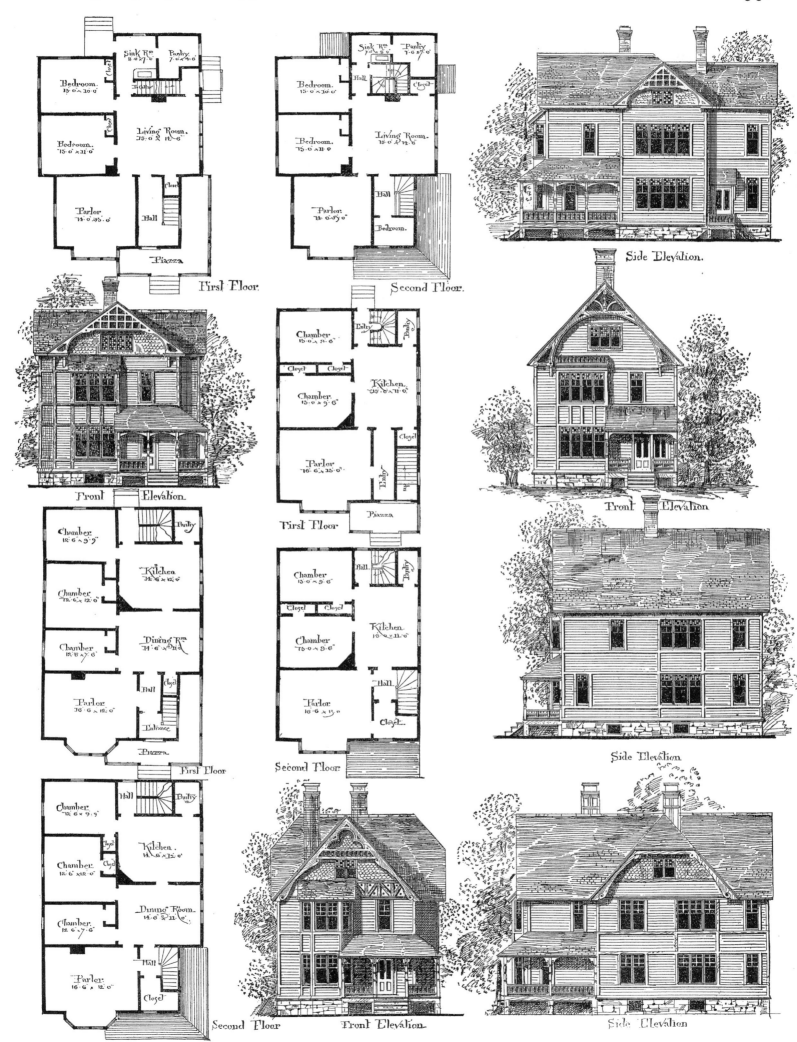

First Floor.

Second Floor.

Side Elevation.

Front Elevation.

First Floor.

Front Elevation.

Second Floor.

Side Elevation.

First Floor.

Second Floor.

Second Floor.

Front Elevation.

Side Elevation.

Design 94 illustrates a compact and square frame cottage the frame of which is sheathed, and lower story covered with narrow clapboards, while the second story is covered with ten-inch matched and grooved boards, and the joints battened with flat three-inch battens. The plan is simple and well arranged giving the greatest amount of room for the least possible outlay. No room is here wasted in useless halls or passages, the whole arrangement is close, compact and cosey—one chimney answers for all and gives facilities for at least three stove-pipe connections—a sink, pump and cistern constitutes the improvements and conveniences in the kitchen part. For water closet, if suitable drainage and water service were convenient, it might be placed in the cellar; if not, it is better to have it at a respectful distance from the house, and then arrange it as an earth-closet which is much preferable to an ordinary privy vault; this makes a very good cottage for quite a large family and is a nice little village home, of which no one need be ashamed to live in for a cost of $1,375.

Design 95 shows a very well arranged and roomy cottage of eight rooms giving a good large living or dining-room, with back kitchen conveniences, the pantry is large, well arranged and lighted, and the stairs so placed that they are accessible from either living-room or parlor; the exterior finish is similar to the preceding design, and having a more broken surface and gable finish, would present for some localities a better appearance than that one; there being two chimneys in the design, and the exterior being more cut up and complicated, the cost is $150.00 higher than last design, or rather there is about that difference between the two plans, finish being equal.

Design 96 gives a very small simple cottage, which is a mansion compared with the ordinary New York City tenement, and for those needing the amount of room and conveniences here shown it is a study that can be looked into with profit and some small degree of pleasure. A little cottage like this is very easy to furnish and does not need a fortune in carpets and furniture, with a cellar under the whole house, a suitable cistern, pump, sink and proper drainage, this house costs to build it about $850.

Design 97 shows a study of a very tasty and neat six-room cottage presenting a very picturesque and pleasing appearance as to exterior. The front entrance hall is very roomy and is lighted by a stained-glass window; the rooms are all of good size and are desirable as to their relations to each other, and with a plain neat interior finish, water, drainage and cellar, such a home can be built under favorable circumstances for about $1,400. All the cottages shown on the plate are of the same general character and design, with variations as to size and general plan, and would all look well painted in the same style. The lower stories look best with a red body, the body of upper parts and gables having an orange buff, and the whole trimmed with bronze green, the sash to be white, and the shingle work of roofs red. These colors are very striking and appropriate in every way.

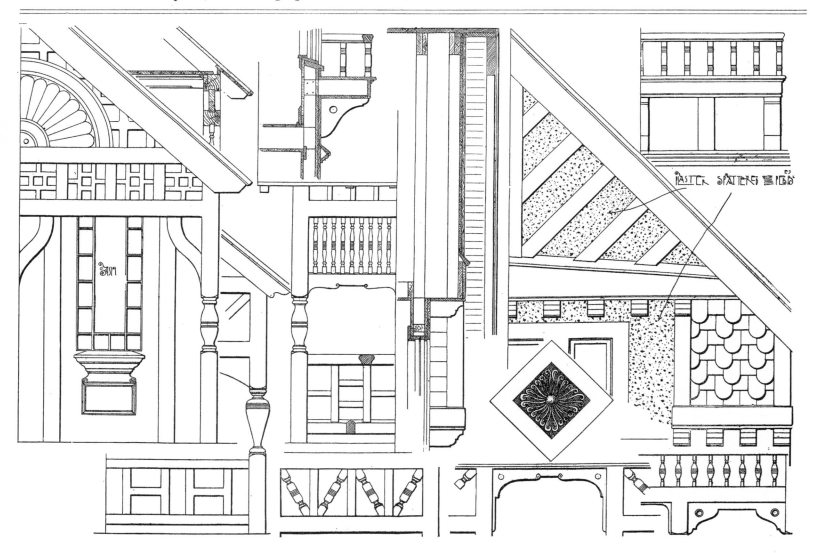

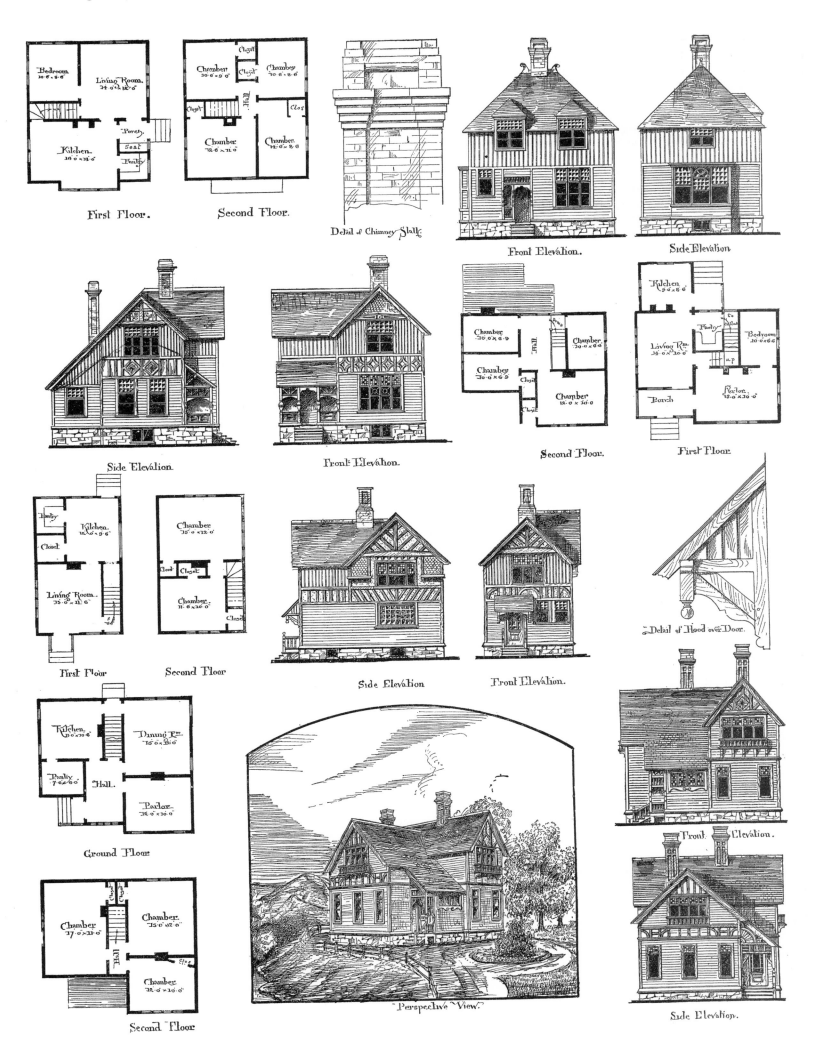

First Floor.　　　Second Floor.

Detail of Chimney Shaft.

Front Elevation.　　　Side Elevation.

Side Elevation.　　　Front Elevation.

Second Floor.　　　First Floor.

First Floor.　　　Second Floor.

Side Elevation.　　　Front Elevation.

Detail of Hood over Door.

Ground Floor.

Front Elevation.

Second Floor.

Perspective View.

Side Elevation.

PLATE 35.

Design 98 shows a rather ordinary type of six-room cottage, having good rooms and being well suited for suburban use and location. The space over the kitchen part on second floor is laid out in one room still it would be large enough for two, if it were so required. With a suitable cellar under the whole house, cistern, sink, pump and drainage, the interior finished in a neat, plain and substantial manner in pine and painted; such a house would cost about $1,200 in its erection.

Design 99 gives a very nice and economical plan of a seven room house which is arranged in very compact form, the three main rooms on the first floor being grouped around a central chimney which answers for all parts of the house. The stairs to the second story are reached from either the sitting-room or the kitchen, while the cellar can be reached from the kitchen by stairs placed under the main stairs. The house has good and roomy closets, and makes a very cosey home for an outlay of about $1,400, varying a little with location.

Design 100 gives a six-room cottage, very handy and conveniently arranged, with good, generous rooms and convenient closets, pantry, etc. One flue answers all purposes being centrally located, and to which two stoves on the first floor and one on the second can be connected. Such a house as this would be very suitable for a mechanic's home, and would always look welcome and inviting if properly treated as to paint and colors, and can be built for about $1,300, according to cir. cumstances, the management brought to bear upon it, etc.

Design 101 gives a good plan for a seven-room house, well arranged and nicely adapted to the needs of quite a large family, giving three good rooms on the first floor and four chambers above. There is no waste or useless room here everything being properly utilized and used up to good advantage. The front porch is a closed one making the front part thoroughly comfortable in cold weather, and in summer, when opened up will be equal to an open veranda. Cost $1,475.

Design 102 is a picturesque little cottage home of seven rooms suitable for the residence of almost any of America's citizens desiring to keep up with modern ideas in the design and building of homes. Cost $1,600. This design can be reversed, can be improved by the addition of a bath room on second floor without much trouble, and in other ways its value enhanced; and, in fact, all the designs in this book can be treated in different ways to suit people's various ideas, requirements, site, depth of pocket, etc., etc. And to make a correct estimate of cost to suit any particular location it is necessary to know the exact circumstances, cost of materials, labor, etc., together with the complete specifications as to improvements, finishes, etc., to be included, as it is a fact that the cost of a house can very easily be varied fifty per cent. or more, according to method of construction, cost of materials finishes adopted and improvements applied, and very often the difference in cost of materials and labor between two localities varies one hundred per cent. or more—as for instance, some of these houses erected in Nova Scotia for $600, would cost in Massachusetts $1,500 and in other States of the West and South $1,000 to $1,200.

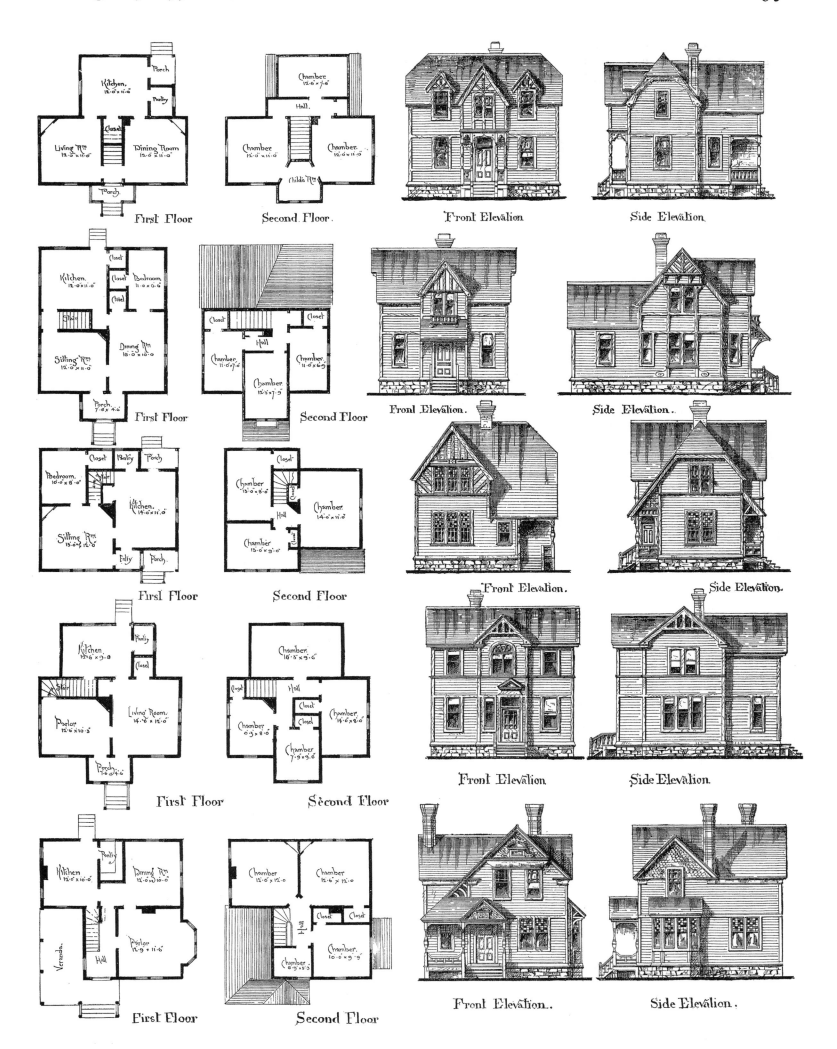

First Floor

Second Floor

Front Elevation

Side Elevation

First Floor

Second Floor

Front Elevation

Side Elevation

First Floor

Second Floor

Front Elevation

Side Elevation

First Floor

Second Floor

Front Elevation

Side Elevation

First Floor

Second Floor

Front Elevation

Side Elevation

Design 103 shows two floor plans, two elevations and general perspective view of a picturesque and cosey one-and-a-half-story cottage in wood, which presents some features in the general composition that cannot fail but be suggestive, both from an economical and artistic point of view. One chimney answers for the whole house, starting from cellar bottom gives an ample flue for connection to heater in cellar, and the kitchen stove or range on first floor. It is economy in such houses as this where there is bath-room and three or four rooms to be warmed to put in the cellar a portable hot air furnace, with the necessary pipes and registers to heat the two main rooms and hall of first floor, and the two main chambers and bath-room of second floor. Such a furnace, with the necessary piping, would not be much more costly than two self-feeding parlor stoves; the actual net cost of such a furnace for a house of this kind only being about $100, and the dirt and dust arising from their heating and warming is thus kept down in the cellar where it can be easily cleaned up and taken care of, much to the comfort and cleanliness of the upper part of the house. The first floor is nicely arranged, and the large entrance hall will furnish up very good and present an appearance that could not fail but impress the new comer very favorably, the small sash and top half of the hall window being in Cathedral glass of many tints, would lend a very harmonious coloring to the whole; same in top lights of the windows of parlor and dining-room. The four bed-rooms are all good and serviceable, easily reached, and in close proximity to each other although not directly connected. The bathroom is very nicely situated in a good warm place, not likely to freeze up and make trouble in winter time (a very important trouble that it is always well to avoid as far as possible, and which when avoided, results in both pleasure and profit to the occupant of the house); with a cellar under the whole house, furnace and hot and cold water, cistern and tank, and the whole work properly carried out in good and workmanlike style as here shown, such a house as this can be built, under ordinary favorable circumstances, for about $2,450. The exterior painting of such a house as this has much to do with the success of the design, and we would suggest red for the body of the lower part, golden bronze for the sides that are shingled, and bronze green for the trimming color. The roof if painted, to be a brown of medium color.

Design 104 gives a very roomy and attractive little home, which to many will embody the wants and needs of a permanent and social residence. The first floor arrangements are on a scale well suited to quite a family, and the parlor and dining-room being closely connected by means of the sliding doors can be made available as one large room on social occasions, or on any occasion for that matter; the bed-room on this floor will make for many who are used to living in the country an indispensable feature, closets and pantry arrangements are well provided for. This house, built in like manner to the preceding design, less the bath-room and the fixtures and expense attending the same, ought to be carried out at a cost of about $2,300. In the painting, such colors as are specified for last design are very suitable for this, and would make a very nice appearance. This style of cottage always looks well when built among suitable surroundings, and to the lovers of nature might be pictured as a perfect paradise when almost enveloped in running vines, rose bushes, lilacs and flowering shrubbery so common to all parts of our country. That such homes are greatly needed cannot be denied, and we trust that these designs may stimulate their erection somewhat.

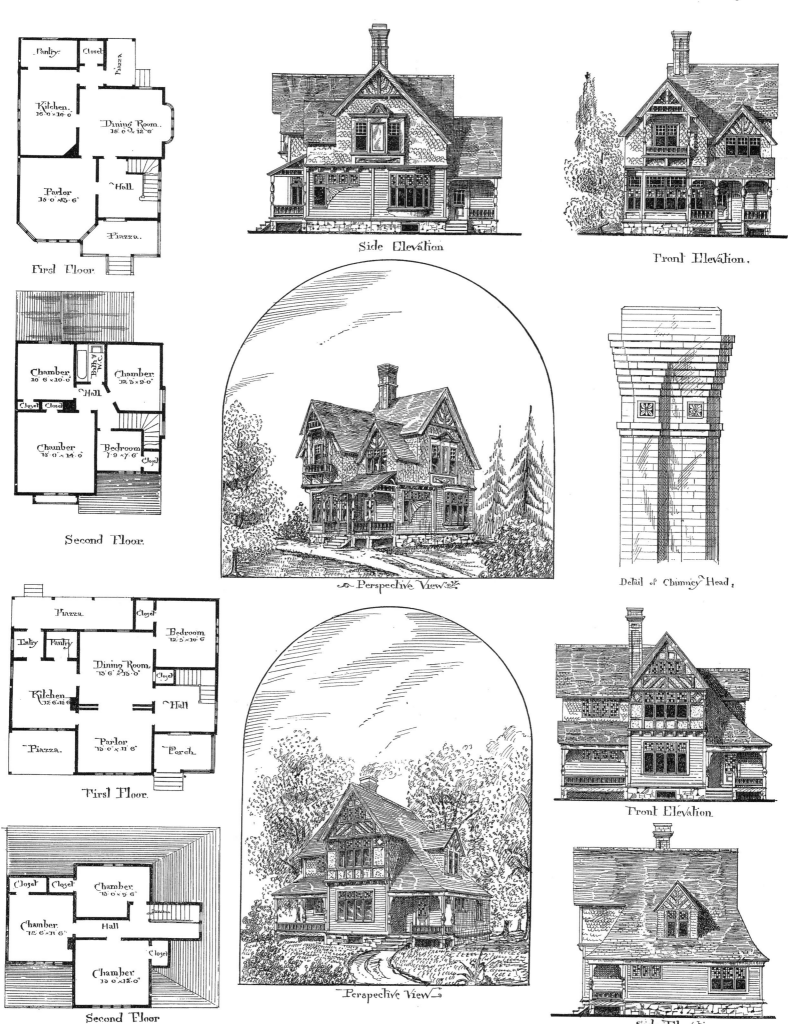

First Floor.

Second Floor.

First Floor.

Second Floor

Side Elevation

Perspective View

Perspective View

Front Elevation.

Detail of Chimney Head.

Front Elevation.

Side Elevation.

This plate shows four plans for two-family houses suited to the needs of one family for each floor. All are designed with a special fitness for using up the least amount of ground possible and are well suited to narrow lots. The designs are all simple in outline, the detail being of a very economical construction giving a suitable finish and character to the general external appearance. In such houses as these room and economy are the watchwords, and when we have provided the first with the most approved conveniences and arrangement of rooms at the minimum of cost, we have accomplished that which thousands are looking for and which many who have built have failed to find. To build well and yet on an economical basis is probably one of the hardest problems in the world to solve, and it requires some experience as well as good business management, as it is a very frequent occurrence to find that in two men estimating, the figures of one will be double that of the other, and still it will be possible for the lowest to do the work at a fair profit. To those not used to these things it may look peculiar; yet to the architect, who is used to this sort of thing, and who has it coming up in his daily experience, it does not appear strange, as he is able to discriminate and judge upon the accuracy of a bid by his general knowledge of the cost of like structures by his past experience gained by actual cost of parallel buildings erected under like circumstances.

Design 105 shows a very convenient plan, both families using the same front and rear entrance doors. This is desirable at times, as it does not give so much the appearance of a two-family house, and, in a general way, it is owned by the party who lives on the first floor and he has his own choice of a tenant for the second, and naturally chooses one that he does not object to mixing with. The kitchen, dining-room and parlor, with the two bed-rooms, make a good tenement, while there is room on attic floor to finish each family two nice small rooms in each gable, the attic being reached by front stairway over main stairs. The two-story veranda gives equal privileges to the family up stairs, and does not interfere with the privacy of the family on first floor. Cost $2,500 to build in ordinary locality.

Design 106 gives a very general type of house as to outward show, each family having a private front entrance and both using back door and stairs in common. One large living-room answers for general kitchen and dining-room, and the other rooms opening into this renders it an easy house to warm, the kitchen stove being ample to heat the whole house, except in very cold weather. We have had such houses as this built for about $2,200, including two rooms in the attic.

Design 107 is a square, compact cottage, very much in use in the New England States, renting for from 12 to 16 dollars per month each floor. Two rooms can be finished in attic, each family use the same front door and have separate back entrances. Such houses as this seldom stand empty, and are always a good investment on the outlay if built in the right locality. Cost of this design does not exceed $2,000.

Design 108 gives a very roomy plan with sliding doors between two main rooms. Each have their own front hall and entrance, and the attic is controlled by the second floor. Such may at times be found best as the owner can live on the top floors and have additional finished rooms in the attic for sleeping purposes. This house is built at a cost of about $2,600. All these designs can be enlarged or in many ways changed to suit individual wants, as those using them may see fit or the case may demand.

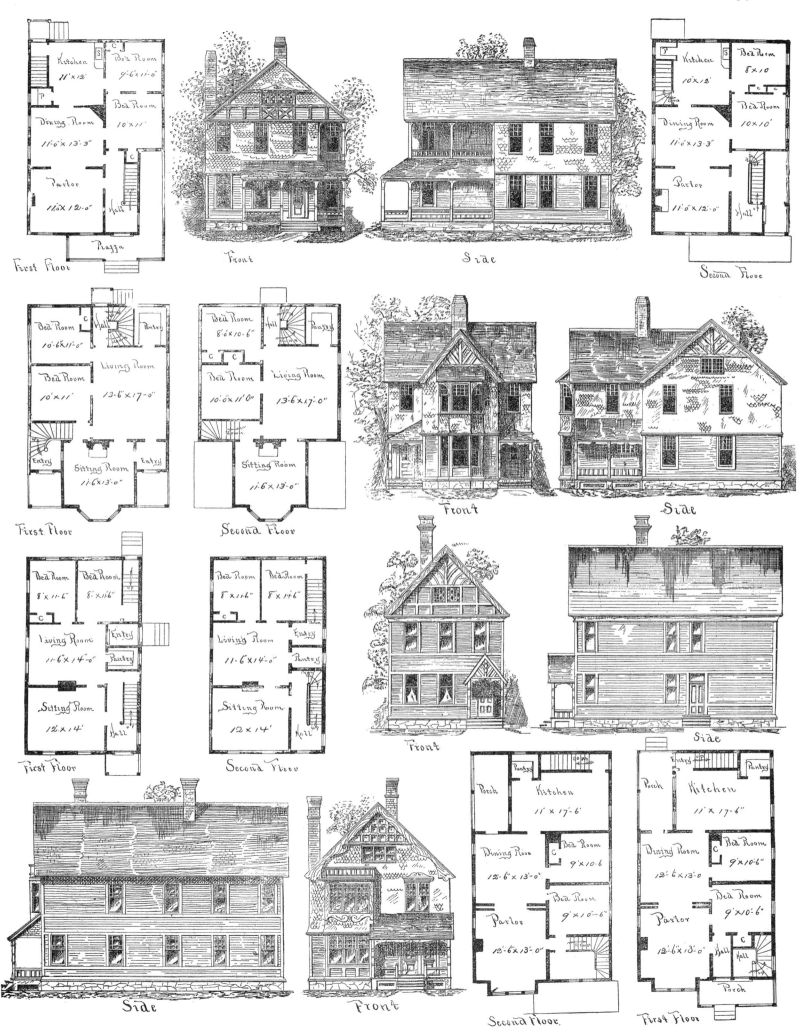

PALLISER'S NEW COTTAGE HOMES AND DETAILS.

PLATE 38.

Plate 38 illustrates one set of floor plans suited to a site twenty feet front, and having light only at front and rear. Such houses as these are in active demand in suburbs or new portions of large towns and cities where ground will soon become too valuable for large lots. The city of Philadelphia is a very fair example as to the general needs of some improvement in its long rows of narrow fronts, all just alike. Almost anything that breaks the monotony of the line would be very agreeable to the eye and would no doubt be largely appreciated by the occupants of such a street. There is certainly no objection to making a long continuous row of house fronts all different in design or of three or four designs, erecting them in alternate blocks of from two to four in each style. This is possible and yet a harmony be retained, and the whole vastly improved in general appearance. It also gives a better variety both for selling and renting purposes, and very materially helps to give a more decided and distinctive character to a man's home, whereby it is possible for his neighbor to distinguish him from the others. Give us variety and plenty of it and if it were possible to never build two buildings at all alike, so much the better, and it is certainly best to vary them as much as circumstances will allow, there may justly be a similarity in the general plan, but it is inexcusable as to outward appearances; even nature will teach us this lesson, and those of the world who will think and study nature as they pass along, may soon see and learn the lesson thereby taught. The plan gives a house 20x42 feet, with four floors, containing ten rooms and bath-room. Such a plan would give very good accommodations for quite a large family and would be a very convenient home to live

in generally; the parlor on the first floor would answer as general reception-room, while the drawing-room on the floor above would give a more retired and pleasant room for general family use. The butler's pantry is nicely arranged in connection with the dining-room, and the little porch on rear which is recessed, could be converted into a plant cabinet or conservatory for use in winter-time. The balconies on second and third floors could also be enclosed with glass in like manner, which would make a warmer house. The twelve designs for front elevations, as given, show quite a variety of outline and are all capable of being carried out in good construction, and could be so arranged that all would look well, even in a block of twelve houses. In some cities there might be objections as to the use of wooden construction, as shown in two of the designs, but with brick backing this would be obviated and it could be made to pass the most rigid building laws. The fronts that are of stone ashlar could be trimmed with brick at the door and window openings which would produce a very harmonious and nice appearance in connection with the brick work. A little terra cotta and nice stone carving, sparingly used with some few bands of moulded brick properly worked in will combine to form an agreeable and consummate whole. The brick work of such fronts as these ought to be laid up with good materials, and the best of pressed brick should be used. White or buff brick can be used to very good advantage and trimmed with red brick, terra cotta and brown stone, would look very nice. Plate glass in the front windows also lend very much to the richness of the whole and a few dollars here spent is money well invested. Cost of such houses are $3,000 to $3,500.

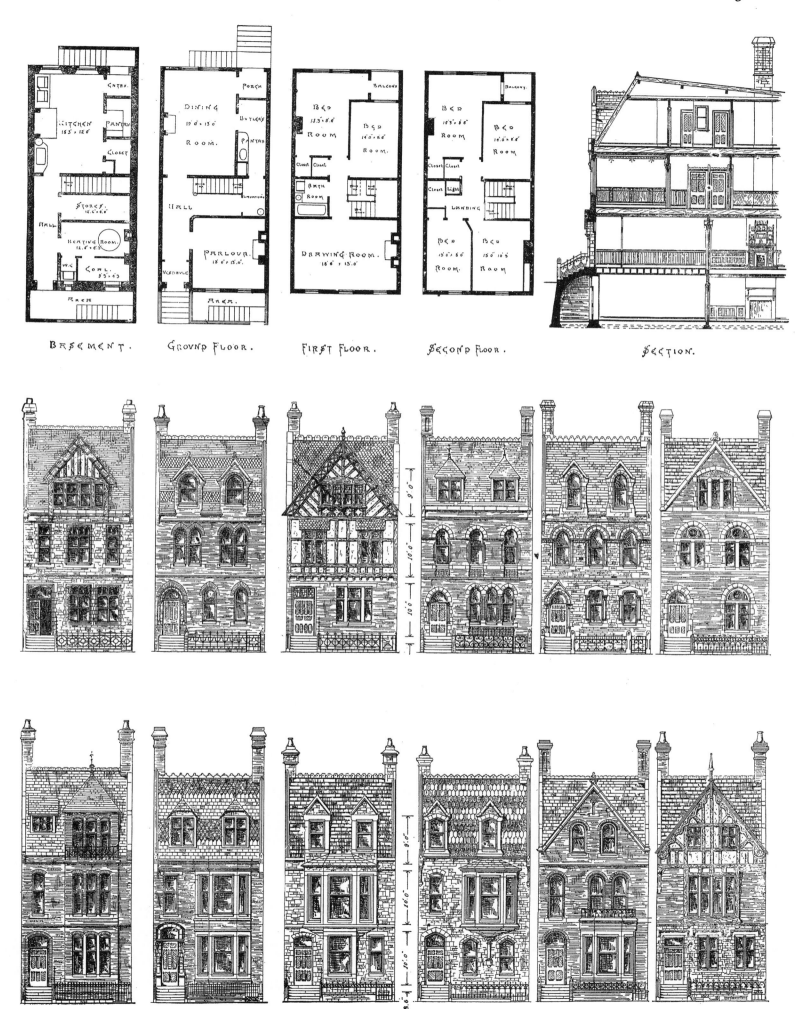

BASEMENT.

GROUND FLOOR.

FIRST FLOOR.

SECOND FLOOR.

SECTION.

Design 121 represents a very solid and artistic-looking house in frame or wood, having a very strong tendency or leaning to the classic features of the renaissance, the details of the front porch and the main gables being particularly good and pleasing, and are such as to be capable of a transplanting process and execution on a house worth several times the cost of this one. This is probably one of the most radical changes of the style so prevalent some few years ago, yet retaining many of the features of that date which can well be utilized even in what we may term these enlightened times. Anything that is good will never die out. It may be passed by and thrown aside for a time to give place to some new innovation which will have its day after which we have time to again look upon and admire the beauties of the classic world. So it is and has been for all time past and to-day we are obliged to admire the elegant and massive proportion of the works executed by the ancients, and which are handed down from generation to generation as examples of the art of architecture never yet surpassed and which are copied and accepted by the best artists as being beyond their improvement in many of their details and fine proportions. The design here shown is fully illustrated by the plans, elevations and details together with the perspective view giving the finished and general effect of the whole when completed and in harmony with its general surroundings. The cellar plan gives a good open cellar and laundry in the part under the kitchen. The first-floor rooms are large and very cosey, well arranged for the comfort and convenience of a small family. The four rooms on second floor give ample sleeping accommodations. The first story is clapboarded, second story shingled with square butt shingles, the panels in gables being finished in plaster and wood; the whole frame is sheathed and covered with paper; the roofs can be either shingle or slate, the latter being somewhat more expensive. The colors we suggest for painting exterior are for first-story, body, a maroon; shingle work of second story, terra cotta red; the panels in gables, etc., orange red; and the trimmings throughout, bronze green; the carved work on cornices, etc., being brought out with chrome yellow; window sash white and the outside blinds green of a lighter shade than the trimmings. The cost of such a house is $3,000.

Design 122 brings us very forcibly back to the days of our great grandfathers and at once puts us in mind of the times of the revolution. The plan is very conveniently arranged and is a very desirable layout, and would provide ample room for a large family, the style of architecture here illustrated is termed by many, "Old Colonial," with the large stone chimneys built on the exterior walls, up which the ivy vine could be trained to good advantage; and the other quaint features here shown we think the aesthetically inclined will in this design find something worth studying. Such a house as this will harmonize finely with nature and properly placed on a suitable site with rocks, trees, and perhaps a running brook to blend in with it, and about two or three acres of nice ground of an uneven nature, nicely undulating, is a home fit for a prince to live in, and the cost is $5,000.

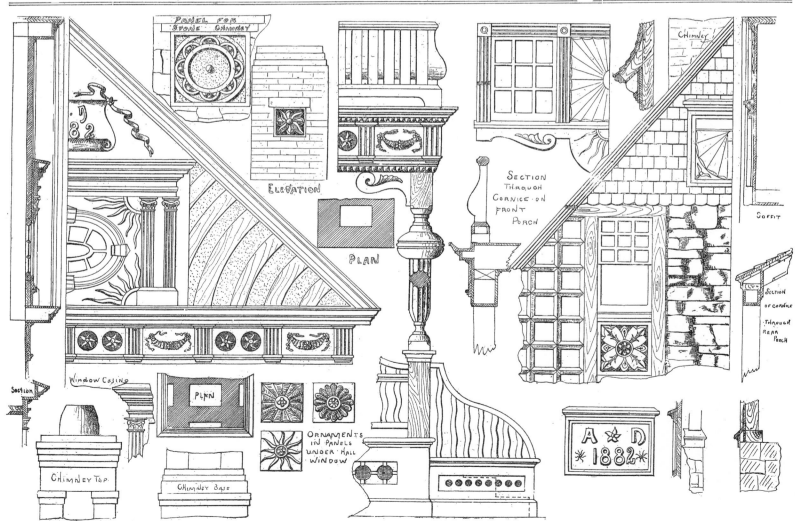

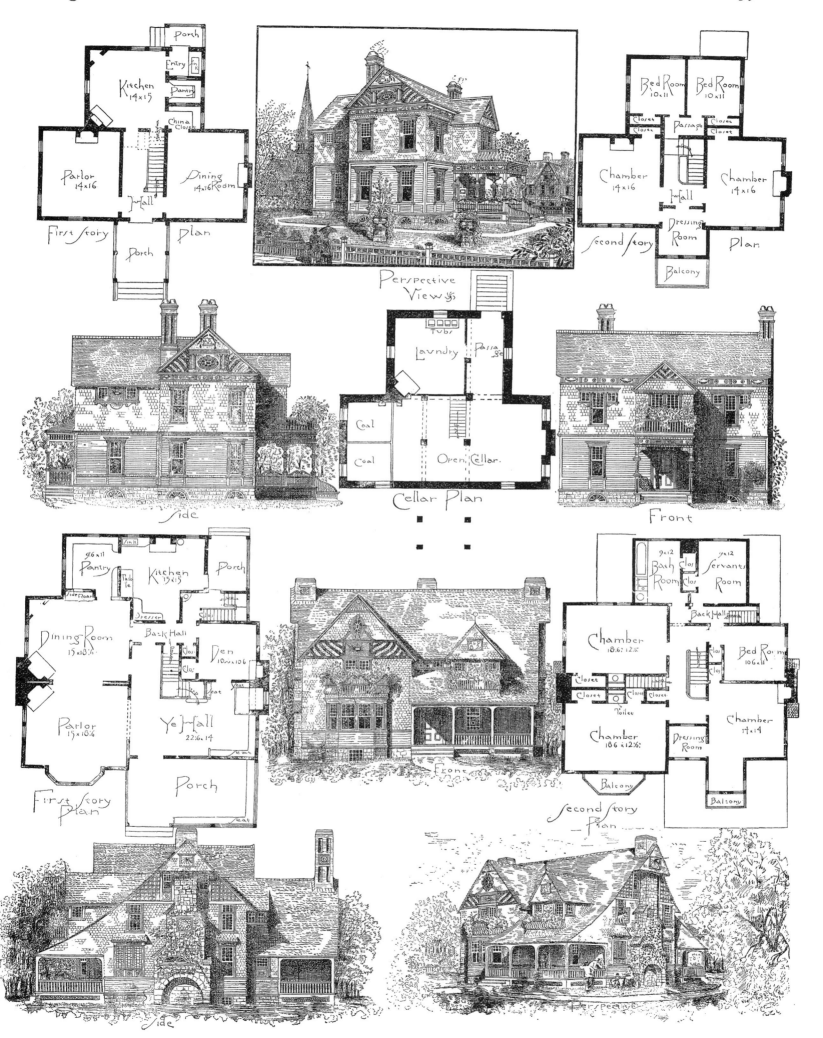

Porch

Kitchen
14x15

Entry   Sink

Pantry

China
Closet

Parlor
14x16

Dining
Room
14x16

Hall

First Story   Plan

Porch

Perspective
Views

Tubs

Laundry   Passage

Coal

Coal   Open Cellar.

Cellar Plan

Bed Room
10x11   Bed Room
10x11

Closet   Passage   Closet
Closet   Closet

Chamber
14x16   Chamber
14x16

Hall

Dressing
Room

Second Story   Plan

Balcony

Side

Front

9x12
Pantry   Kitchen
15x15   Porch

Side Board

Table

Dresser

Back Hall

Dining Room
15x18:6   Closet   Den
10x10.6

Seat   Seat

Parlor
15x18:6   Ye Hall
22:6.14

Porch

First Story
Plan

Seat

9x12
Bath
Room
Clo.   9x12
Servants
Room
Clo.

Back Hall

Chamber
18.6:12:6   Bed Room
10.6x11

Closet   Closet   Closet
Closet   Closet   Closet

Toilet

Chamber
18.6x12:6   Dressing
Room   Chamber
14x14

Second Story
Plan

Balcony

Balcony

Front

Side

Perspective

Design 123 shows a very pleasant and nicely planned house of seven rooms—four on the first and three on the second floor—all well laid out and as convenient as they can be considering the amount of money it costs to build. The external appearance is very tasty and desirable. This design is well adapted to a suburban lot 50 feet front, and is well suited to a family of taste and refinement. A bath-room can be easily worked in on the second story at an added cost of about $250. With a neat painted finish internally and the cellar under the whole house, we have had such houses built for inside $2,100, still there are localities in our knowledge where it would require as much as $2,800 to build.

Design 124 gives a first-floor plan and front elevation of a very nice little one-story cottage, giving four nice rooms well adapted to the wants of a small family. Such a home as this is worth about $550 to build it, and would fill the wants of a large class of people who want to own their own home, no matter how small it may be.

Design 125 shows a very roomy plan which is well suited to the wants of a large and growing family. The dining-room is large and would be the general living part of the house, the whole arrangement of rooms and conveniences in connection therewith being specially happy in their relation to each other and the exterior giving a suitable covering to the whole; this house should have a cellar under with a stone wall well laid in mortar and neatly pointed. On exposed surfaces a well-sheathed frame papered before the finish is applied, and a good shingle roof. It will make a warm, comfortable house at a cost of about $2,800.

Design 126 is a one-and-a-half story six-room cottage, very

simple and economical in its appointments and yet of considerable pretension to artistic effect which is obtained in a very legitimate way and not by any expensive means. The layout of the rooms is good and in every way suited to the house and its style. No waste room; but every inch of room counts towards the strictest economy and comfort of the family to be sheltered. The cost of such a cottage as this does not exceed $900 to $1,000, including cellar, cistern, pump, sink and proper drainage. As to what constitutes the latter a large book might be written and then justice not be done to the subject. The circumstances vary so much with different locations and sites that a special treatment is very necessary to suit each individual case. On some grounds where not built up thickly and with a gravelly bottom, a leaching cesspool placed fifty to seventy-five feet from the house might safely be used with a four or six-inch pipe running from the house to it. All pipes in the house ought to be of iron and to a distance of three to six feet outside where the iron pipe connects to the earthen tile in the ground. A running trap and fresh-air inlet on the house side of the trap ought to be connected and the iron waste pipe run up through the house and out two or three feet above the roof, and be there capped with a neat galvanized iron ventilator. All the plumbing fixtures should be trapped with the most approved anti-siphon traps, or if ordinary traps are used they should be ventilated from top of same and connection made from the vent pipes into the iron wastes, care being taken to make them well above the highest waste connection. This would prevent all bad effects from the traps, and if the work was properly done with good materials would make a first-class sanitary job and be practically safe.

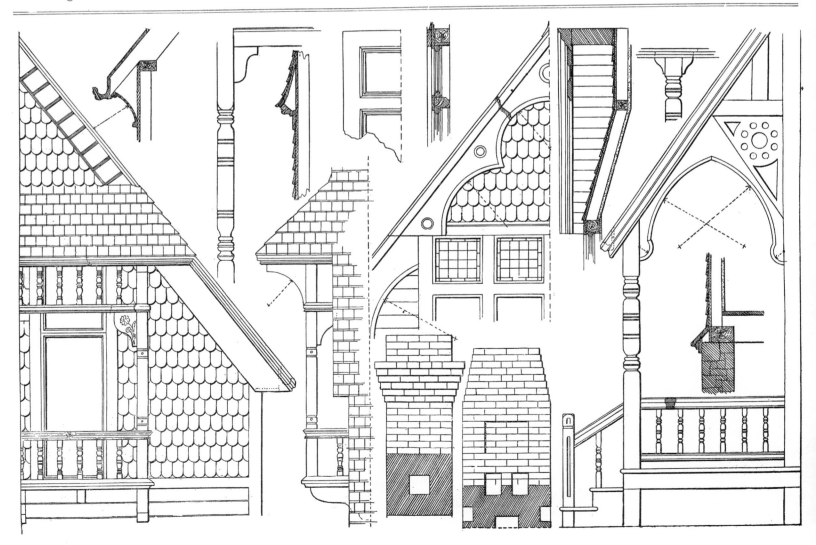

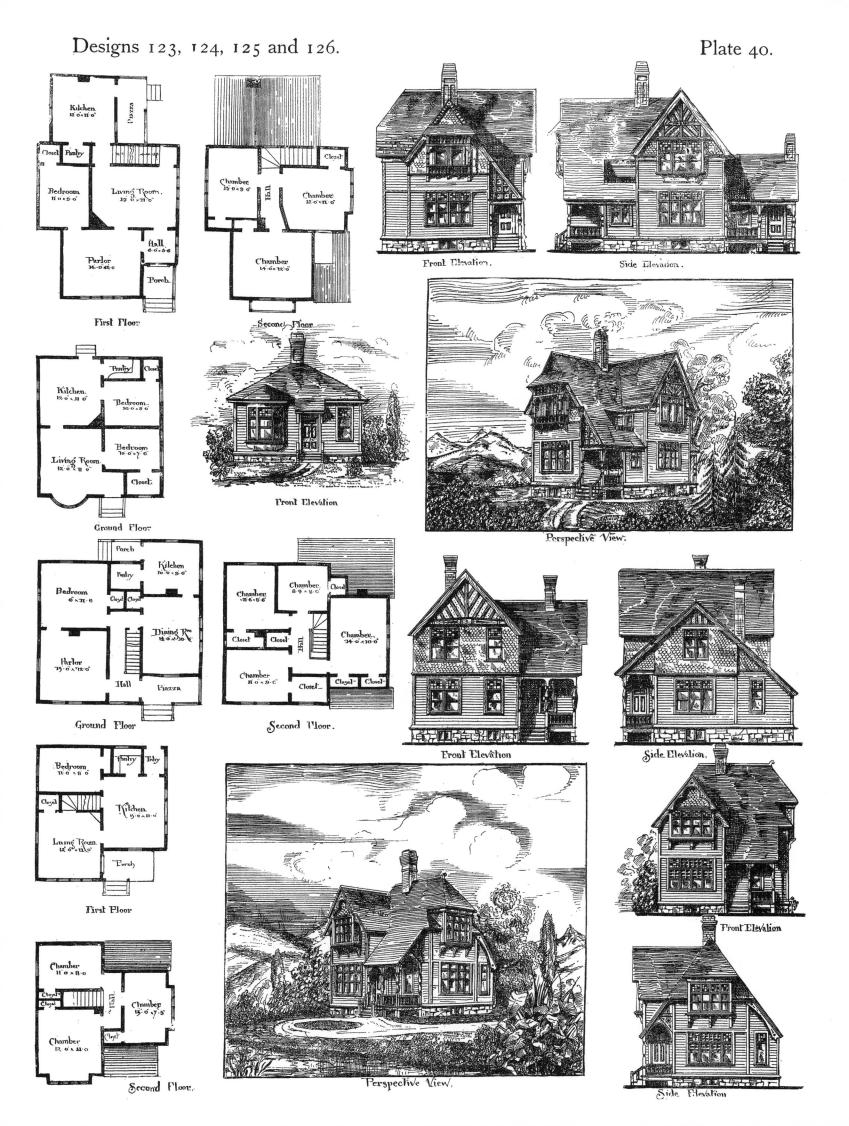

First Floor

Second Floor

Front Elevation.

Side Elevation.

Ground Floor

Front Elevation

Perspective View.

Ground Floor

Second Floor.

Front Elevation

Side Elevation.

First Floor

Perspective View.

Front Elevation

Second Floor.

Side Elevation

Design 127 shows plans and elevations of a well-arranged eight-room two-story cottage, which is designed in the popular style often called Queen Anne. This house is very suggestive for a country home where fair sized rooms and comfort are looked for more than style in the largeness of halls and general internal beauties that are so largely made for show. The perspective view here shown gives a very good idea of the external appearance of the house when erected, and shows the advantage of having a view of this kind, in connection with the plans and elevations, as it enables those who are not at all versed in plans, and who cannot tell what a geometrical elevation will look like when built, to know and study the appearance to their full benefit and satisfaction. The house here shown, in cost, is about $3,000, varying somewhat as to location and general management displayed.

Design 128 illustrates a square one and a half-story cottage, with quite a picturesque exterior, giving four good rooms on a floor and very simple and economical in plan. To many people needing a home, room is the first consideration, and the second item the cost; and to accomplish the one within the compass of the other is often a very hard and difficult problem to solve, and although it is often apparently an impossibility for the architect to bring the two extremes together, and make the minimum of cost cover the maximum of room, still the only way to do is to persevere and not aim too high, nor be too particular about the building of a monument to one's own skill, but to produce one based on the ability of the client to pay, and the room needed. If this is safely done the result is invariably satisfactory, and the client made happy; and when the architect has so far succeeded as to do this his own peace of mind, cannot help but prove right as a duty faithfully done and conscientiously executed to the satisfaction of all concerned, is one of the most agreeable things that can be worked for, and makes life pass pleasantly and smooth. Tis, alas, only too true that often the architect is hampered to a great extent by the unreasonableness of his client, in which case it is far better to quarrel outright, and get through with each other as soon as the trouble is found out, unless the client can be brought to a realization of his error. We have known many of these cases, and have had one or two instances in our own practice in one case we were plain, and told the client we were positive we would not be able to suit him, and we preferred him to settle for what we had done, and get some one else. He did so, much to our great relief; and, as he found out afterwards, much to his great disappointment. It so happening that we had two clients who built one on each side of him; the one house we designed in stone and brick for first story and wood above, which was built at a cost of $9,000; the other was all frame, a very fine house in every respect, and was built at a cost of $5,000. Both of these houses were large and roomy, and had the front door in the centre of fronts, had each five rooms on the first story, with halls 9 feet wide (between) and elegantly finished inside, while the house built by our former client had a narrow front, only one room to the street, not as much room in it or nearly so well arranged as the less expensive one planned by us; back stairs dark and no light on them; bath-room built over a porch so as to freeze up every winter, which has not failed to happen, we have been informed, and the whole house is pointed out as one of the most expensive houses of its size, and the most illy-contrived possible, and looks like an ordinary $4,000 house, while in reality it cost the most of the three, and is to-day a standing advertisement of the difference in the abilities of the architects employed, and the way the clients co-operated with them. A unity of purpose between architect and client is necessary to success in such cases.

Front Door

Water Table

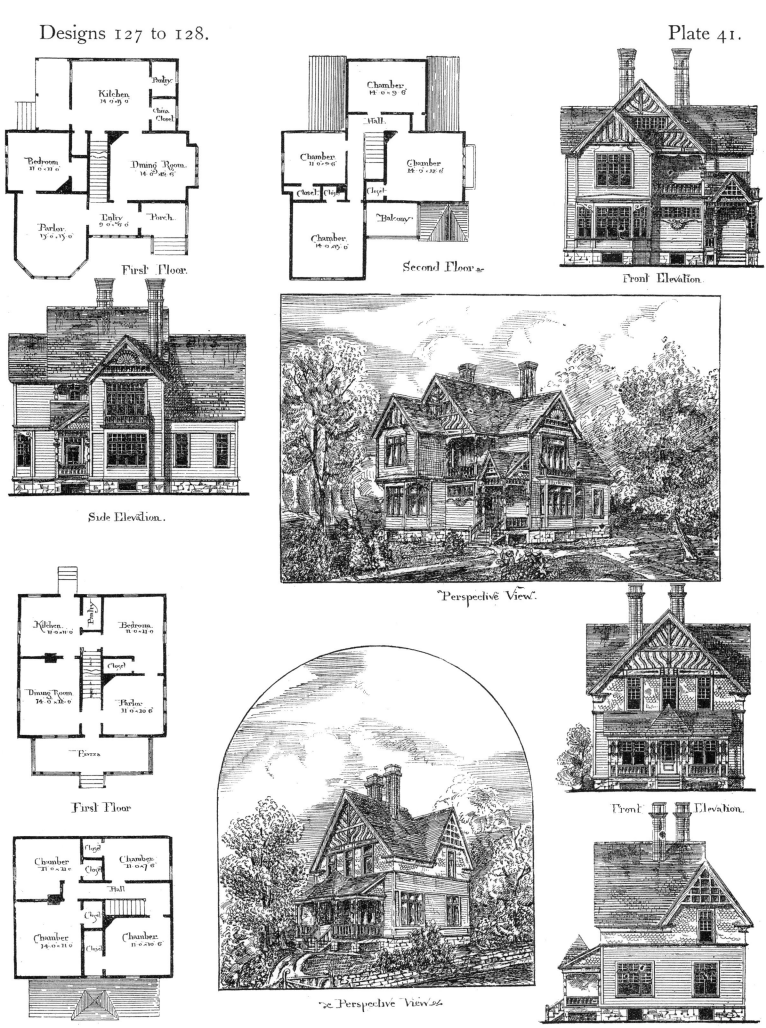

Kitchen
14-0×13-0

Pantry

China Closet

Bedroom
11-0×11-0

Dining Room
14-0×12-6

Parlor
15-0×15-0

Entry
9-0×6-0

Porch

First Floor.

Chamber
14-0×9-6

Hall

Chamber
11-0×9-6

Chamber
14-0×12-6

Closet Closet

Closet

Balcony

Chamber
14-0×13-0

Second Floor

Front Elevation.

Side Elevation.

Perspective View.

Kitchen
11-0×11-0

Pantry

Bedroom
11-0×11-0

Dining Room
14-0×13-0

Closet

Parlor
11-0×20-6

Piazza

First Floor

Chamber
11-0×11-0

Closet

Chamber
11-0×7-6

Closet

Hall

Chamber
14-0×11-0

Closet

Chamber
11-0×20-6

Second Floor

Perspective View.

Front Elevation.

Side Elevation

PLATE 42.

Design 129 gives full plans and details of a very good country house, which is well laid-out and in every way suitable for a first-class and permanent residence. The main hall is very large and the stairs being placed well back from the front door, makes a very spacious inner-room, from which the other rooms open. This is well lighted by the stained-glass windows on the stairs, which shed a mellow and subdued light throughout the halls of first and second floors. A very good vestibule is arranged, also well lighted by stained-glass windows on sides and transoms over the doors. This would give ample room on one side for an umbrella stand and a seat on the other. The hall is also a good shape for furnishing both economically and artistically. The sitting-room and parlor at left of hall are well arranged. The alcove in sitting-room is a very pretty feature, giving a nice opportunity in furnishing as well as helping the outlook from the room. The portiere across the partition between the two rooms is, in this case, undoubtedly preferable to the ordinary sliding doors—saves room and is more economical and convenient, as the two rooms will be largely used as one or together. The dining-room is nice in shape and size; fire-place being in the corner, is entirely out of the way, and the sideboard is placed to good advantage, being recessed in the front wall and having a small window filled with art glass through the centre, makes a very effective as well as a useful article of furniture in the room. To build a sideboard in the dining-room of a first-class house is the proper thing to do, and in scores of cases we have done this within the last few years, always designing the sideboards with a special reference to the requirements of the room and in harmony with the mantel pieces, and other trimmings showing in connection therewith. A sideboard recessed into the wall does not interfere with the room, and frequently two feet can be saved in the width or length of a room by this method. The kitchen pantries and connection from kitchen through butler's pantry to dining-room are admirably laid out; pantries are large and well fitted for the purposes

intended. The kitchen range comes directly under the bath-room, and the pipes to latter come in very nicely where there are the least amount of them and not liable to freeze up or cause trouble. The back stairs are very nicely situated, going up directly from the kitchen and down from the entry-way between front hall and kitchen. This is a good feature, as it enables anyone in the house to pass down to the cellar without disturbing the privacy of the kitchen, a feature that is very often appreciated by the members of a household who have the welfare of the family at heart. The washbowl under the stairs in main hall is convenient for general toilet purposes. The second story gives four good chambers, six closets, bath and dressing-rooms, and the front stairway runs on up to the attic, where there is ample room to finish four or five good rooms, if required. The cellar would contain laundry with stationary wash-tubs, furnace and fuel room, store and cold cellar, and is about seven and a half feet high, walls built of good stone and the bottom well cemented; the furnace large enough to heat the whole house without any forcing, as a large furnace run with ease at a slow-going fire is much more effective and economical than a smaller one, that has to be forced to do the work required of it. For the internal finish of this design we suggest, oak for front hall, stairs, etc.; ash or birch for dining-room; cherry for sitting-room and parlor; the floors of hall and dining-room of oak with a neat cherry strip for border; the kitchen part of yellow pine, and other parts of white pine, all filled and finished on the wood. For the exterior finish the design shows clearly what is best—chimneys of good red brick in red mortar (fire-places laid up in pressed brick and trimmed with tile and brass on facings), first story painted maroon for body, second story red and third story orange yellow, trimmed throughout with bronze green; the roofs brown, window sash white and blinds green is a very happy combination. The cost of this we place at $6,500, varying with location, etc.

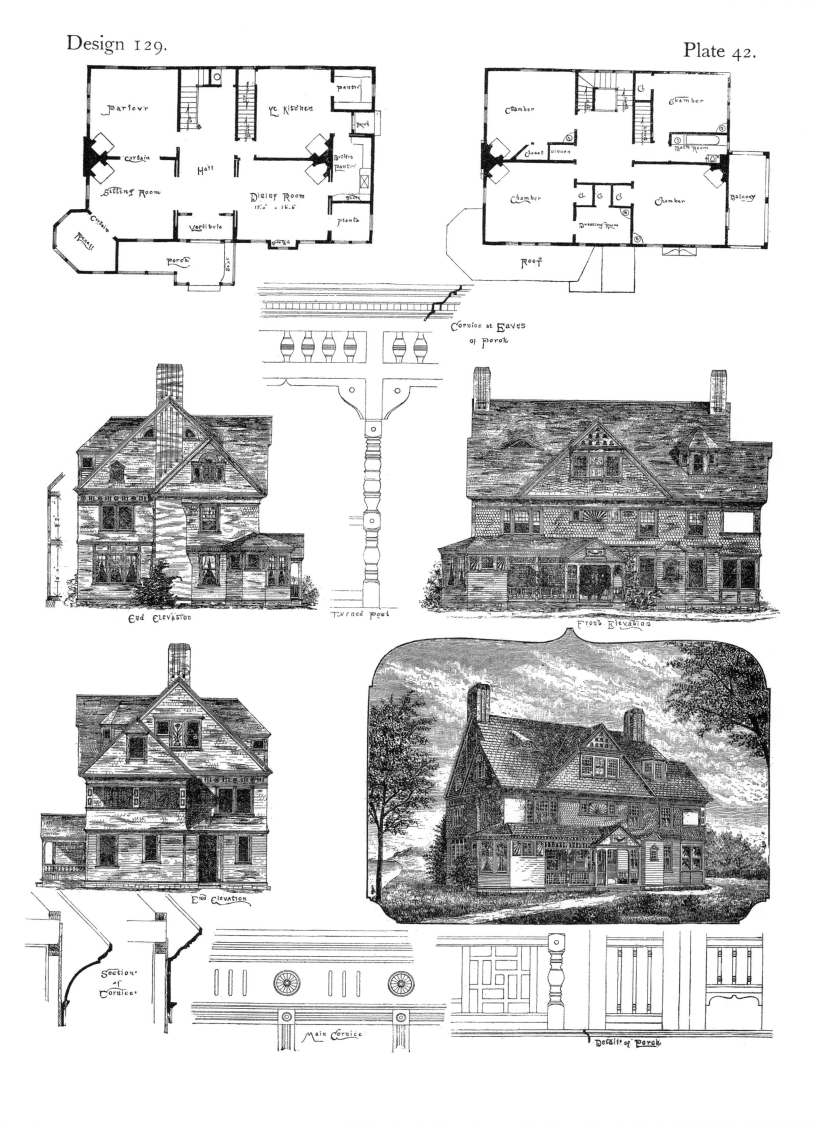

Parlour

Ye Kitchen

Pantry

Curtain

Porch

Hall

Butlers
Pantry

Sitting Room

Dining Room
15'0" × 16'6"

Curtain

Recess

Vestibule

Shed

Plazza

Porch

Chamber

Chamber

Closet

Linnen

Bath Room

Chamber

Chamber

Balcony

Dressing Room

Roof

Cornice at Eaves
of Porch

End Elevation

Turned Post

Front Elevation

End Elevation

Section
of Cornice

Main Cornice

Detail of Porch

Design 130 gives a plan of a very roomy, well arranged house, which would suit a great many people living in the country who are not in the habit of having their work, etc., done by hired help. A very good plan for a farm house, and has some good features both in plan and exterior design that cannot help but fall into play at times. That there is very great diversity of opinion on the question of house planning, and what suits one man and is his meat is very apt to be poison to the next one who comes along cannot be denied; that our aim has been to meet this diversified opinion, and that we have fairly succeeded we shall leave to the reader to judge, hoping that said reader will be one of the many who will profit by our endeavors to meet the wants of such a large class as the designs and ideas as illustrated in this work are intended for. The plan here shown has no waste room, every part being well utilized for the rooms; the stairs are simple box stairs about 3 feet, 4 inches wide, and are very well located so as to get upstairs from the kitchen and dining-room as well as from the entry at their foot from outside, while the cellar is reached from the passageway which answers as a press or But-ler's pantry between the dining-room and kitchen. The kitchen pan-try is large and nicely located, well away from the heat of the range. This is an important feature in a house of this kind, a large cool room for the proper storage of the kitchen crockery, eatables and such articles as must always be kept within reach of the careful housekeeper, the sliding sash connection from pantry to passageway is so fixed as to save many steps, a feature that every house wife will appreciate. The plan of the three rooms on first floor being such as to throw them into one room by opening the sliding doors, gives ample room for the social element of the household, and furnishes the necessary space for any entertainment the young folks may have on hand; a provision very much overlooked in the planning of many country houses, although one that tends in no small extent to the general pleasure and great enjoyment in many farming districts where it is the custom to have pleasant social times amongst them-selves at their residences. Certainly this is a feature that can be cultivated in all country neighborhoods to the mutual advantage of all concerned. Such a house is capable of many changes, and will no doubt serve as a key note to many as to what are their needs, and thus assist them by the many suggestions gleaned from it. Such a house ought to have a cellar under the whole of it, and be built at a cost of about $2,750 in any favorable locality.

Design 131 illustrates a very cosey and comfortable cottage, very good in its appointments, and withall very suitable for erection as a neat and attractive country home. The elevations are low; still the rooms on second floor are desirable, being cut on external sides only about one-third the height of walls. The large hall and main stairs therein, also the addition of a fire-place, makes this a fine sit-ting room, and connecting as it does with parlor and dining-room, and the latter joining together with sliding doors, is very desirable. The drive-porch is a feature that in many houses of this size would not be necessary, still there are many instances where it could be utilized to very good advantage, the location and the family wants of those occupying being the guide. This house costs, to erect complete, with neat finish and shingle roof, $2,300. The details of this plate are very suggestive as to chimney-tops, gable-porch and balcony finish.

Blessed is the man who owns a home.

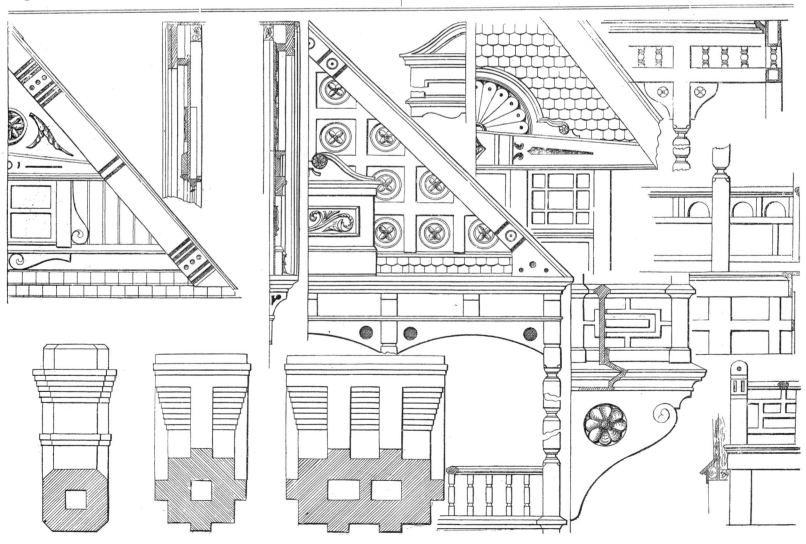

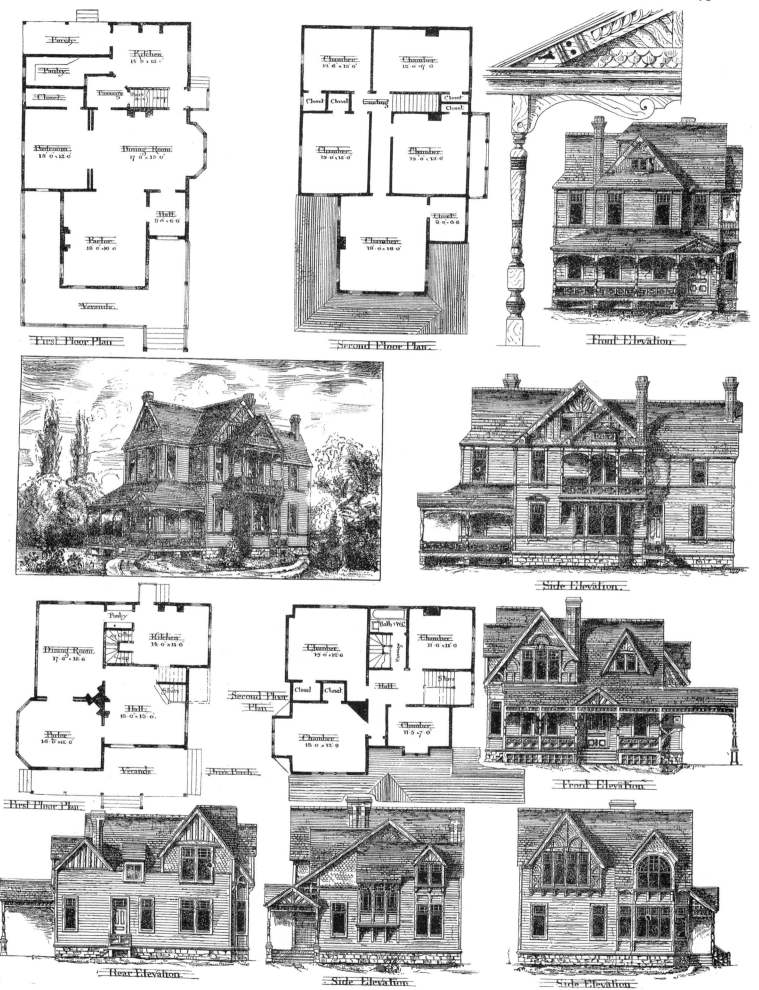

Designs 130 and 131.

Plate 43.

Porch

Kitchen
15·0 × 12·0

Pantry

Closet

Passage
5

Stair Way

Bedroom
15·0 × 12·0

Dining Room
17·6 × 15·0

Hall
8·0 × 6·6

Parlor
18·0 × 16·0

Veranda

First Floor Plan

Chamber
12·6 × 12·0

Chamber
12·0 × 7·6

Closet Closet

Landing

Closet

Closet

Chamber
15·0 × 12·6

Chamber
15·0 × 12·6

Closet
9·0 × 6·6

Chamber
18·6 × 16·0

Second Floor Plan

Front Elevation

Side Elevation.

Pantry

Office

Kitchen
14·0 × 11·6

Dining Room
17·6 × 12·6

Stair

Hall
15·0 × 15·0

Parlor
16·0 × 12·0

Veranda

Drive Porch

First Floor Plan

Bath & W.C.

Chamber
15·0 × 12·6

Chamber
11·6 × 11·6

Closet Closet

Passage

Hall

Stairs

Chamber
15·0 × 12·9

Chamber
11·3 × 7·6

Second Floor
Plan

Front Elevation

Rear Elevation

Side Elevation

Side Elevation

Design 132 gives a type of suburban cottage well adapted for erection on a fifty foot lot and excellently suited to the wants of the thrifty and sensible mechanic whose wife will not be above the point where she is willing to contribute her help by a proper and economical care of her own household wants and duties. It should be the duty of every mechanic to strive to own his own home, and undoubtedly a great help to this attainment can be meted out by the prompt and efficient co-operation of the better-half, whose duty it is to help her husband in the saving of his earnings for the common weal of the family. The large kitchen 13x15 feet in size, gives ample room for all domestic living purposes, the dining-room being a better and general sitting-room for family uses, while the parlor gives a nice, cosey room in which the modest parlor organ and neat parlor suite will help smile a sweet welcome to the company of the young folks and in which they can entertain themselves to the full enjoyment and mutual benefit. The five bed-rooms on second story gives ample sleeping accommodations with a sufficient supply of closet-room. A sink, pump and cistern would constitute the full complement of the modern improvements so essential to family wants, and a cellar under the whole house is the right thing in that line. Such a house cost to build it, $2,475.00. The small bedroom could be made into a Bathroom if so desired.

Design 133 gives a large amount of room on first and second floors, with a sensible lay out, well adapted to the needs of a large family. This cottage has a number of good features to commend it—first, an absence of waste room in hallways, the stairs also being accessible from all parts of the house. Very good pantry conveniences and closets on the first floor, nice verandas and good, airy well-lighted rooms. The exterior is a good model, and makes a very pleasing perspective. It is a good plan, and as a whole will no doubt, fit and groove in with the ideas of a great many people. To build such a house the cost is $2,850 in any convenient locality.

Design 134 shows a very pretty cottage, only one and a half stories high, containing six fine rooms, good closets, and is a very handy little home, well suited to any one needing a house of this size. This cottage, as to quantity of materials with which to construct it, is reduced down to a minimum, the detail is very simple, easily constructed and is such that good results emanate from it, both in an artistic and sensible point of view. Such a house would make a pleasant home for the young married couple just starting out in life, and would be capable of enlargement at any time should the family needs require it. Cost of this design to execute, $1,560.

Such houses as are illustrated in this work if erected in the suburbs of our cities would add very much to the value of the ground they stand on and pay a handsome rate of interest on their cost, better than any other class of building investments, as the supply falls far short of the demand. Business men, clerks, mechanics and others wishing to reside out of the city need just such homes as this, and we wonder capitalists and real estate owners do not make money for themselves and others by erecting such tasteful, yet inexpensive, suburban homes.

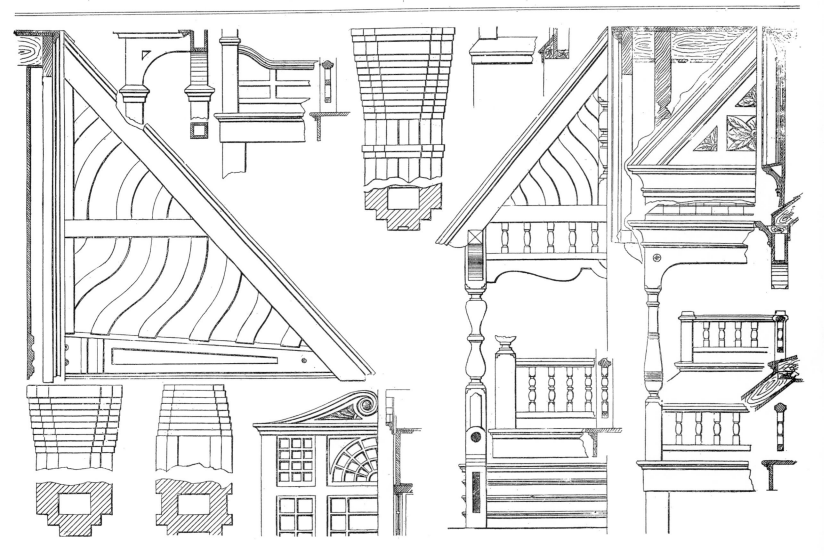

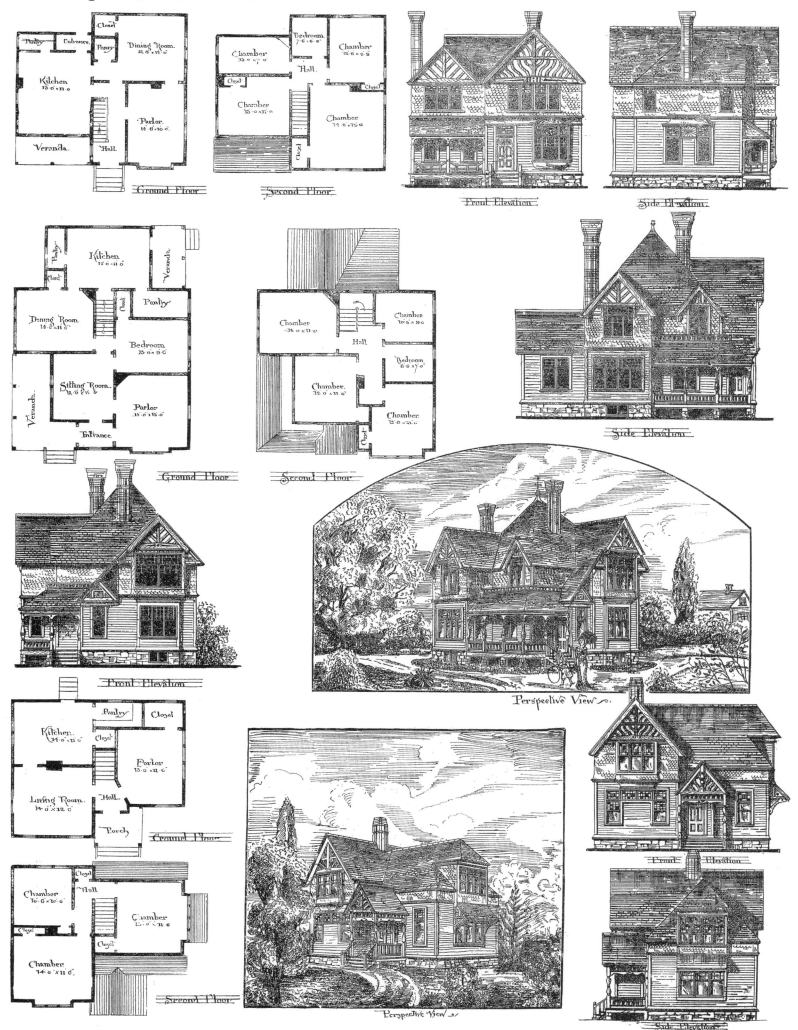

Ground Floor

Second Floor

Front Elevation

Side Elevation

Ground Floor

Second Floor

Side Elevation

Front Elevation

Perspective View

Ground Floor

Second Floor

Perspective View

Front Elevation

Side Elevation

PLATE 45.

Design 135 gives us a house, although in plan of a somewhat ordinary type, and in its many arrangements a commonplace character, yet presenting an exterior and general make-up that is quite artistic and unique in its varied detail. The arrangement of the parlor chimney, placing the same on the outside of the wall and facing the exterior work up with rough stone, makes a very good feature and one that will commend itself as being good in its convenience, thus leaving the parlor a square room without the addition of a large chimney breast to use up a large part of the available space, as is usually the case in houses of this class. The first floor arrangement is particularly good in the disposition of the rooms. The parlor and dining-room being connected with sliding doors makes a roomy and open house and one that would be pleasing and give a fine impression to the visitor upon entering the parlor door. The front veranda is very wide; much more so than the same is usually on ordinary houses. The library is pleasantly situated and is such that it could be used as a bedroom, should it be desirable. The rear hall and stairway gives access to the second floor and cellar as well as provides a closet—a very great convenience—in which to hang wet wraps, leave one's overshoes, umbrella, etc., and which might be provided in every house of any pretension to very good advantage. The kitchen, pantry and closet arrangements are good and desirable and well suited to the domestic family wants of the inmates to be sheltered. The second story gives four roomy bed-rooms, two dressing-rooms, bath-room, large linen closet and a good closet in every room. There is also ample room to finish three or four rooms in attic which would be desirable. This house should have a furnace to heat it, a brick set range in kitchen and ought not to cost over $4,300.

During the past ten years, P. T. Barnum, the greatest and most successful showman on earth, has erected large numbers of cottage homes from our plans. In this respect he has done a great deal toward helping along the improvement of the town of Bridgeport, Conn., where he makes his home. His ideas were always carried out with a view to making money, he would acquire large tracts of land at low figures, lay the same out into lots and displayed originality of mind by the method of bringing his lots into market. Some of the lots were thought to be inferior in value to the rest. On these he caused houses to be built, relying on an old idea which some men entertain who prefer to buy a house ready built than build for themselves.

> "He who builds a house
> Pays for every pin;
> He who buys one ready built
> Gets the pins thrown in."

He sold part of his grounds to such buyers as wished to become immediate owners of house and lot. Other lots found ready purchasers at constantly advancing prices.

P. T. Barnum has become a wealthy man, making much money out of his real estate and building operations, and at the same time has benefited hundreds of other people.

Every town and city of consequence presents like opportunities for the land speculator to put up tasty, well-built homes and bring his ground into market at a handsome profit.

Design 136 is an admirable design for a suburban residence, with a sensible plan, well suited for a small family. In external finish this house presents a very quaint and old-time look; still, with a new, fresh and inspiring temper. Old-time houses of fifty or seventy years ago were built far better than many of their more modern prototypes, as evidenced by their ability to stand the test of time. Still, it is possible to do as good work to-day as then, as we have better facilities now to do it and do it well; the difference in cost between a good and poor job is never over five to ten per cent., and frequently at the same price, the difference lying very often in the selection of a builder. Get a good builder, by all means, pay a reasonable price, and then you get a good job. Such a house as this can be erected for about $2,000.

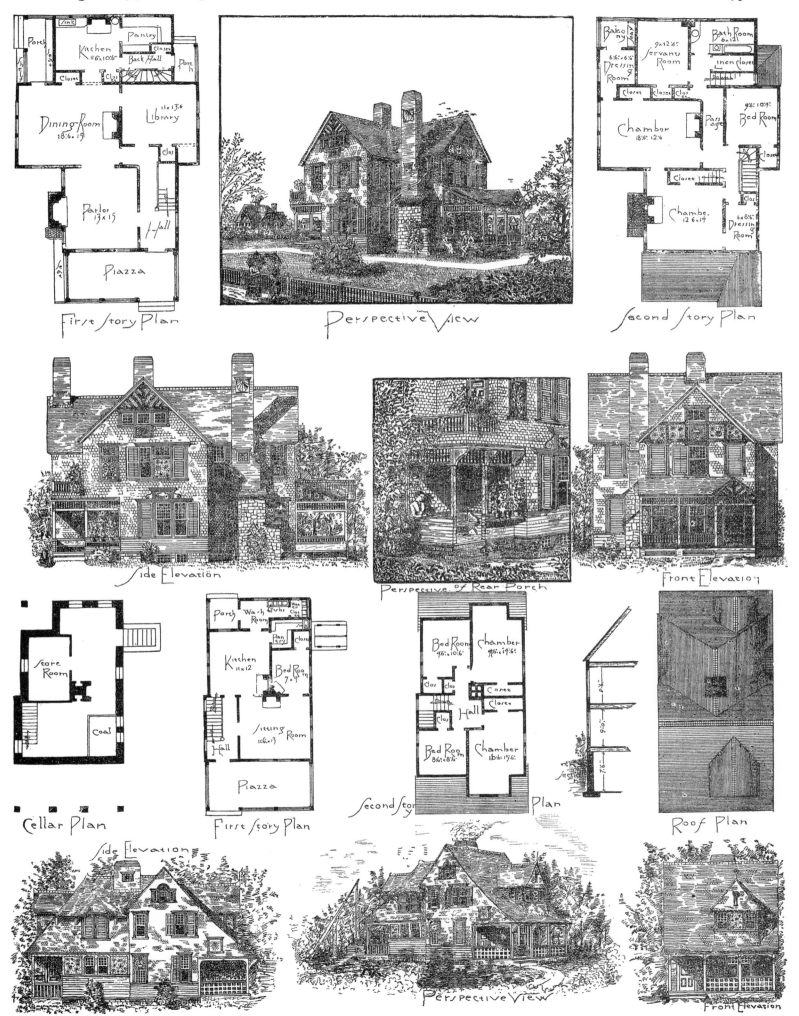

First Story Plan

Porch
Kitchen 11.6 x 10.6
Pantry
Closet
Back Hall
Porch
Seat
Closet
Clos
Dining Room 18.6 x 15
Library 11 x 13.6
Clos
Parlor 13 x 15
Hall
Piazza

Perspective View

Second Story Plan

Balcony
6.6 x 6.6 Dressing Room
9 x 12.6 Servants Room
Bath Room 6 x 12
Linen Closet
Closet Closet Clos
Chamber 18.6 x 12.6
Passage
Bed Room 9.6 x 10.9
Closet
Closet
Chamber 12.6 x 14
Clos
6 x 8.6 Dressing Room

Side Elevation

Perspective of Rear Porch

Front Elevation

Cellar Plan

Store Room
Coal

First Story Plan

Porch
Wash Room
Tubs Clos
Pantry Closet
Kitchen 11 x 12
Bed Room 7 x 9
Hall
Sitting Room 16.6 x 13
Hall
Piazza

Second Story Plan

Bed Room 9.6 x 10.6
Chamber 9.6 x 14.6
Clos Clos
Closet
Closet
Clos Hall
Bed Room 8.6 x 8.6
Chamber 16.6 x 15.6

Section

Roof Plan

Side Elevation

Perspective View

Front Elevation

Design 137 gives us a house that, no doubt, will fill the eye of a great many people. In looking over a book of designs like this, no doubt the reader will find something he would like; but the reader will please remember that it is easier to build castles in the air than in reality, and to the man who contemplates the erection of a home there is some sensible thinking to be done, and it does not do to theorize too much; but he must carefully count the cost, and then count the room to come within this limit of cost. All architects will agree that the greatest bane of their professional labors is brought about by the adverse wills of their clients, who, after they have delivered themselves and their minds by giving the information as to their limit of cost, then go on and specify the size and number of rooms they must have, and the many things that are indispensable to their existence in the structure to be erected, until they have gone two or three times over their limit, and still they won't cut down, but insist the architect must and can give them what they ask for at their price. Verily it is no wonder that architects seldom live to be old. This design is a model of its class and in every way a sensible, roomy house, well adapted to a large family who may be happily enough fixed to live in luxury and such ease as a house of this style warrants. The rooms on first floor are of a nice size and so connected together as to open up practically into one. The entrance hall is very nicely arranged, the recessed fire-place under stairs, fully illustrated in section, through hall being a pleasant feature, giving an air of warmth and welcome to those entering which could not fail but be cheerful. The roomy conservatory on the rear connecting the sitting-room or parlor, is a good and pleasing arrangement. Second floor is well planned for good chambers, closets and bath-room. The back stairs extending to attic gives access to four or five good rooms on that floor, and good storage attic-room. Cellar walls of stone, first story of brick—second story shingled, gives an external variety of construction very desirable. A good heating apparatus, a slate roof, good plumbing and hard wood finish on the first floor would be appropriate and bring the cost of such a structure up to about $7,500, this amount being varied by finish, location and general management.

Design 138 gives us a very attractive cottage of one and a half stories in height, which in arrangement of plan is capable of furnishing many good suggestions. The children's play-room on ground level, reached from back hall, is a nice idea and utilizes this space under the conservatory which is on a level with stair platform, half way between first and second story to very good advantage, this location for the conservatory being very desirable. The external design of this cottage is pleasing and of such a unique character as to meet the ideas of those wanting a small house of an artistic order, the style being such that will wear and grow upon those seeing it the most. The sides of first story are paneled and clapboarded, second story shingled and the roofs could be covered with shingles painted red and very effective. Should it be desirable to enlarge or get more room, the plan is capable of changes to meet this end. To execute it about as shown, with the necessary conveniences, the cost is $3,750.

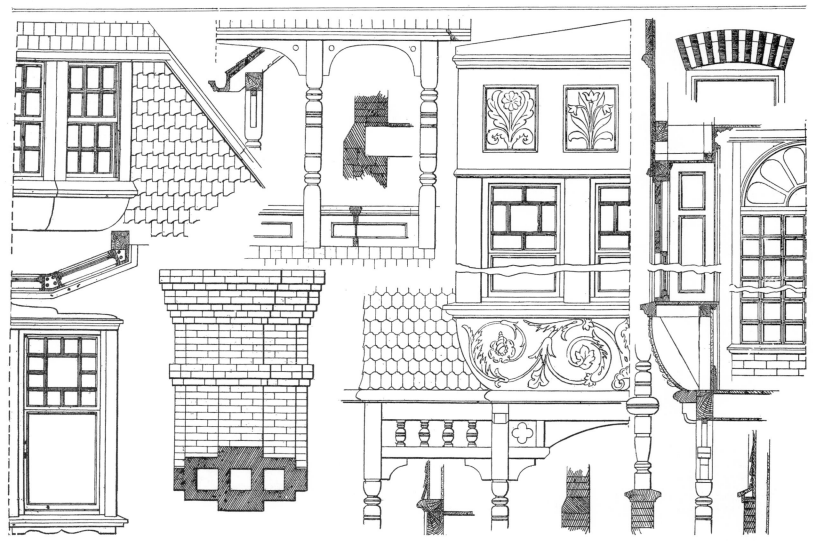

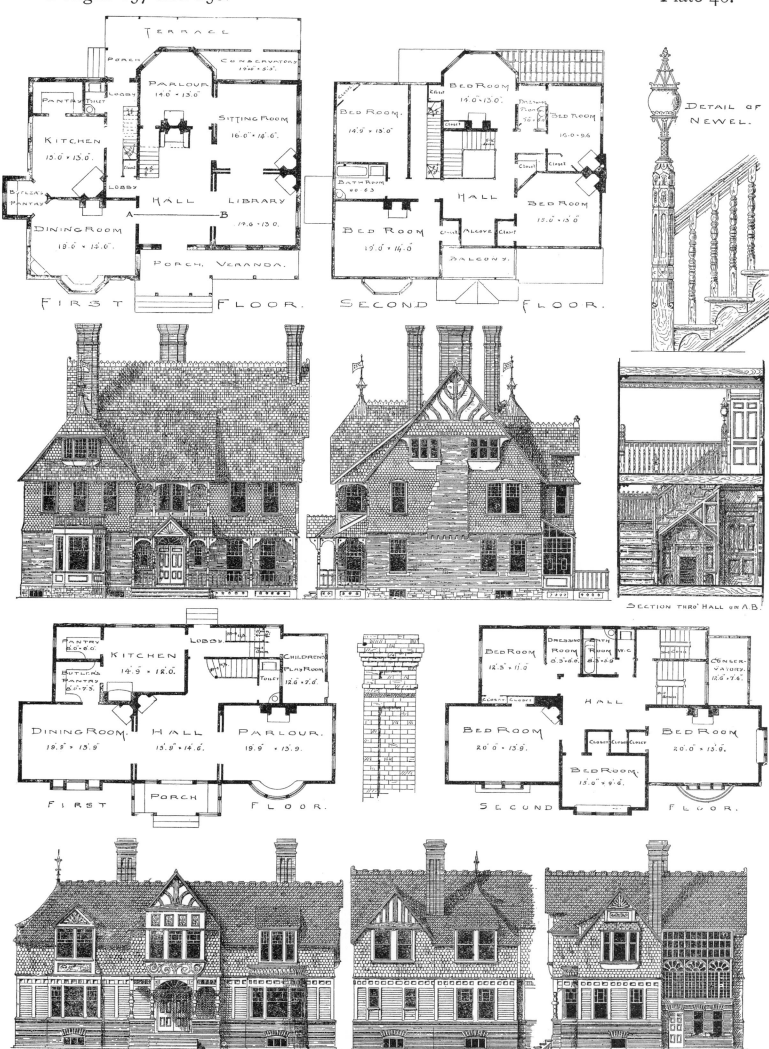

TERRACE

PORCH CONSERVATORY 19'.0" × 5'.3"

PARLOUR 14'.0" × 13'.0"

PANTRY TOILET LOBBY

SITTING ROOM 16'.0" × 14'.6"

KITCHEN 15'.0" × 13'.0"

BUTLER'S PANTRY LOBBY

HALL LIBRARY 14'.6" × 13'.0"

A B

DINING ROOM 19'.0" × 14'.0"

PORCH. VERANDA.

FIRST FLOOR.

BED ROOM 14'.0" × 13'.0"

BED ROOM 14'.9" × 13'.0"

Closet DRESSING ROOM 10'.0" × 5'0"

BED ROOM 16'.0" × 9'.6"

BATH ROOM 10'·63

Closet Closet

HALL

BED ROOM 15'.0" × 13'.0"

BED ROOM 19'.0" × 14'.0"

Closet ALCOVE Closet

BALCONY.

SECOND FLOOR.

DETAIL OF NEWEL.

SECTION THRO' HALL ON A.B.

PANTRY 8'.0" × 6'.0"

LOBBY

KITCHEN 14'.9" × 12'.0"

CHILDREN'S PLAY ROOM 12'.6" × 7'.6"

BUTLER'S PANTRY 8'.0" × 7'.3"

TOILET

DINING ROOM 19'.9" × 13'.9"

HALL 15'.9" × 14'.6"

PARLOUR. 19'.9" × 13'.9"

FIRST PORCH FLOOR.

BED ROOM 12'.3" × 11'.0"

DRESSING ROOM 8'.3" × 6'.0"

BATH ROOM 8'.3" × 5'.9"

W.C.

CONSER- VATORY 12'.6" × 7'.6"

Closet Closet

HALL

BED ROOM 20'.0" × 13'.9"

Closet Closet Closet

BED ROOM 20'.0" × 13'.9"

BED ROOM 15'.0" × 9'.6"

SECOND FLOOR.

Design 139 is a type of house well adapted to suburban erection. The lower story is of brick, and could well be done with four inches of brick work laid up on the outside of the frame work and anchored to same. This method of construction is known as brick veneering, and is a good way of giving a brick appearance with very little material and at little cost, compared with having to build a twelve-inch wall, which would be the ordinary way of doing it. The frame work of second story is covered with shingles. This exterior is very plain and simple, both in detail and construction, yet gives a sensible and pleasing structure, which, when complete and properly painted, would present to the view of the passer-by an appearance that would strike the beholder as being what common sense would naturally apply in the erection of a house of that size. Some one has said you can always know a man by the house he lives in. Still, we do not think this applicable in all cases, though to a very large extent it may be true, as a tasty and artistic mind will generally try and keep his home surroundings in keeping with his artistic ideas, and have it, at least, present a clean and tidy appearance; and nothing embellishes a house at little cost more than a well-arranged front yard and garden. A few flowers and flowering shrubs, and occasionally a group of evergreens, if the grounds are large enough to admit of it, judiciously distributed, and so planted with a view to their best effect from the windows, as well as from the street—these always come in and help out the artistic effect and add to the personal enjoyment and contentment of the inmates of any home. Nature is a great satisfier, and flowers and plants always lead the mind into bright and pleasant channels, no matter how worried or tired one may be. We cannot help but love nature, as displayed in these beautiful things, that come for the season and brighten and cheer our way through life. Such a house as this, with creeping vines climbing and running over the brick work of the first story, always looks well, and is a thing that should be more encouraged and done. We commend this house for its simplicity, and trust that it will be honored for the good there is in it. Cost, $4,800.

Design 140 is a house well adapted for a residence by the seashore or elsewhere, for summer use; gives a liberal amount of piazza accommodation, for living outdoors; and the arrangement of hall through centre of house, with doors from piazza at both ends, and its general arrangement, with the principal rooms all connecting with it, makes the whole living portion of the house, for the purposes it is intended, "a model," and one that any person will be perfectly safe in following after. The locating of the kitchen and its entrance have been carefully studied, so as to make the communication to the other portions of the house perfectly convenient and desirable in every respect and at the same time keep that portion of the house isolated to as great an extent as possible. There is a cellar under the whole house. The rooms are large. Five bed rooms and bath room, with a liberal closet to every room, are provided on second floor, with a linen closet in hall, and the attic gives four sleeping rooms and trunk room. Perfect earth closets, properly ventilated and furnished with simple, mechanical dust-sprinklers, make a perfect sanitary system. A good storage closet on rear piazza is found to be a great convenience for keeping together all the implements connected with the sports of the lawn and field. Cost of construction is $3,000.

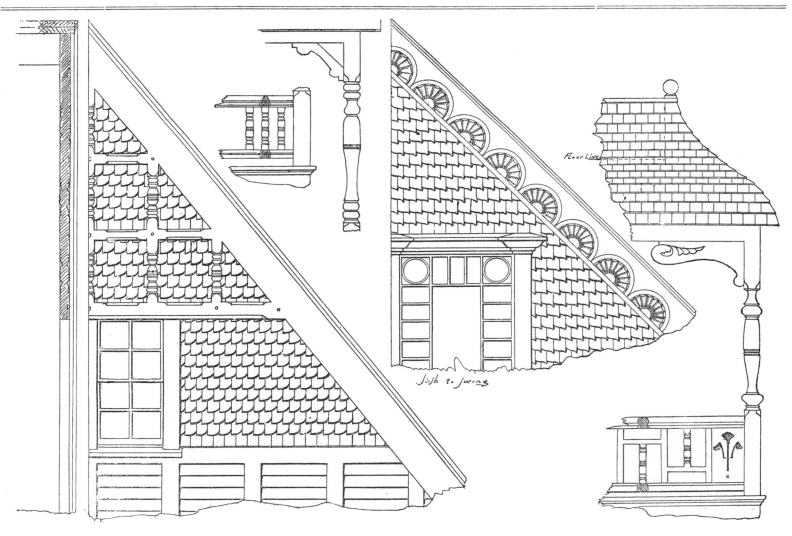

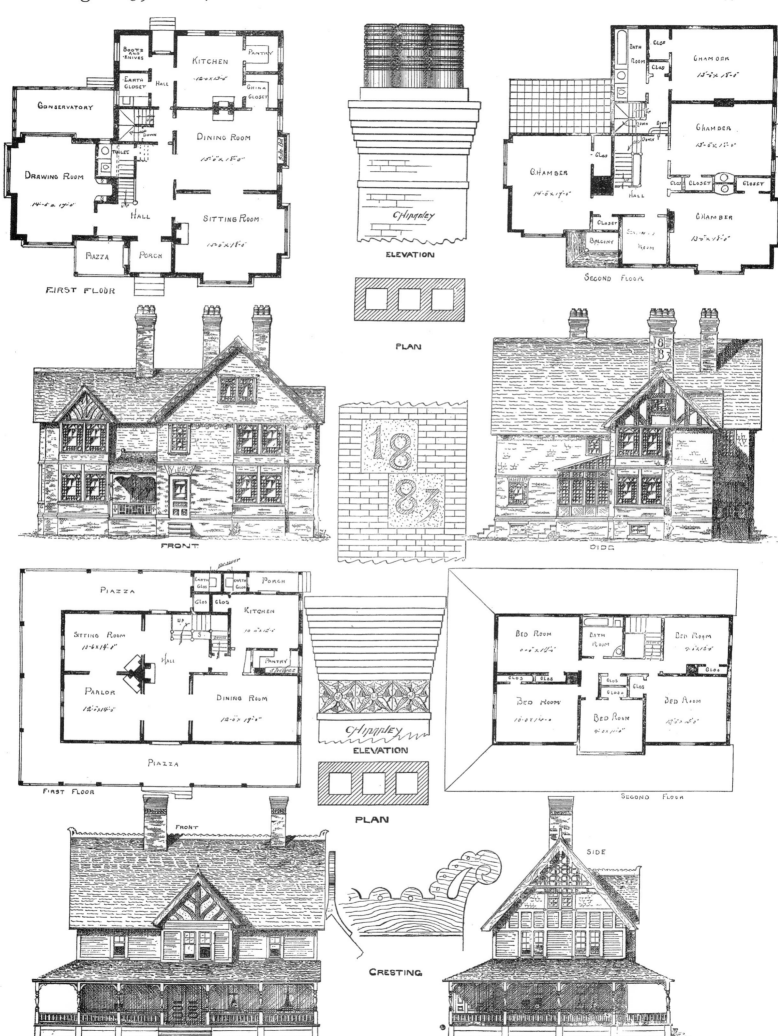

FIRST FLOOR

ELEVATION

PLAN

SECOND FLOOR

FRONT

SIDE

FIRST FLOOR

ELEVATION

PLAN

SECOND FLOOR

FRONT

CRESTING

SIDE

We show on this and the opposite page, illustrations of economical and stylish houses built in pairs. The elevations given fairly represent the fronts and sides of the different structures, except, of course, that the colors are not shown. Of the latter, olive greens, grays and reds predominate, strongly contrasting with each other, and clearly defining the detail; but we do not like to see two persons owning such houses who cannot agree in all matters pertaining to the improvement of their premises, and especially so in regard to colors for painting, and we could name several instances where owners of double houses have actually been very bitter towards one another as to the colors they should adopt, and we have seen one-half of such houses painted white while the other was brown, and the owners and occupants were brothers at that.

The double house is one of the many ways by which it is possible to obtain a large amount of room at a small outlay giving the necessary accommodation for separate families. One lot, one roof, one wall, etc., etc., is made to do the duty of two but unless two persons come together in owning such houses as can agree in all matters, it is better that they should be the property of one man, as then he can live in one-half and rent the other, and do as he pleases with the whole.

We think that these designs cannot fail to please the most fastidious double-house critics and in the New England States there are many of them.

Design 141 gives each family a two-story and attic dwelling with three good liberal rooms and hall, with nice staircase, well lighted on first floor; a pantry and rear entry is also well placed for convenience and economy on this floor. Second floor gives four good bed-rooms, with closets and bath-room, and the attic has two bed-rooms and space for storage. Cellar under the whole house, frame is balloon, sheathed throughout and clapboarded in the main

with ornamental shingle work, shingle roofs; interior finish—first story in natural wood, second story painted. Cost $2,250 each house.

Design 142 has parlor, library, dining-room and kitchen with pantry, toilet-room and hall on first floor; main entrance is through a recessed porch at the side; on second floor are four bed-rooms, sewing-room and bath room; on attic floor three bed-rooms. Underpinning of stone, first story walls of brick, faced with selected brick of even color laid in red mortar; second story, shingled, roof slated. Cost, $3,500.

Design 143 contains on first floor main entrance in front through double doors to the hall, which is 8x16 feet square, containing platform stairs placed well back, and has double doors leading to the parlor; passage to kitchen is through two doors, and from this passage the cellar, laundry and furnace is conveniently reached. Dining-room, pantry and kitchen and the rear entrances as located are especially good in arrangement. There are four good-sized chambers and bath-room, with closets, and also rooms in attic for servants, etc. Cost $3,100.

Design 144 has a good front entrance hall 8x11 feet square, with a flight of box-stairs, well out of the way, ascending to second floor. Parlor and dining-room are large rooms and connected to hall. Cellar stairs are reached from both dining-room and kitchen; a side piazza at end of dining-room which can be closed with glass for conservatory if desired is quite a feature. The second floor gives three good bed-rooms with closets, bath-room and sewing-room and the attic floor has two bed-rooms. Cost, $2,300.

For the suburbs of large towns and cities there can be no better style of houses built than these that will give as good returns on the investment; business men in moderate circumstances need just such homes and they will rent for $30 to $50 a month easily.

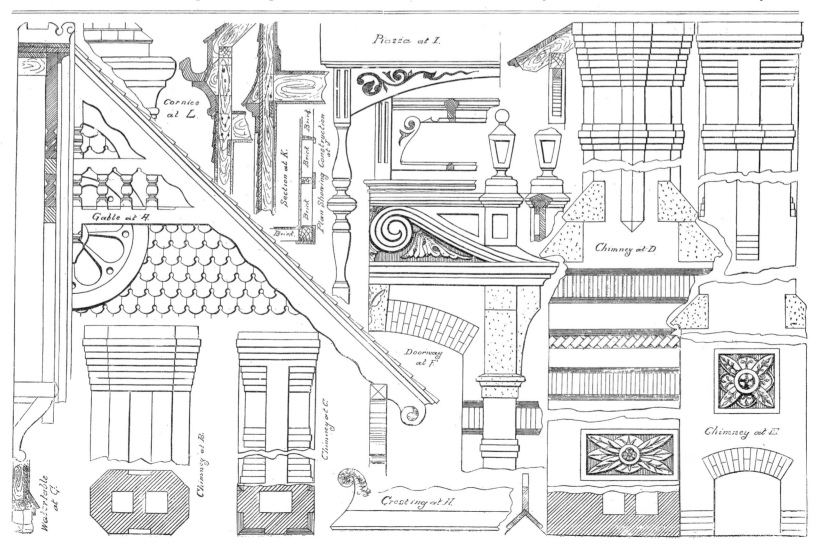

Piazza at I.

Cornice at L.

Section at K.

Plan Showing Construction at J.

Brick. Brick. Brick.

Gable at H.

Brick.

Chimney at D

Doorway at F.

Chimney at B.

Chimney at C.

Water-table at G.

Cresting at H.

Chimney at E.

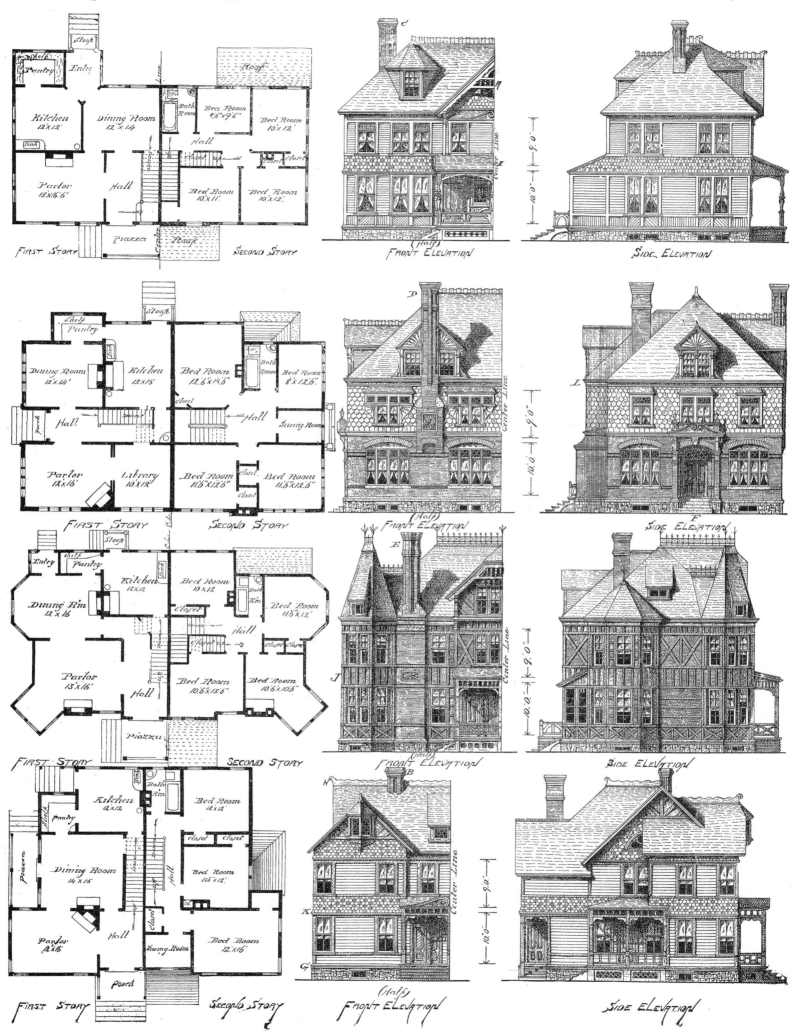

Design 141

FIRST STORY
- Kitchen 12'x12'
- Dining Room 12'x14'
- Parlor 13'x16.6'
- Hall
- Pantry
- Shelf
- Entry
- Stoop
- Sink
- Piazza

SECOND STORY
- Bath Room
- Bed Room 6.6'x9.6'
- Bed Room 10'x12'
- Hall
- Bed Room 10'x11'
- Bed Room 10'x12'
- Roof
- Closet

FRONT ELEVATION (Half)   SIDE ELEVATION

Design 142

FIRST STORY
- Dining Room 12'x14'
- Kitchen 12'x15'
- Parlor 12'x16'
- Library 10'x18'
- Hall
- Pantry
- Shelf
- Stoop
- Porch

SECOND STORY
- Bed Room 12.6'x15.6'
- Bath Room
- Bed Room 8'x12.6'
- Hall
- Sewing Room
- Bed Room 11.6'x12.5'
- Bed Room 11.6'x12.6'
- Closet

FRONT ELEVATION (Half)   SIDE ELEVATION

Design 143

FIRST STORY
- Dining Rm 12'x16'
- Kitchen 12'x12'
- Parlor 13'x16'
- Entry
- Pantry
- Shelf
- Hall
- Stoop

SECOND STORY
- Bed Room 10'x12'
- Bath Rm
- Bed Room 11.6'x12'
- Closet
- Hall
- Bed Room 10.6'x13.6'
- Bed Room 10.6'x10.6'
- Closet

FRONT ELEVATION (Half)   SIDE ELEVATION

Design 144

FIRST STORY
- Dining Room 14'x15'
- Kitchen 12'x12'
- Parlor 12'x16'
- Pantry
- Hall
- Piazza
- Porch

SECOND STORY
- Bed Room 12'x12'
- Bath Rm
- Bed Room 11.6'x12'
- Closet
- Hall
- Sewing Room
- Bed Room 12'x16'

FRONT ELEVATION (Half)   SIDE ELEVATION

PLATE 49.

Design 145. We here present the reader with a substantial, plain, yet very good-appearing brick and shingle country house, with accommodation for a family of a dozen or more persons, and its style is thoroughly in keeping with the character of a rural neighborhood and is suggestive of comfort and cheerfulness.

The outlines of each elevation, the materials of the different stories and the window and door openings are arranged to be dissimilar in form; strong and decided contrasts of color are applied to different parts and tinted glass of various shades are used for the smaller lights of the sash. There is an absence of large verandas with their roofs so generally found on houses of this class and which are so apt to shut out the genial sunshine, so much wanted in homes in the cold season, and to effectually shut out the same must result in weakness and death to the occupants.

The liberal front porch connecting with the large main hall makes a cool retreat for summer, and in winter the porch is arranged to be effectually closed up by the aid of sashes and a storm door so that the cold can be excluded from the house.

The floor plans explain themselves; kitchen has a dresser built into recess. Dining room has a sideboard in recess and a hall stand is built in recess in the main hall and all in a thoroughly convenient and practical manner. The arrangement of the office or business room, with its outside private entrance, and the conservatory located above on a level with platform of stairs will, we are sure, commend itself to many persons who wish for both these in a country house; and there are many reasons why a special room for business should be provided not only for the large farmer, politician or medi-cal man, but also for those who, doing business in the city, make their family home in the suburb or adjacent rural neighborhood.

The third story supplies necessary accommodation for the hired help. Cost of erection $7,000.

Design 146. This is perhaps in style a more ambitious house than the preceding, although smaller in plan, and may be adapted to a similar domain.

The materials of which it is built is brick for the first story, which could be of stone, and for second story, timber construction, with plastered filling of cement between the timbers which requires careful work to make a good and perfect job; and this rough casting of panel work is coming more and more into favor, and mechanics will therefore become more familiar with the modes of carrying out the same in a workmanlike manner, although it is a fact that nearly all mechanics working at masonry trades discourage and condemn the adoption of anything out of their ordinary routine of brick and mortar, and we have known cases where the downright pigheadedness of a mason has spoiled many a good piece of work that he might have otherwise made a reputation on, if he only had had the sense to see his own interests.

A veranda on the south side of this house is a pleasant feature, and at the same time does not shut out the sun from living and dining rooms, both of which are well exposed and are large and elegant for living apartments.

The porch shields the front hall in winter by enclosing the same; and for an elegant convenient house to live in this house can be recommended to the reader. Cost, $4,000.

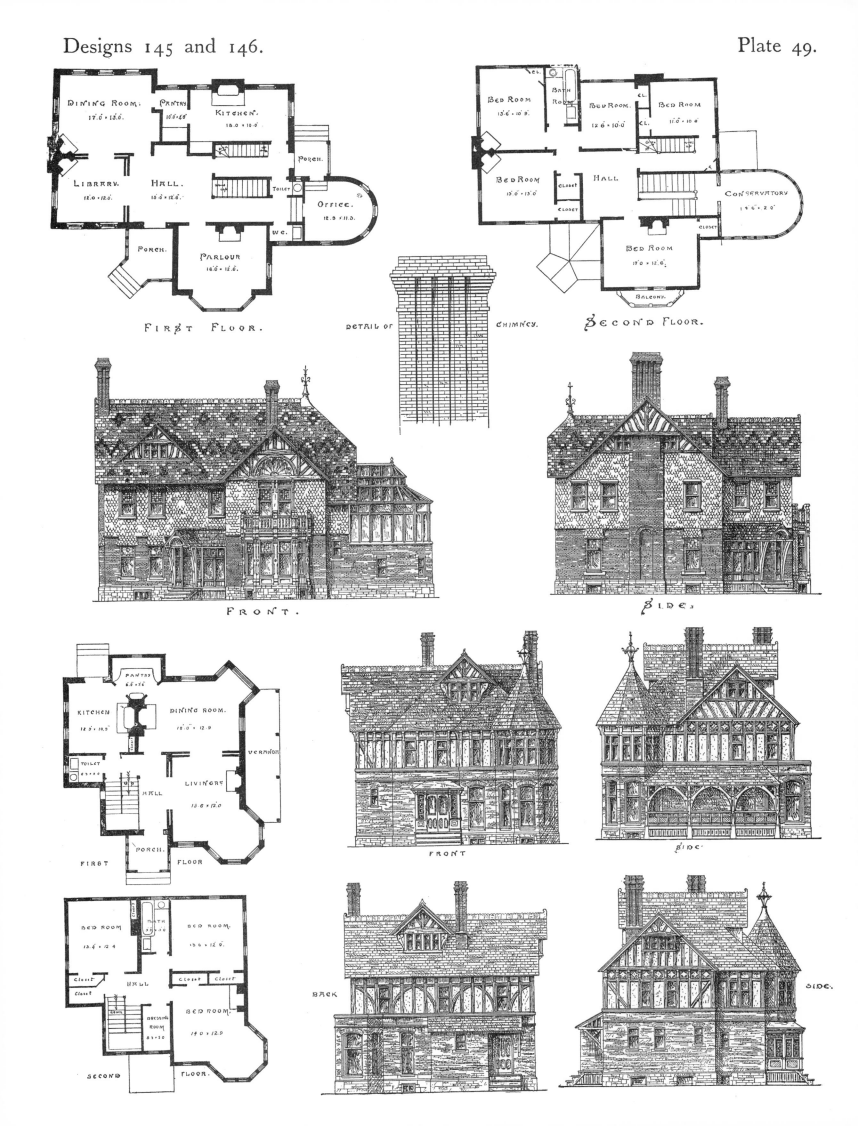

DINING ROOM.
17.0 × 15.0.

PANTRY
10.0 × 6.0

KITCHEN.
18.0 × 10.0.

PORCH.

LIBRARY.
12.0 × 12.0.

HALL.
15.0 × 12.0.

TOILET

OFFICE.
12.3 × 11.3.

W.C.

PORCH.

PARLOUR
16.0 × 12.0.

FIRST FLOOR.

DETAIL OF CHIMNEY.

BED ROOM
15.6 × 10.9.

BATH ROOM

BED ROOM
12.6 × 10.0.

BED ROOM
11.0 × 10.6

BED ROOM
15.0 × 15.0

CLOSET

CLOSET

HALL

CONSERVATORY
14.6 × 12.0

CLOSET

BED ROOM
17.0 × 12.6.

BALCONY.

SECOND FLOOR.

FRONT.

SIDE.

KITCHEN
12.9 × 10.3

PANTRY
6.6 × 7.6

DINING ROOM.
18.0 × 12.9

TOILET
6.5 × 6.0

VERANDA

HALL

LIVING RM
15.6 × 12.0

FIRST FLOOR

PORCH.

FRONT

SIDE.

BED ROOM
13.4 × 12.4

BATH
7.0 × 5.0

BED ROOM
15.6 × 12.9.

CLOSET

CLOSET

CLOSET

HALL

CLOSET

DRESSING ROOM
8.3 × 5.0

BED ROOM.
14.0 × 12.9

SECOND FLOOR.

BACK

SIDE.

PALLISER'S NEW COTTAGE HOMES AND DETAILS.

PLATE 50.

Designs 147 and 148 are of such a class of houses as answer a popular demand, embracing, as they do, at a low price the long-prized excellencies of the old-fashioned country and suburban house, with hall through the centre and doors at both ends to give ample ventilation in warm weather. With all the progress that has been made in architectural taste and conveniences, we doubt if the central hall and direct communication from it to every room has been much improved on. The finest country and surburban houses with which our associations are connected, and which are remembered for their comfort and elegance, have the spacious hall running through the middle.

It will be observed in these designs that as far as possible the construction is planned for straightforward, square work. The rooms are pleasantly located, easily reached and, for economy, are as compact as any plans that may be devised of similar area. The exteriors are plain, but at the same time they look well and will wear well, and while without the prevalent numerous irregularities that afford variety of light and shade, they are also without the expense connected with them.

Design 147 contains on first floor four good rooms and all the requisite conveniences ; the hall is spacious and contains seat and stand at foot of stairs. Dining-room has a recessed fire-place with seats on each side. A passage through china pantry, between kitchen and dining-room, cuts off the smell of cooking, and the doors through this passage are hung with spring hinges and without locks or other fastenings ; they are opened with the foot and close immediately after passing. The domestic can pass from the kitchen to dining-room with the service of the table, while flies and the aroma of cooking have little chance of getting into the main part of the house. On second floor there are five rooms, bath-room and plenty of closets, and on third floor are four rooms. Exterior is clapboarded throughout. Cost $3,600.

Design 148 gives about the same accommodation as the preceding design, but of different arrangement, and with the addition of a conservatory for those who love to gratify their taste for flowers. This conservatory is in rear of dining-room with windows looking into same, forming a splendid background and effect, and the entrance is convenient from hall via rear veranda. Exterior of this house is simple but yet good in detail. First story is clapboarded, being mitred at corners. A band 2 feet, 6 inches deep of shingles comes in between the windows of first and second stories, and the second story is ceiled and panels formed on face, which with the panelled and shingled gables, makes a very effective finish. Cost, $4,000.

To make houses warm in winter and cool in summer, an air chamber for confined or dead air is formed between the outer sheathing on the frame and the lath and plaster of the inside. The old method of filling in with soft brick laid on edge in mortar has been discarded some time ago, and where special provision is made, on account of an exposed situation, for securing warmth in winter, in addition to the sheathing and papering of the exterior of frame, a system of filling in with sawdust, or of mineral wool, or of back plastering or lathing between studs is usually adopted—nailing of rough pieces or of lath against strips fastened to each side of the studs and covering with coarse mortar, and this has been found very serviceable, but this also is being rapidly superceded by sheathing up the inside of the frame, before plastering, with a patent sheathing lath, a combination of sheathing and lath, which makes a perfect and tight job, and is made ready for plastering by the operation ; and the Byrkit Sheathing Lath is something that will be shortly used in the construction of all buildings, and is already highly recommended by architects and builders.

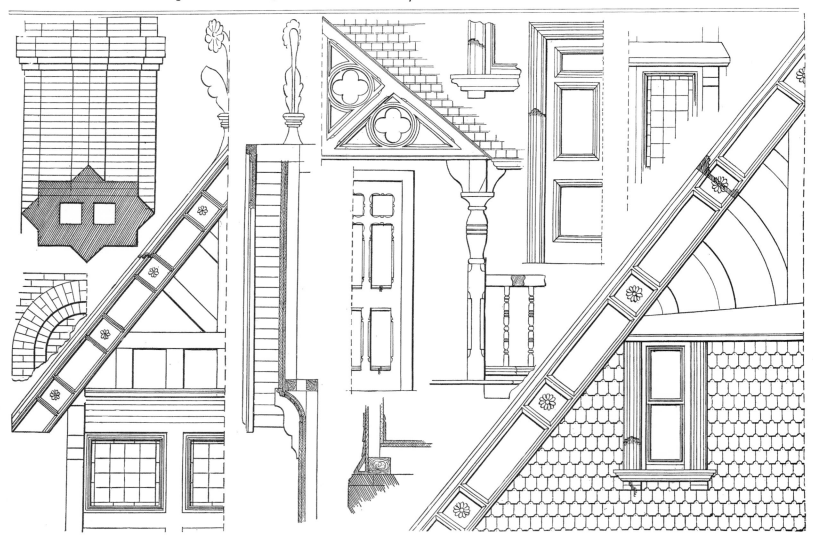

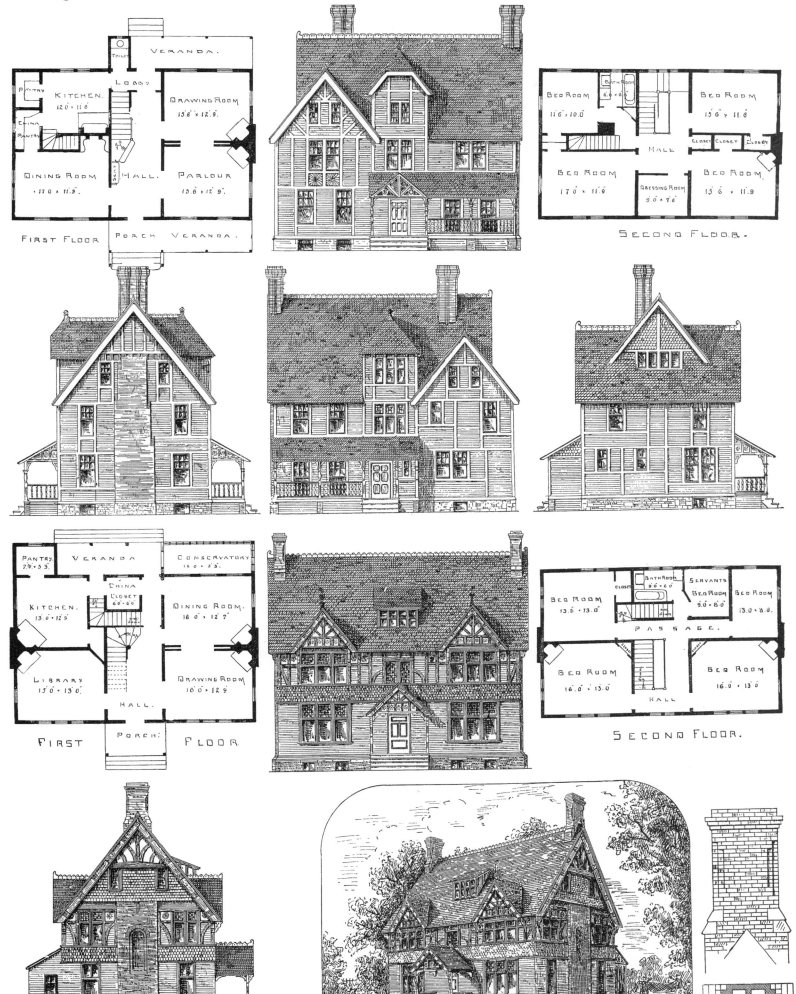

FIRST FLOOR

Pantry

Kitchen.
12.0 × 11.6

Loggy

Toilet

VERANDA.

China
Pantry

Dining Room
17.0 × 11.9

Hall.

Drawing Room
15.6 × 12.9

Parlour
15.6 × 12.9

FIRST FLOOR   PORCH   VERANDA.

SECOND FLOOR.

Bed Room
11.6 × 10.0

Bath Room
6.0 × 6.0

Bed Room
15.6 × 11.6

Hall

Closet Closet Closet

Bed Room
17.0 × 11.9

Dressing Room
9.0 × 7.6

Bed Room
15.6 × 11.9

Pantry
7.0 × 5.3

VERANDA

Conservatory
16.0 × 5.3

Kitchen.
13.0 × 12.9

China
Closet
6.0 × 6.0

Dining Room.
16.0 × 12.7

Library
15.0 × 13.0

Drawing Room.
16.0 × 12.9

Hall.

Porch.

FIRST   FLOOR.

SECOND FLOOR.

Bed Room
13.0 × 13.0

Bath Room
9.0 × 6.0

Closet

Servants
Bed Room
9.0 × 8.0

Bed Room
13.0 × 8.0

PASSAGE.

Bed Room
16.0 × 13.0

Bed Room
16.0 × 13.0

Hall.

The designs given on this plate are for houses specially adapted for erection in Florida, or by the sea shore, for summer occupancy, and we have designed, from time to time, a large number of such houses for permanent and winter residence at the South and summer residence at the North; they have no cellars under them; no mason work is required in the walling of underpinning, etc., but they are supported on posts set in the ground, and admit of a free circulation of air. The post holes should be dug about one foot larger than the post, and the space around filled in with water-lime concrete, being careful to bring the concrete above the level of the finished grade, and to slope it off in such a manner as to form a water shed around the post on the surface of the ground; this will prevent the post from rotting at the ground line and will insure its preservation for many years. The ground under the house should be rounded up to the centre and graded from that and sloped down on all sides, then a substance of coarse gravel, ashes and water-lime mixed so as to form a concrete should be spread over the surface under the house, thus preventing damp and malarious vapors from rising up into the house. A little foresight will render such houses healthful and wholesome, but as a rule such matters are never thought of and are carelessly neglected, and, as a consequence, sickness and other distress follow which could easily have been prevented.

Design 149 has a large hall, parlor and dining-room, with kitchen properly isolated from the other rooms, though easily reached from dining-room; piazza and porch room is liberal, and there is every opportunity of getting through the house all the breeze there may be about; five bed-rooms and closets, also a balcony are obtained on second floor. Cost $1,000.00.

Design 150 contains a like amount of room as the former, but distributed a little differently, yet meeting all the requirements of climate and wants of the people. Cost $800.00.

Design 151 gives a somewhat different plan from the other two, though very convenient, and, as will be seen by careful study, is well adapted to the purposes for which it is intended. Cost, $900.

Balloon framing is technically as well as sarcastically applied to a system of putting together frame buildings, that had its origin in the early settlement of our prairies, where it was impossible to obtain heavy timbers and skillful mechanics, and its simple, effective and economical manner of construction has been of great benefit in building up of new territory and sections of this country, and being stronger than any other method of framing has led to its universal adoption for buildings of every class throughout the United States. In olden times, before the portable saw mill, or easy transportation by railroad of timber and lumber usurped the functions of the broad-axe, the skillful framing of a building required no inconsiderable talent and practice. He indeed was considered a boss carpenter who could "in his mind," with magic scratch awl, indiscriminately "lay out" mortices and tenons in cabalistic characters upon a confused accumulation of dimension sticks, which on "raising day" without hinderance of mismatched jointing, assorted and assembled themselves into a harmonious whole, from sill to roof-tree. Such was the building practiced forty years ago. Now, in these days of cheap things, substantial frames are, as it were, knocked together, and men who appear to indifferently wield hammer and saw, are employed in the carpentering.

The balloon frame is a characteristic American invention, and like all successful improvements, has thrived on its own merits, the balloon frame has passed through and survived the theory, ridicule and abuse of all who have seen fit to attack it, and may be reckoned among the prominent inventions of the present generation, an invention neither fostered nor developed by any hope of great rewards, but which plainly acknowledges its origin in necessity.

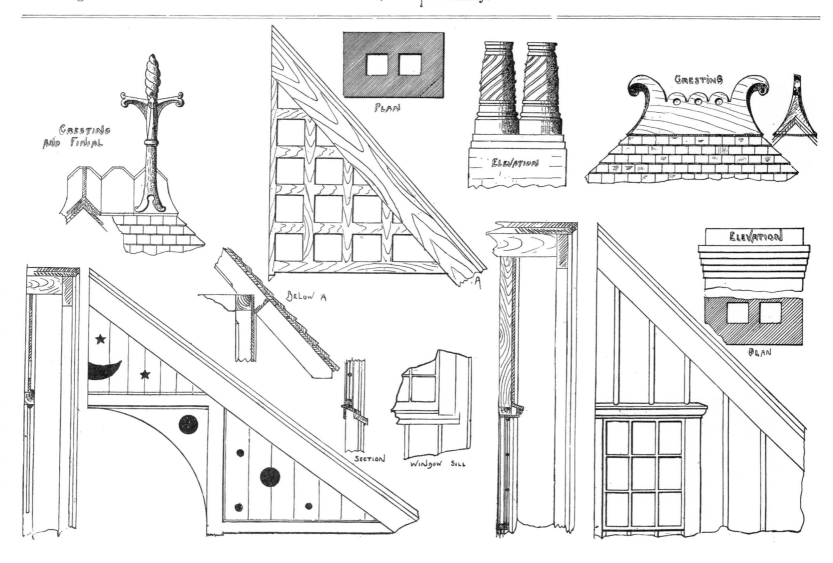

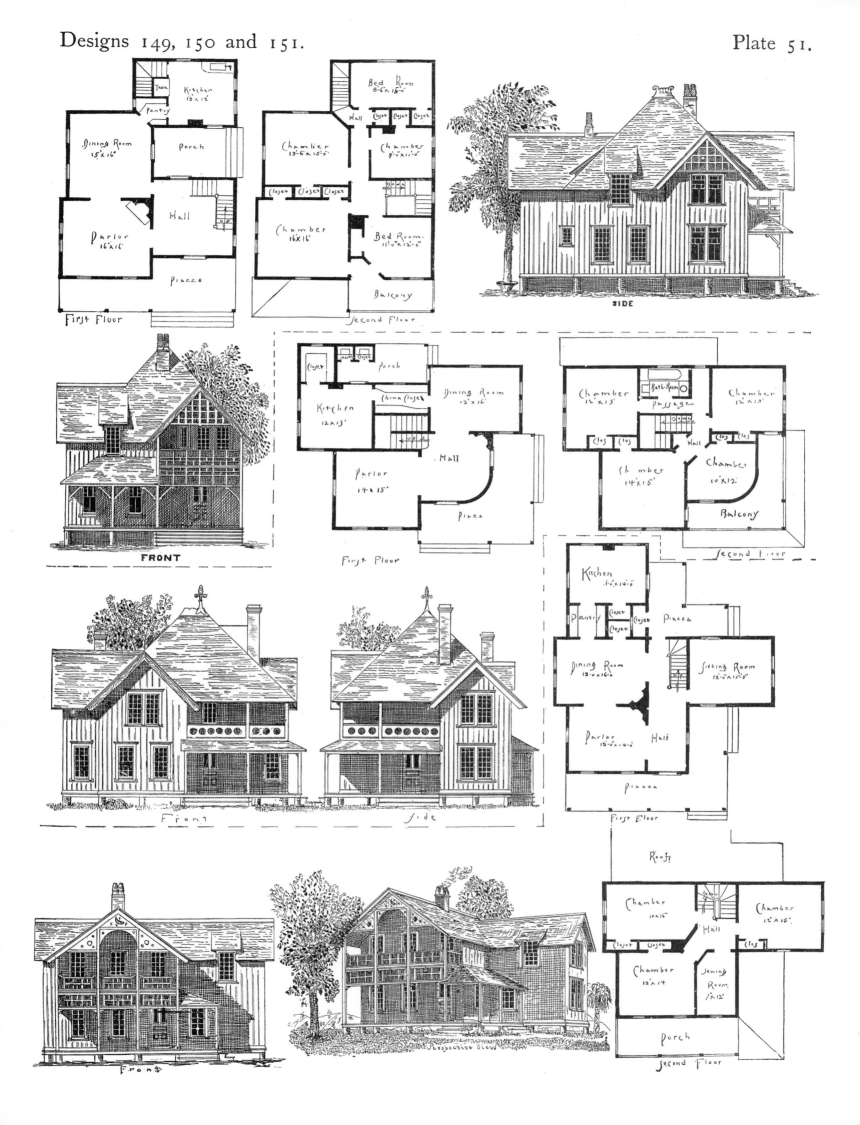

Kitchen 12' x 12'

Table

Pantry

Dining Room 15' x 16'

Porch

Parlor 16' x 16'

Hall

Piazza

First Floor

Bed Room 8'-6" x 15'-0"

Hall

Closet Closet Closet

Chamber 13'-6" x 15'-5"

Chamber 9'-0" x 11'-0"

Closet Closet Closet

Chamber 16' x 16'

Bed Room 11'-0" x 12'-0"

Balcony

Second Floor

SIDE

FRONT

Closet

Porch

Kitchen 12' x 13'

China Closet

Dining Room 12' x 16'

Hall

Parlor 14' x 15'

Piazza

First Floor

Chamber 12' x 13'

Bath-Room

Passage

Chamber 12' x 13'

Clos Clos

Hall

Clos Clos

Chamber 14' x 15'

Chamber 10' x 12'

Balcony

Second Floor

Kitchen 12'-0" x 14'-0"

Pantry

Closet Closet

Piazza

Dining Room 12'-0" x 16'-0"

Sitting Room 12'-0" x 15'-0"

Parlor 12'-0" x 14'-0"

Hall

Piazza

First Floor

Front

Side

Front

Perspective View

Roof

Chamber 10' x 16"

Chamber 12' x 16'

Hall

Closet Closet

Clos

Chamber 12' x 14

Sewing Room 7' x 12'

Porch

Second Floor

Design 152, while it presents a unique cottage for a summer residence suitable for the Adirondack region or the Thousand Islands of the St. Lawrence River, is also a good plan for a permanent country or suburban residence. If built for the former, the design here shown should be followed. The framing is all dressed and is exposed in the rooms. The covering is of narrow, matched pine boarding, put on outside of frame, laid horizontally and well nailed to every stud. The floors and partitions are constructed in like manner, the boarding in all cases being dressed on both sides, thus doing away with the use of plastered walls and allowing of a quick construction, which is very often desirable when one wishes to put up a shore or mountain cottage, at the opening of spring, for occupancy in a month or two after deciding to build it. The interior arrangements of this cottage are all that a family of refinement would wish for. The main hall is liberal in size, has a floor of narrow hardwood, with neat border; an open fire-place, in which to burn wood when the air is damp. Stairs are well located and out of the way; the parlor and dining-room are good rooms and are well placed and connected; ample piazza and balcony accommodation are provided, for cool retreats, and on second floor are three good chambers, two dressing rooms and bath, and in attic servants' room. Cost, $1,500.

Design 153 gives a cottage of like construction as the above described, and has a very large piazza for living outdoors, and a large living room inside, adapted for general use of the family, and is a good and economical arrangement. Four bed rooms are provided on second floor, and to any one needing a simple cottage, easily and quickly constructed, this design should be a help,

and for a summer residence, where every breeze is desirable, it is a good one. Cost $1,000.

Design 154 provides, in like manner as the others, a cottage that is a little gem, and for a small family a very desirable one to live in for a few months of the summer, amid mountains or lake scenery, and but a small amount of money is needed to erect it, so that the cost is but little more than one would pay out for his family expenses for a season's sojourn at a fashionable resort, putting up at a hotel. It gives large hall, dining-room and kitchen on first floor, with open fire-place in both hall and dining-rooms, and four bed rooms and bath on second floor. Cost, $1,000.

During the summer months it adds much to the comfort of a house to protect all the doors and window openings by neat wire window screens, which do not obstruct air or sight and does keep out flies, mosquitoes and other little pests that this season of year brings. The method of adjusting these screens to their position is very simple, and they can be stored through the winter in a closet or attic, and by their use cleanliness and comfort of an open country-house can thus be enjoyed, fresh air can be had in abundance, and a feeling of comfort insured which those who have once tried it will never be without.

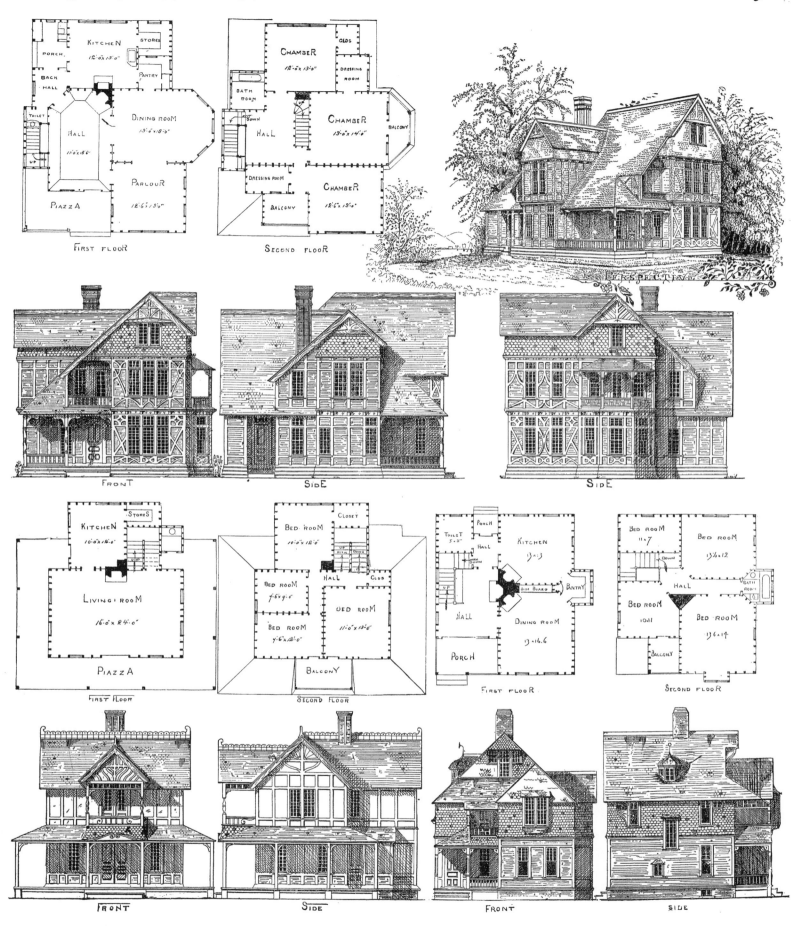

Design 152 — First Floor: PORCH, KITCHEN 12'0" x 13'0", STORES, BACK HALL, PANTRY, TOILET, HALL 11'0" x 18'6", DINING ROOM 13'0" x 18'0", UP, PARLOUR 18'6" x 13'0", PIAZZA — FIRST FLOOR

Design 152 — Second Floor: CHAMBER 18'0" x 13'0", CLOS., DRESSING ROOM, BATH ROOM, DOWN, HALL, CHAMBER 13'0" x 14'0", BALCONY, DRESSING ROOM, CHAMBER 18'6" x 13'0", BALCONY — SECOND FLOOR

PERSPECTIVE

FRONT   SIDE   SIDE

Design 153 — First Floor: KITCHEN 10'0" x 18'0", STORES, UP, LIVING ROOM 16'0" x 24'0", PIAZZA — FIRST FLOOR

Design 153 — Second Floor: BED ROOM 10'0" x 12'0", CLOSET, UP, BED ROOM 7'6" x 9'0", HALL, CLOS., BED ROOM 7'6" x 12'0", BED ROOM 11'0" x 13'0", BALCONY — SECOND FLOOR

Design 154 — First Floor: TOILET 5' x 11', PORCH, HALL, KITCHEN 13' x 13', UP, DOWN, HALL, SIDE BOARD, PANTRY, DINING ROOM 13' x 16'6", PORCH — FIRST FLOOR

Design 154 — Second Floor: BED ROOM 11' x 7', BED ROOM 13'6" x 12, DOWN, HALL, BATH ROOM, BED ROOM 10'11, BED ROOM 13'6" x 14, BALCONY — SECOND FLOOR

FRONT   SIDE   FRONT   SIDE

PALLISER'S NEW COTTAGE HOMES AND DETAILS.

PLATE 53.

Design 155.—This design is quite compact and works up into one of the neatest and prettiest houses it is possible to get up and there are many good reasons for it. The front entrance or reception hall with its unique staircase, its toilet conveniences, its open fire-place, etc., is all that can be desired. The parlor, dining-room and conservatory arrangements and connections are attractive and good. The library is in a quiet and easy corner of the house, and the rear portion of house, of the kitchen, back stairs and hall are especially good. The second floor gives five bed rooms, dressing room, bath room and necessary closets. The front bed-room could be made six feet larger by leaving out the dressing room. Two rooms are also provided on third floor. Cost, $4,600.

On the exterior we give by way of variety the hipped or truncated gable, a style of finish which needs to be carefully used, but answers well in some places, and where there is not a disposition to do too much of it. We remember a place where it was introduced on a building some years ago, and the fashion thus set was persistently followed in all manners until it became quite a disagreeable feature there abouts. Better make ordinary gables pointed.

Design 156 is for a cosey, suburban house, such as is wanted by an employee of a bank, office or store, with a considerable family, who desire all the comforts and conveniences of a home suited to people in moderate circumstances of life, yet possessing a degree of taste which could be shown up by them in such a cottage residence as this one, being very good, both in interior arrangement and exterior design. The roofs are covered with

California redwood shingles stained to give them the appearance of English tile, thus obtaining a unique and picturesque roof which is very agreeable to the eye; the second story is also covered with these shingles and the first story clapboarded. The interior wood-work throughout is also of this California mahogany or redwood, which is a beautiful wood when rightly finished up and costs less in the New York market than good, clear, white pine, and it is a wonder that more of it is not used, and we presume it will now come rapidly into favor, and much of it is capable of taking the place of mahogany in color and grain, and at one-third the cost. Cost of building this house $3,500.

Every frame erected for a habitation should be well protected and braced by sheathing it either horizontally or diagonally on same. The latter is the strongest and best method. Each edge of the sheathing boards should be well nailed through to every timber of the frame; yet with all these modern ideas we find many houses put up for rent or sale, and some for occupancy by the owners and builders that are actually with no outer sheathing on frame, without papering or any other protection except a covering of clapboards or novelty siding, and a common lathing and plastering on the inside, thus giving both wind and rain every chance to penetrate, while a few rough boards and some paper laid all over the boarding and well lapped under all casings and corner boards would afford at a cost of a few dollars means of protection that would save fuel and doctors' bills, exceeding the amount in one year, to say nothing about the promotion of both comfort and health of the occupants.

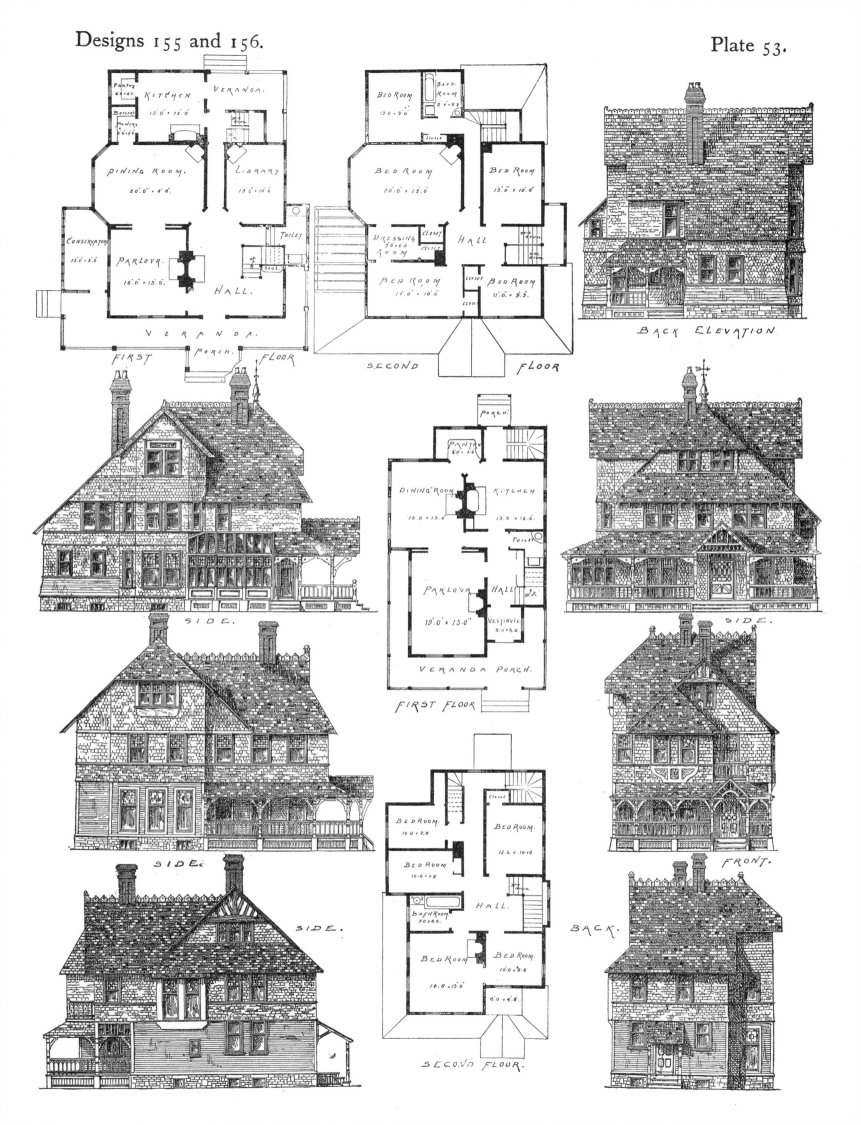

PALLISER'S NEW COTTAGE HOMES AND DETAILS.

PLATE 54.

Design 157.—We here show a design for a brick residence adapted for erection in the suburbs of a city, which always seems to require more ornate styles than are suited to the broad and open country. The evidences of the position and taste of the occupants of such houses and their proximity to the city seem to justify a special treatment and elaboration in their design, which, however, is not necessarily to be of an expensive character, and in this case effective treatment has been obtained by the broken front, its veranda and the expressive chimney-stacks, together with a little color in the brickwork carefully worked in so as to avoid a shoddy or cheap appearance, and, of course, it is no more costly to lay a brick of one color than it is of another. Such effects are worthy of careful study by all who are engaged in building. The environs of London, particularly Bedford Park and St. John's Wood, are studded with handsome places and pretty cottages, well arranged for the purposes of the life for which they were built. In fact, Europe is full of them, while in this country the suburban villa is too often dragged right into the heart of the city, with a house too large for the small grounds and to whimsical for contrast with the forms around, and wanting a large, cheerful lawn and a background of trees to set it off to advantage ; and in turn the city house is frequently taken out into the suburbs or country and set up with its bare straight sides, sloping roof to rear, nearly flat, and three windows in front. And we contend that a man has no right to disfigure some grand scene by an inharmonious dwelling. How often this has been done, those who have rambled on the banks of the Hudson and in the vicinity of all large cities can testify.

The villa or suburban residence should always be built on a lot of good width and with a depth of 150 feet, so that it can stand well back from the street and have a retired appearance, and an opportunity for a lawn and shrubs, which are necessary adjuncts. The arrangement of first floor provides veranda in front which is the southern exposure, and a hall in the centre of house, with staircase, having a platform rendering the ceilings of the front portion of the house two steps higher than the rear or kitchen part, an arrangement which is often very desirable when one wishes to keep the roof at the rear lower down than that of the main part. The dining-room or living-room of the house is of large size and shapely, has passage through entry to kitchen, and conveniently arranged, while on the other side of the hall are parlor and bed-room, the latter being placed on this floor by special request, together with bath room. The kitchen and pantry occupy the northern exposure. The second story contains four bed-rooms, with good closets, and two rooms are provided in attic. Cost, $4,500.

The cost of houses, according to circumstances, will range all the way from 50 to 100 per cent., and this difference exists in nearly all classes of buildings, according to the section of country in which they are built, the facility of getting materials and the business management brought to bear. As prices constantly change, a good way is to show the nearest good mechanic the style of house you have decided on to adopt. Tell him, as near as possible, your wishes, and he can generally give you an approximate estimate of the amount of money you will need to carry out your wants and wishes.

Design 158 is a somewhat plain structure, though, with sufficient character in outline to give it some distinction among the class of house to which it belongs—viz., the residence of a working man who believes in owning his own comfortable home, containing all the necessary rooms and suited to his family wants, and of such arrangement as to be convenient and avoid unnecessary steps in the carrying out of the household duties attended to by his wife and family, and the bath room, so often left out on the score of economy, is not lost sight of in this instance, but is constructed into the building at the outset ; and the whole cost is $2,050.

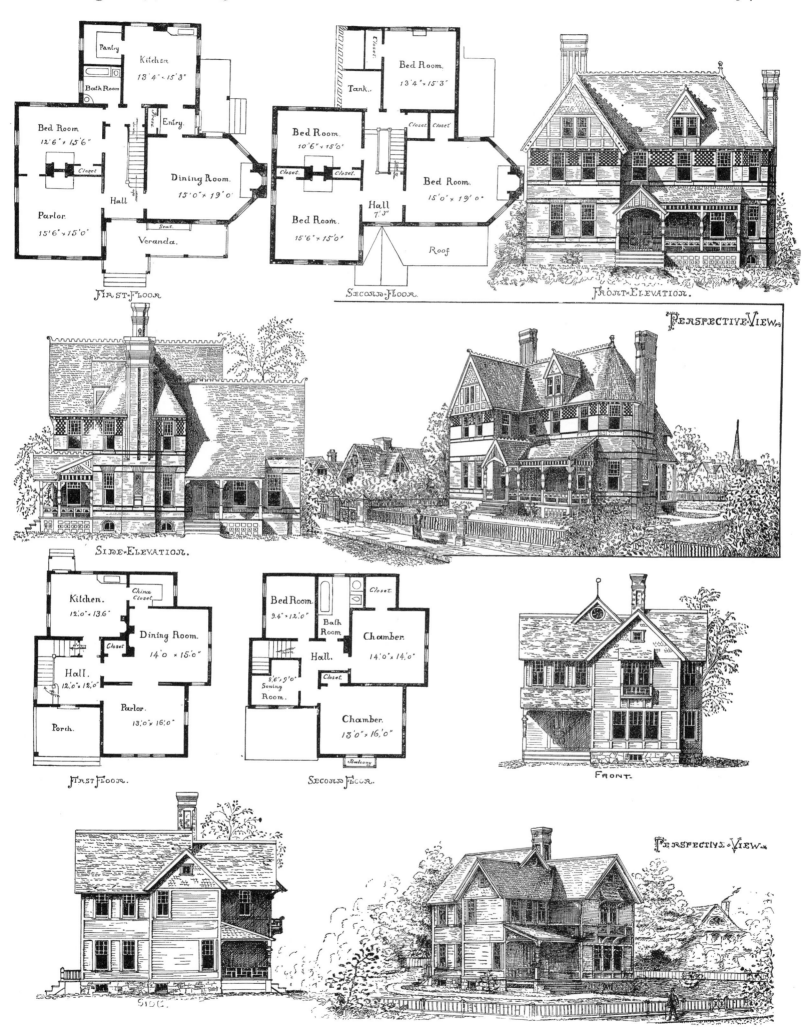

First Floor.

Pantry
Kitchen.
13'4" × 15'3"
Bath Room.
Entry.
Bed Room
12'6" × 15'6"
Closet
Hall
Dining Room.
15'0" × 19'0"
Parlor.
15'6" × 15'0"
Veranda.
Seat.

Second Floor.

Closet
Tank.
Bed Room.
13'4" × 15'3"
Closet Closet
Bed Room.
10'6" × 15'0"
Closet Closet
Bed Room.
15'0" × 19'0"
Hall
7'3"
Bed Room.
15'6" × 15'0"
Roof

Front Elevation.

Perspective View.

Side Elevation.

First Floor.

Kitchen.
12'0" × 13'6"
China Closet
Dining Room.
14'0" × 15'0"
Closet
Hall.
12'0" × 12'0"
Parlor.
13'0" × 16'0"
Porch.

Second Floor.

Bed Room.
9'4" × 12'0"
Closet
Bath Room
Chamber.
14'0" × 14'0"
Hall.
8'6" × 9'0"
Sewing Room.
Closet
Chamber.
13'0" × 16'0"
Balcony.

Front.

Side.

Perspective View.

Design 159, which is for a pair of dwellings will answer well for a country gentleman ; or two of them, for a farmer and his son to live in, or for two city business men to occupy for their families in summer as their country home; it presents good variety and is considered attractive, home-like and picturesque in exterior effect and well suited to almost any surroundings of a rural nature. It is worthy of careful study and we will here state that the principles upon which architectural beauty was obtained in the village and country houses built fifty or sixty years ago, and which are now so much admired, principles which apply equally well to buildings of to-day were simplicity, reality and intention. Their importance cannot be too strongly insisted on and so impressed therewith should architects be that in devising any plan they should mentally train themselves to reply to a question that should be the query of the present age,—is it honest ? In a few years, how beautiful may this country be made by its rural architecture. No country in the world is so favored by nature, and by reason of the unfettered freedom for expression of individual taste, the lack of restraint by any well defined style or precedent, and the presence of a common sense which will teach us to judge of a thing only by its intrinsic merits. No land on the face of the earth has such opportunities for the advancement of art. The interior arrangements are well worth a close examination by any one who needs about the room that either side of this house provides, whether they wish to build jointly with some one else, or all alone by themselves. The hall makes a good living-room, and as all houses have their luxuries, we may safely say that this is indeed that portion of the house which is elegant ; and the rooms opening from it are so placed as to help its utility as well as assist its elegance. Piazzas and porches are liberal for out-door living, and the whole arrangement for its purposes are good. Six bed-rooms and bath room with good closets are provided on each side on the floors above. Cost, $4,500 a side. Though, an ingenious farmer who can supply from his farm a considerable portion of the materials, do his own hauling, and with the aid of a skillful mechanic and one or two handy laborers, if the work is not to be pushed too fast to completion, could execute this and similar designs by the use of very little money and discount the cost above by considerable, and we have assisted many all over the country to build at extremely low figures either by getting material furnished from the proper markets at first cost or in some other way to get what they could not furnish reasonable, and by lumping out the labor to say two or three men to do the various mechanical work requiring skilled labor.

A great many conflagrations throughout country districts are caused through carelessness in construction around fire-places and chimneys, and the common expression is "it was caused by a defective flue." The timbering and wood-work should be kept well away from any fire-place or flue, and should be carefully framed around them and protected by the proper use of incombustible material, and too much careful inspection of such work cannot be given to even the very best mechanics doing such work as this. Great care should also be taken in constructing chimneys, and their flues, as fuel gases will disintegrate the mortar joints of the best constructed brick flues, and if a spark escapes through either, the fuel is ready and waiting the conflagation in all dwelling houses—our homes—whether the occupants are asleep or awake. Think of this.

While nothing adds more to the outward appearance of a dwelling than the style of its chimneys, they should be built solid above the roof, and where exposed to the elements so as to avoid the falling to pieces in two or three years, and therefore they should be more than one brick thick and aside from the architectural beauty obtained by the use of good bold chimney stacks properly studied and in keeping with the general effect they denote good cheer, social firesides and a generous hospitality within, features which should always mark the country dwelling, and more particularly that of the farmer or country gentleman. Our illustrations throughout this work show them of very many kinds, generally cheap in construction, yet expressive in their treatment.

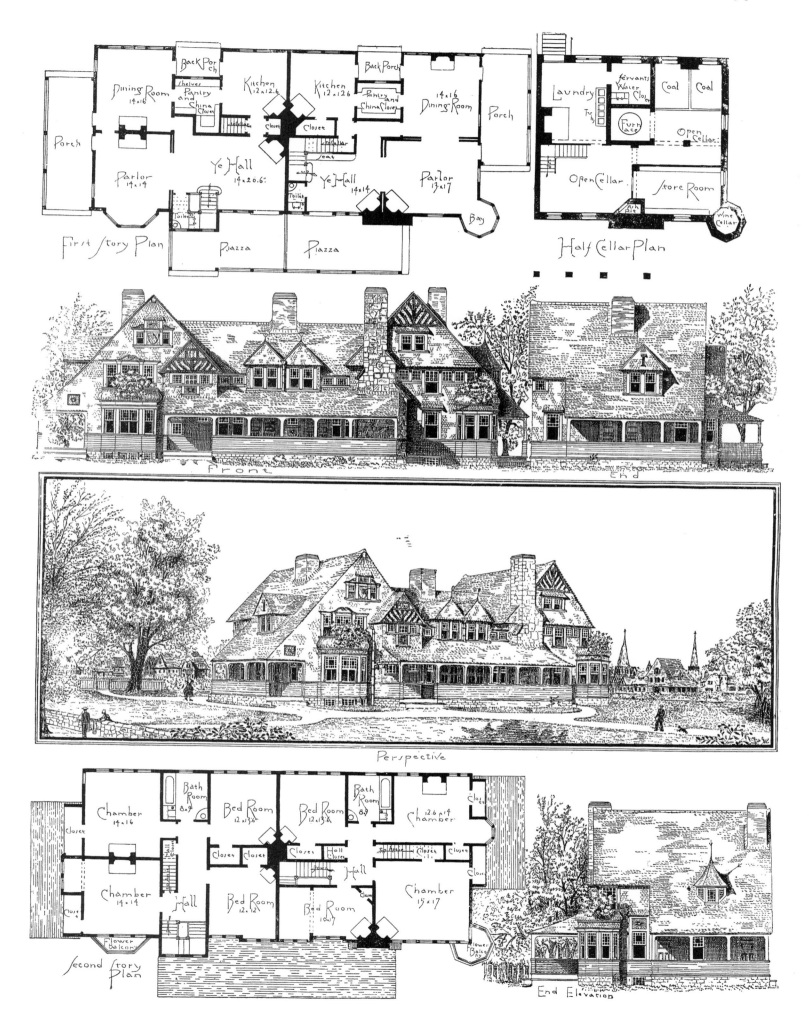

First Story Plan

Porch

Dining Room
14×16

Back Porch

Shelves

Pantry and China Closet

Kitchen
12×12.6

Kitchen
12×12.6

Back Porch

Pantry and China Closet

Dining Room
14×16

Porch

Parlor
14×14

Closet

Closet

Ye Hall
14×20.6

Ye Hall
14×14

Parlor
13×17

Toilet

Toilet

Bay

Piazza   Piazza

Half Cellar Plan

Laundry

Tub

Servants Water Closet

Coal

Coal

Furnace

Open Cellar

Open Cellar

Store Room

Ash Pit

Wine Cellar

Front

End

Perspective

Second Story Plan

Chamber
14×16

Bath Room
8×9

Bed Room
12×13.6

Bed Room
12×13.6

Bath Room
8×9

Chamber
12.6×14

Closet

Closet

Closet

Hall Closet

Closet

Closet

Closet

Closet

Chamber
14×14

Hall

Bed Room
12×12

Bed Room
10×17

Hall

Chamber
15×17

Flower Balcony

Flower Balcony

End Elevation

Design 160 is of a house built of good common, hard-burned brick, selecting the best and even-colored ones for the facing of the outside walls, which are laid up in red mortar, and when properly cleaned down with a correct solution and stain, makes work equal in appearance and certainly less harsh than is usually obtained by the use of pressed brick. The trimming-bands of brick are of a different or darker color, and the whole exterior is very pleasing with wood-work painted bronze green and red, with white for sashes. The arrangement of rooms throughout the first and second floors is excellent, as will be seen by a study of the plans, and servants' rooms are obtained in attic. The halls are especially deserving of attention, and the conservatory is a feature of this house that is both a pleasing and useful addition appreciated by very many people nowadays. Cost, $6,600.

Design 161 presents a house having good features in its out-lines, which are just sufficiently broken to give it the requsite character without making it expensive or whimsical; in fact, it is of the good, common-sense order of architecture, adapted to the wants of many people requiring the amount of room that it gives; the hall in the centre, with parlor and dining-room on either side, connecting all together by means of sliding-doors, is the features of this house. The dining-room and kitchen arrange-ment is good; and with back stairs and the liberal veranda adds much to the whole house.

The arrangement of second floor, giving five good bed-rooms, is all that can be desired. Cost, $3,650.

Every cellar under a dwelling-house should be sweet and clean at all times, and no excuse allowed for its being foul. Ventilate and purify it always. Decaying vegetation should not be tolerated in it. The floor should be well grouted in cement, walls and ceilings should be whitewashed, and ceiling, if possible, plastered; and one flue of the chimney should start from and open into the cellar for ventilation. In fact, pure air and enough of it is the cheapest blessing one can enjoy, and to deny ones self so necessary an element of good health is the sheerest folly, if not criminal. Yet thousands who build at much expense to pro-tect their health and that of their families, as they allege and sometimes suppose, by neglecting the simplest of all contrivances in the work of ventilation, invite disease and infirmity from the very pains they so unwittingly take to ward off such afflictions. Their memory carries them back to their boyhood days, prehaps, and the old homestead with its fire-places, scarcely throwing off sufficient heat to warm one side of a person at a time, withplenty of good air coming in at ill-fitting doors, windows, etc., which they did not regard as much of a luxury, but which, however, made them healthy and vigorous, and they say to themselves that their children shall be made comfortable, so that in their house building they take extra pains and expense to make a tight, warm house. They discard the open fire-place, perhaps, entirely, and put in an air-tight furnace or air-tight stoves in the various rooms, and provide no means of carrying off the bad air, and the rooms, as a rule, become overheated; windows and doors are sometimes opened to cool a room, and as a result all sorts of bodily afflictions follow in the family, and they wonder what is the matter, but never dream that day after day they are breath-ing decomposed air, which cannot escape, because there is no means for it to do so, and go where you may into houses that are without fire-places, and you will invariably find the subject of ventilation entirely overlooked.

Health and comfort depend on proper ventilation, which ought always to be considered carefully. In connection with the heating, the air in the room must be kept in constant circulation, and there is no better ventilator than an open fire-place with a fire; this will carry off the chilled, foul air as it falls to the floor, and keep the purer air circulating, and the fire-place even with-out a fire will aid in this way to equalize the temperature.

In all rooms that have no fire-places there should be a vent opening with register in the inner wall near the floor. Another vent opening and register near the ceiling is also desirable, that the room may be cooled when too hot and avoid draughts and also for the purpose of summer ventilation. These openings should be connected with tin pipe carried up to attic and to a hot, tight flue in chimney. Closets, pantries and bath-rooms are seldom ventilated even in houses of considerable pretention, yet it can be done at a very small cost by a tin pipe with an area of four inches square with an opening near the ceiling carried up to the ventilating flue.

PLAN

ELEVATION

BLACK BRICK

CRESTING AND FINIAL

PLASTER

PLAN OF CONSERVATORY

SECTION   PART ELEVATION

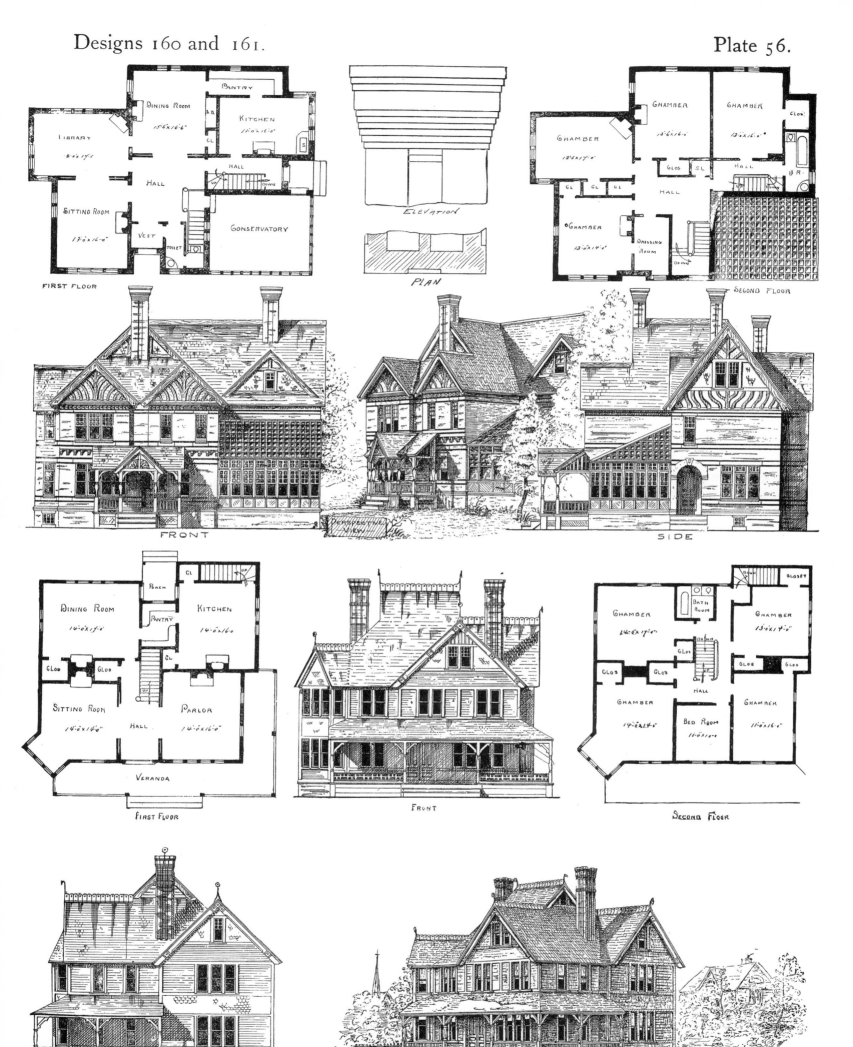

FIRST FLOOR

LIBRARY 13'-0"×17'-0"
DINING ROOM 15'-6"×16'-6"
PANTRY
KITCHEN 15'-0"×16'-0"
HALL
SITTING ROOM 13'-6"×16'-0"
VEST
TOILET
CONSERVATORY

PLAN

ELEVATION

SECOND FLOOR

CHAMBER 13'-6"×17'-0"
CHAMBER 15'-6"×16'-0"
CHAMBER 13'-0"×16'-0"
CHAMBER 13'-0"×14'-0"
DRESSING ROOM
HALL
B.R.

FRONT

PERSPECTIVE VIEW

SIDE

FIRST FLOOR

DINING ROOM 14'-0"×17'-0"
PORCH
PANTRY
KITCHEN 14'-0"×16'-0"
SITTING ROOM 14'-0"×16'-0"
PARLOR 14'-0"×16'-0"
HALL
VERANDA

FRONT

SECOND FLOOR

CHAMBER 14'-6"×17'-0"
BATH ROOM
CHAMBER 13'-0"×14'-0"
CHAMBER 14'-6"×17'-0"
HALL
BED ROOM 15'-0"×19'-0"
CHAMBER 15'-0"×16'-0"
CLOSET

SIDE

PERSPECTIVE VIEW

Design 162 shows a double house adapted for two families to live on each side, the owner of his side could occupy basement and first floor and rent the upper floors, thus helping him in his investment. The style of exterior is like many we have designed for erection by mechanics in New England towns and cities, and embody all that can be wished for. Large numbers of such houses are built throughout New England by people of means for purposes of investment and give probably as good returns as any real estate will do.

The main front entrances on each side are used by both families, while the family on second floor has its own back porch and back stairs and separate cellar entrance at rear, and the family on first floor has its back door from basement, where they have dining-room, kitchen, pantry and cellar. The plan explains fully the arrangement. Cost, $2,800 a side.

Design 163 gives a pair of houses, each for a single family, giving them the same amount of room, but not of the same arrangement, and avoiding in a measure that appearance of the double house so common, and which some genteel people like to get rid of as far as possible when building and intending to occupy one themselves. Such houses as these are good property to own, and bring in a rental in New England cities of $25 to $30 a month, and in the suburbs of New York a considerable advance on this, if located where they can be reached inside of an hour by railroad. Cost, $2,250.00.

Chimneys are an important feature of the exterior design of a dwelling, and we like to see them treated boldly, and of sufficient height above the roof as to overlook all other obstructions, and thus insure a good draught.

Design 164 gives an inexpensive double cottage, adapted for a farm or other country estate, for the housing of workmen connected therewith, or wherever ground can be obtained cheaply. This plan could be adopted by mechanics who wish to get a home of their own at a small outlay of money, and secure to themselves the blessings of home comfort and the privileges of being their own landlords, which is a desirable thing to be, and the American mechanic is not slow in this matter, but is making rapid strides in that direction, and no other country in the world can show a like advancement and helpful condition in this direction as the United States.

A parlor, dining-room and kitchen with pantry, nice hall and staircase, with convenient access from kitchen to cellar and two doors between hall and kitchen and between kitchen and dining-room; china closet in the dining-room; front and back porch are given on first floor, and on second floor three bed-rooms with good closets, a sewing-room or child's bed-room, make this a cosey and desirable residence at a cost of $1,200 a side. The rooms as shown on the plan would probably be better if increased in size, though if one undertakes to build low-priced houses we must adhere firmly to the plan—a little here and a little there, will, when all bills are paid, be found to double the cost.

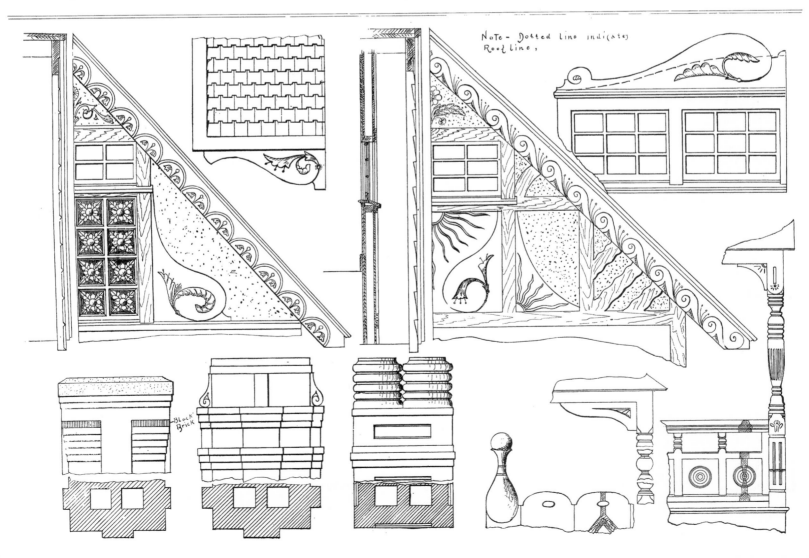

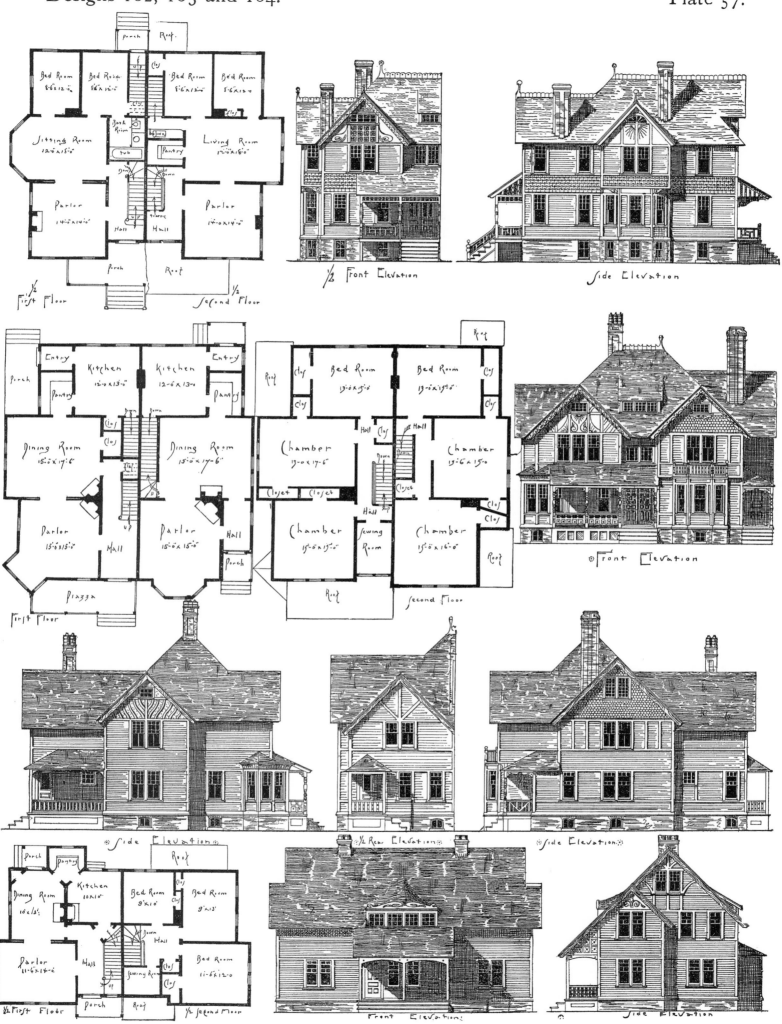

½ Front Elevation

Side Elevation

½ First Floor

½ Second Floor

Front Elevation

First Floor

Second Floor

Side Elevation

½ Rear Elevation

Side Elevation

½ First Floor

½ Second Floor

Front Elevation

Side Elevation

The designs on this plate are for city brick houses for a block of three, and are such as give variety of outline to the fronts and at the same time preserving a quiet dignity in their make-up.

The first design shows but one house, viz.: The left hand one, the one on the right hand to be the same reversed, and the centre house is intended to finish up with a tower having an ogee-shaped roof.

The second design shows the three houses just as they appear in the block, giving a very solid and massive appearance, and one that would strike the observer in the street of almost any ordinary town or city.

The third design shows the centre, and right hand house, the left hand house to be the same as on the right side but reversed, and makes a very elegant and attractive block of houses.

These houses are built on twenty feet of ground each, underpinning of basement story is laid up with dark blue granite, rock-faced ashlar, laid in irregular courses, level beds and plumb joints, and this kind of work is by far the handsomest of any and far ahead of the smooth cut faced stone work that one sees so much of in the larger cities. The water table, sill courses, etc., are of red stone, and the main walling of brick; fronts faced with pressed brick, with a little effect from terra cotta, very sparingly used; the steps and platforms are of hard red stone.

The plans of the several floors explain themselves fully and provide cellar, dining-room, kitchen, laundry, parlor, sitting-room, six bed-rooms and bath-room, with closets and other requisites. Cost, $5,000 to $7,000 each.

"In wall and roof and pavement scattered are full many a pearl, full many a costly stone."—*Artosto.*

A gentleman writing us for advice with regard to plans for a dwelling-house, says: "I have heard that it is possible to build without employing an architect; what would you advise?" Our reply was to the effect that a well-developed and matured set of building plans, with details and specifications drawn in such a manner as to get the best, most practical and generally pleasing results, by a competent and practical architect, is usually money saved to the client. By means of such plans he knows just what he is going to get, and just what it will cost him, and should he require any changes in the plans, or should the estimates on the work run higher than he contemplates, he can easily make the changes or modify his plans before putting the work under contract.

On the other hand, if he attempts to build a house or other building without well-matured plans, and without having first counted the cost, he is almost sure to become involved in a greater expense than he intended; and he has no redress, but is likely to get deeper and deeper in the bog, the more he struggles to get out. It goes without saying that a systematized method of doing business is preferable to a haphazard, "rule of thumb" way. The fact that it pays to employ an architect is becoming more and more appreciated by the general public, and we find that owners who have employed an architect once, do not hesitate about it when they build a second time. Where several years ago it was necessary to spend a great deal of time in argument in order to convince the owner that the services of the architect would be profitable to him, and would save him much trouble and annoyance, now no such importunity seems to be needed. The public is becoming educated in matters of art and architecture. We knew, some ten or fifteen years ago a young architect, just starting in business for himself, who solicited a commission of a gentleman of his acquaintance who contemplated building a house. Now the said gentleman had never built before, and although an intelligent man and well informed on many other subjects, had never interested himself in architecture, and consequently knew very little about the methods employed by architects in the development of working-plans, specifications, etc., nor the amount of mental labor therein involved. On accosting this gentleman, the architect said: "I understand Mr. ———, that you intend to build a house. Cannot I make arrangements with you to prepare your plans?" "No!" replied the gentleman very decidedly; "I have no use for your kind of work; I don't want any pictures"—contemptuously; for he was a very plain practical sort of man, with little respect for art. "I have my plans all in my head, and I expect to employ men by the day, and tell them just what I want as we come to it." About an hour's conversation between Mr. ——— and the architect, however, resulted in securing the commission for the latter. The plans were made, the building erected, and after its completion the gentleman came to the architect and made the following statement: "I have now learned what an architect's business is; my house has not cost me a dollar more than I intended when I started out, and I am converted to the custom of employing an architect. And I want to say that if I ever have occasion to build again, even if it should be nothing more than a chicken-coop, I shall have all my plans, specifications, etc., drawn and prepared before starting out with the work."

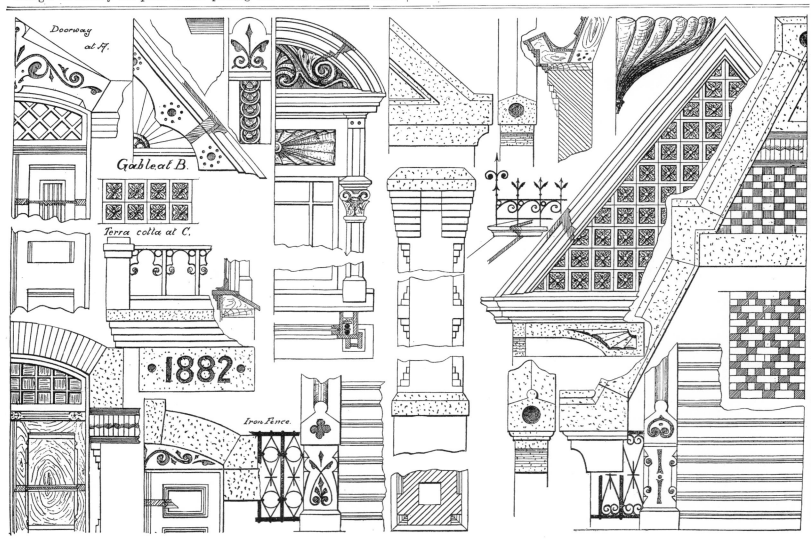

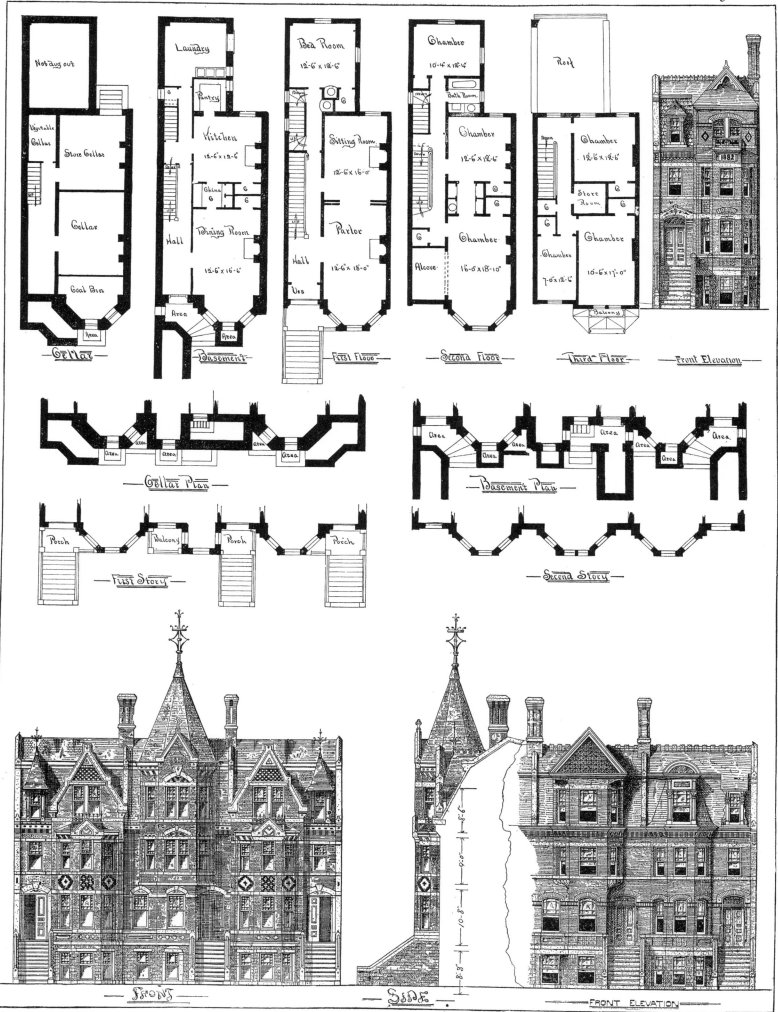

Cellar

Not dug out

Vegetable Cellar

Store Cellar

Cellar

Coal Bin

Area

Basement

Laundry

Pantry

Kitchen
12'-6" x 12'-6"

China

Hall

Dining Room
12'-6" x 16'-6"

Area

Area

First Floor

Bed Room
12'-6" x 12'-6"

Sitting Room
12'-6" x 16'-0"

Hall

Parlor
12'-6" x 18'-0"

Ves.

Area

Second Floor

Chamber
10'-4" x 12'-4"

Bath Room

Chamber
12'-6" x 12'-6"

Chamber
16'-6" x 18'-10"

Alcove

Third Floor

Roof

Chamber
12'-6" x 12'-6"

Store Room

Chamber
7'-0" x 12'-6"

Chamber
10'-6" x 17'-0"

Balcony

Front Elevation

1882

Cellar Plan

Area

Basement Plan

Area

First Story

Porch

Balcony

Porch

Porch

Second Story

Front

Side

Front Elevation

PLATE 59.

Design 168 is a cottage that gives a good deal of room for a small amount of money; is compact and well arranged; it gives parlor and library connected together by sliding doors, while the dining-room is on the other side of hall and communicates only with hall and through china closet to kitchen, being away from the other rooms; this arrangement of the dining-room, it is contended by many, is the proper one for many reasons, and is frequently insisted on by many people in building as the only one that is satisfactory to them. The second floor contains four bed-rooms, closets and bath-room, and the exterior, which is shingled throughout, makes a perfect picture with its colors of orange, red and green, and is both simple and picturesque. Cost, $2,300.

Design 169.—Stone for building purposes is the most durable in the long run, the cheapest, and, as a consequence, the best material which can be furnished for the walls of a dwelling, and especially so if the walls are low, as the expense of erecting high and strong scaffolding, and of raising the stone up to a great height is often too great to allow of its use in dwellings for more than one story, and in this way houses are made from necessity far more picturesque than would be the case if the walls were built entirely of stone up to the roof. Rock faced rubble masonry without dressing or working beyond what is necessary in fitting, which can be done with a stone hammer, is the best for country houses of small expense, and over this work vines may be trained and add further to the effect.

This design is of a farm cottage built of stone for first story and shingled above, is plain but neat and a veranda can be added across the front at any time the owner sees fit or is able to have it done.

The arrangement of plan is of a kind that will please many people and contains no waste room and the stairway is reached directly from hall and porch at rear, and four good bed-rooms are provided on second floor. Cost, $2,250.

Design 170 is a good one for the country or sea shore, and the living hall and dining-room, with all the necessary conveniences, tell their own story, and will be found unique. There is plenty of porch room and on second floor are three large bed rooms and balcony, while the exterior is as good as possible to get up, all things considered; first story clapboarded and second story shingled. Cost, $2,000.

Design 171 gives a unique octagon hall, a nice, easy stairs, parlor, dining-room, conservatory, kitchen, pantry and china closet on first floor, and on second floor three bed-rooms with closets. The exterior is plain but attractive and in every way suitable for the country.

It is difficult to persuade people who live in the country to place their dwellings on the best and most sightly part of their grounds; they will invariably keep in a close proximity to the road, the passing vehicle or traveller being a very acceptable sight for those who see but few people in their vicinity, but it should ever be remembered that the great charm of a country home in pleasant weather is its surroundings, and the dwelling should be so placed as to make the most of them, but if one must build near the road, as a matter of taste, it is best to have a broad and roomy foreground between the house and road. It gives a finer effect to the house and an opportunity for enhancing its value and appearance when properly taken care of, and it should not be allowed to exist under any other circumstances.

Window (a) Jomb

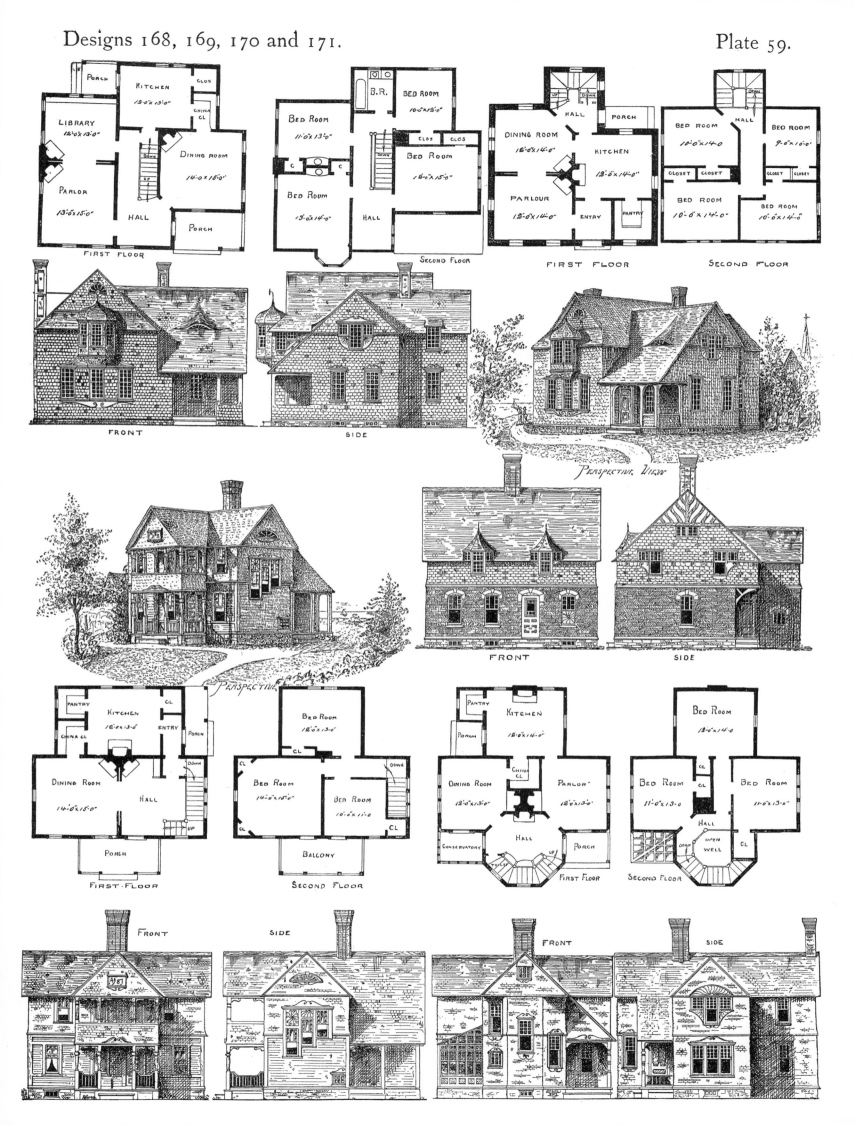

Design 168

PORCH — KITCHEN 12·0"x13·0" — CLOS — CHINA CL
LIBRARY 12·0"x13·0" — DINING ROOM 14·0"x15·0" — DOWN — UP
PARLOR 13·6"x15·0" — HALL — PORCH

FIRST FLOOR

Design 169

B.R. — BED ROOM 10·6"x12·0"
BED ROOM 11·0"x13·0" — CLOS — CLOS
C — C — BED ROOM 13·0"x15·0"
BED ROOM 13·0"x14·0" — HALL

SECOND FLOOR

Design 170

UP — DOWN
HALL — PORCH
DINING ROOM 12·0"x14·0" — KITCHEN 12·6"x14·0"
PARLOUR 12·0"x14·0" — ENTRY — PANTRY

FIRST FLOOR

Design 171

DOWN
BED ROOM 10·0"x14·0 — HALL — BED ROOM 9·0"x10·0"
CLOSET — CLOSET — CLOSET — CLOSET
BED ROOM 10·6"x14·0" — BED ROOM 10·0"x14·0

SECOND FLOOR

FRONT   SIDE   PERSPECTIVE VIEW

PERSPECTIVE   FRONT   SIDE

PANTRY — KITCHEN 12·0"x13·6" — CL — ENTRY — PORCH
CHINA CL
DINING ROOM 14·0"x15·0" — HALL — DOWN
PORCH

FIRST FLOOR

BED ROOM 12·0"x13·0" — CL
CL — BED ROOM 14·0"x15·0" — BED ROOM 10·0"x11·0" — DOWN
CL — CL
BALCONY

SECOND FLOOR

PANTRY — KITCHEN 12·0"x14·0"
PORCH — CHINA CL
DINING ROOM 12·0"x13·0" — PARLOR 12·0"x13·0"
CONSERVATORY — HALL — UP — PORCH
TOILET

FIRST FLOOR

BED ROOM 12·0"x14·0
CL
BED ROOM 11·0"x13·0 — CL — BED ROOM 11·0"x13·0
HALL — DOWN — OPEN WELL — CL

SECOND FLOOR

FRONT   SIDE   FRONT   SIDE

PLATE 60.

Design 172 is for a southern house, many of which are now being built at the South by northern people for residence there so as to escape the severe winter weather at the North during a few months of the year; similar houses can also be used at the summer resorts of the North for residence during the heated term, and thus one might be like the bird of migration, and be able to avoid almost wholly the worst of any weather and take things comparatively comfortable all the year round; this can be and is carried out to a considerable extent by invalids and others who have leisure and wealth.

This kind of house is however more often built by the planter and people who are going South to build up the country and make for themselves permanent homes; the design is therefore plain, unpretending, devoid of ornamentation, but such as can be readily executed out of the materials at hand, and therefore inexpensive in construction and the arrangement of rooms with door and window openings at both ends, plenty of piazza on both floors, kitchen away from the living rooms, etc., are all calculated to give as cool a house as possible, and this plan fills the wants of the people and meets their case as to climate, etc. Cost, $700.

Design 173 provides three living-rooms on first floor and a large amount of piazza. The kitchen is not shown as it is intended to be located in a separate shed at rear of the piazza. The second floor gives three bed-rooms and a large porch. Cost, $800.

Design 174 contains on first floor a large living-room with recessed fire-place and seats, kitchen and pantry at the rear, a good piazza, and on second floor two bed-rooms and large balconies, making in all a desirable southern home. Cost, $600.

It may strike the reader that the two last described houses have a lavish appropriation of piazza. In regard to this it may be remarked that no feature of the house in a southern climate can be more expressive of easy, comfortable enjoyment, than a spacious veranda. The habits of southern life demand it as a place of exercise in wet weather, and the cooler seasons of the year, as well as a place of recreation and social intercourse during the fervid heats of the summer. Indeed, many southern people almost live under the shade of their verandas. It is a delightful place to take their meals, to receive their visitors and friends; and the veranda gives to a dwelling the very expression of hospitality, so far as any one feature of a dwelling can do it. No equal amount of accommodation can be provided for the same cost. It adds infinitely to the room of the house itself, and is, in fact, indispensable to the full enjoyment of a southern home.

As to the use of materials in the construction of such houses, it is generally simply a matter of calculation with him who needs them to figure the first cost of any material he has at hand and adapted for the buildings he wishes to erect, and adopt the cheapest he can find is not by any means the result of a pinched pocket, but it is purely business considerations which control the people who need the buildings and study up all matters connected therewith to the spending of as little money as possible, which in its results is the most advantageous to his interests, provided the main points are attained and the time being provided for and taken care of, and, therefore, wood may be said to be the best material to use, as it is usually abundant and easily obtained at the South, is worked with greater facility than brick, and on many accounts is the cheapest material, for the time, of which a building can be constructed, but, of course, it is perishable and requires every few years a coat of paint, and is associated with the idea of decay, but then everything is, to a greater or lesser degree.

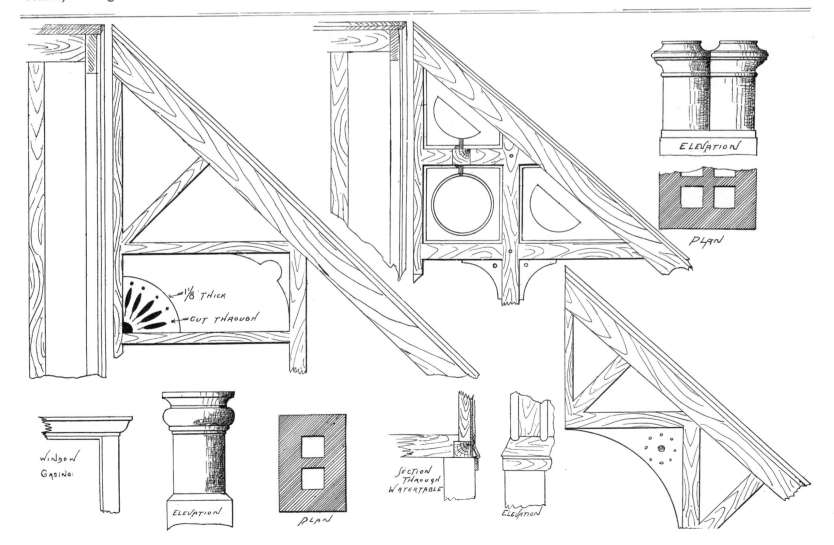

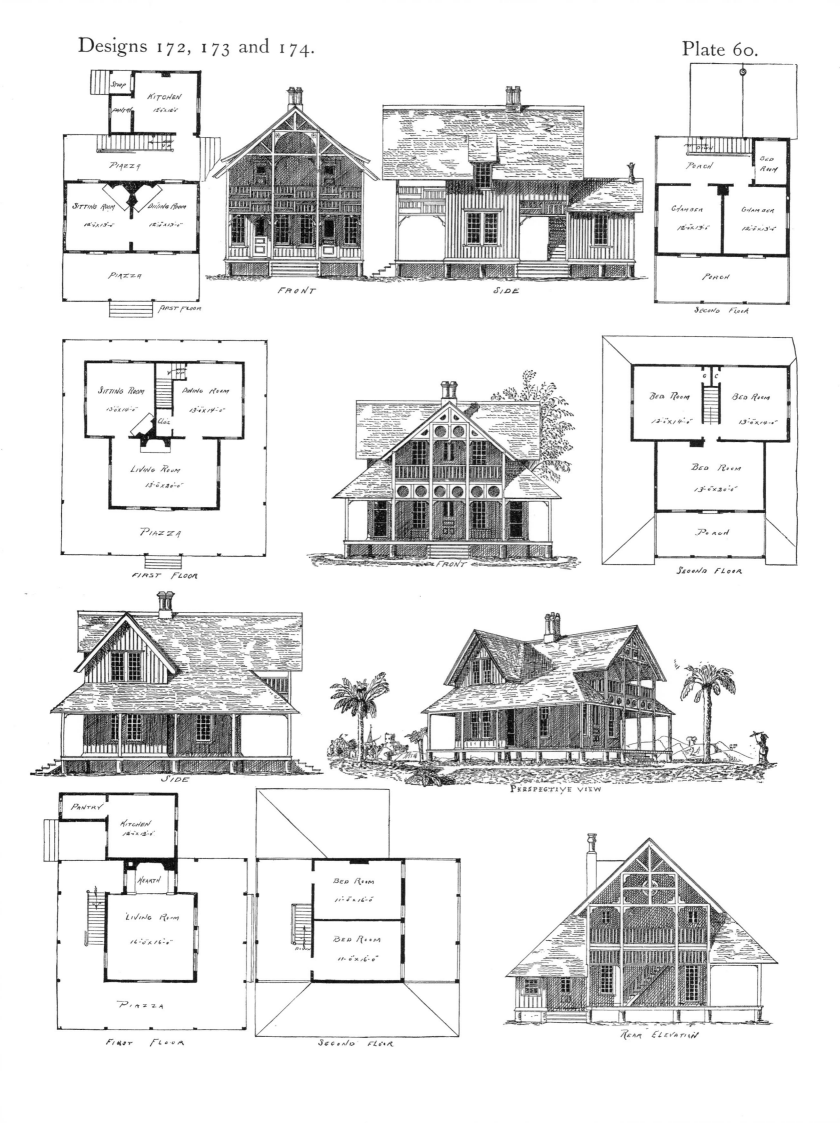

STOOP

KITCHEN
15'0"x16'0"

PANTRY

PIAZZA

SITTING ROOM
18'0"x13'0"

DINING ROOM
12'0"x13'0"

PIAZZA

FIRST FLOOR

FRONT

SIDE

PORCH

BED ROOM

CHAMBER
12'0"x13'6"

CHAMBER
12'0"x13'4"

PORCH

SECOND FLOOR

SITTING ROOM
13'0"x14'0"

DINING ROOM
13'0"x14'0"

CLOS

LIVING ROOM
13'0"x20'0"

PIAZZA

FIRST FLOOR

FRONT

BED ROOM
13'0"x14'0"

BED ROOM
13'0"x14'0"

BED ROOM
13'0"x20'0"

PORCH

SECOND FLOOR

SIDE

PERSPECTIVE VIEW

PANTRY

KITCHEN
18'0"x12'0"

HEARTH

LIVING ROOM
16'0"x16'0"

PIAZZA

FIRST FLOOR

BED ROOM
11'0"x16'0"

BED ROOM
11'0"x16'0"

ROOM

SECOND FLOOR

REAR ELEVATION

PLATE 61.

Design 175 provides, on account of the situation, a broad front in a locality where there is plenty of ground, and can be set off to the best advantage in the country, answering well for a farmer or country gentleman, the room marked "Den" being the master's business or smoking room, but if the house was otherwise used, would do for a sewing-room or for any purpose that the occupants might see fit. The hall with its handsome staircase at the end gives one a hospitable welcome on coming within the front doors. The dining-room is a very pleasant room, and the kitchen offices are all that can be desired. On the second floor, four bedrooms and bath-room are provided. Cost, $2,800.

We have always maintained and advised that the two principal fronts of a house should face east and south, and where the ground is laid off in narrow plots, the front is best to be towards the east, but it is said that Carl Vogt, the eminent scientist of Geneva, Switzerland, by experiment, established the fact that, leaving the north side of a building out of the question, the south side is found during the summer months to be always the coolest, the east side following next in degree of temperature, while the west side he found to be the warmest. The direct effect of the solar rays upon the eastern and western walls of a house he found to be greatly stronger than upon the southern walls, this difference being accounted for by the different angles of incidence of the solar rays falling upon the walls. On the east and west sides, the said angle reaches its maximum size of ninety degrees, while the south walls are struck at an acute angle, hence the effect is much slighter. Vogt for the first time called attention to the problem of computing scientifically how our dwelling houses should be placed to insure for them a sufficient quantity of solar heat and light. Although the idea would not seem to be of much practical value when applied to our customary city dwellings, surrounded, as they are, by other buildings, it must be conceded that in its application to detached dwellings it is deserving of careful consideration at the hands of the professional architect.

As long as nineteen hundred years ago, Vitruvius, the Roman architect, laid stress on the principle that in planning cities the streets must not be laid parallel with the direction of the prevailing atmospherical currents. In Germany, the prevailing currents are northeast and southwest; hence her towns, if laid out on the rectangular plan, should have streets running from east to west and from north to south. This plan has actually been followed in a number of cases, for instance, the cities of Mannheim, Darmstadt and others. Supposing a house so placed, it is evident that the prevailing northeast winds must strike the sides of the house at angles of incidence averaging forty-five degrees. Other winds striking the walls squarely, or nearly so, are usually of short duration, blowing only for a few hours at one time.

It will be observed that if we locate our homes on the principle advocated by Vitruvius, we are, at the same time, fulfilling the requirements demanded by Professor Vogt. During the summer months, the sun rising in the northeast and setting in the northwest, the east and west walls of a house will be heated to a greater, and the south wall to a lesser degree since the rays of the sun then being at its greater declination, fall more obliquely upon the latter than they do upon the former. On the other hand, during the winter months, the sun rising in the southeast and setting in the southwest, it is the south wall which is exposed to rays thrown upon it almost at right angles by the sun, which then is at its minimum declination, whilst both east and west walls receive oblique rays only only. Hence, if your house is so planned that one side greatly exceeds in length the other, place its long side on a line running from east to west to insure for the same greater warmth in winter and less heat in summer, whilst the short side can better afford to be the cooler side in winter and the hotter one in summer, just because it is the shorter side.

Design 176 is suited to a suburban lot of fifty or more feet in width, or might be adapted to the open country or seaside, having a large amount of piazza room, and a compact and economical arrangement of rooms that is taking, and fully explained by the plans. In addition to the bed-rooms on first floor, there is also one provided in the attic. Cost, $2,400.

Design 177 gives a good plan adapted for a farm house, with liberal hall and connections to parlor and dining-room, making a grand house for the open country, and we know of no reason why a farmer, because he is a farmer, should occupy only an uncouth, outlandish house, as many of them do, any more than a professional man, a merchant or a mechanic. Is it because his occupation in life is degrading, his intellect ignorant or his position low? Surely not. Yet, in many of the plans and designs got up for his accommodation, all due convenience, to say nothing of the respectability or the elegance of domestic life, is as entirely disregarded as if such qualities had no connection with the farmer or his occupation.

This plan and the many others submitted in this work for the farmer are intended to be of the most practical kind: plain, substantial and applicable throughout, to the purpose intended, and such as are within the reach, each in their kind, of every farmer in our country. Cost of erecting this house, $3,100.

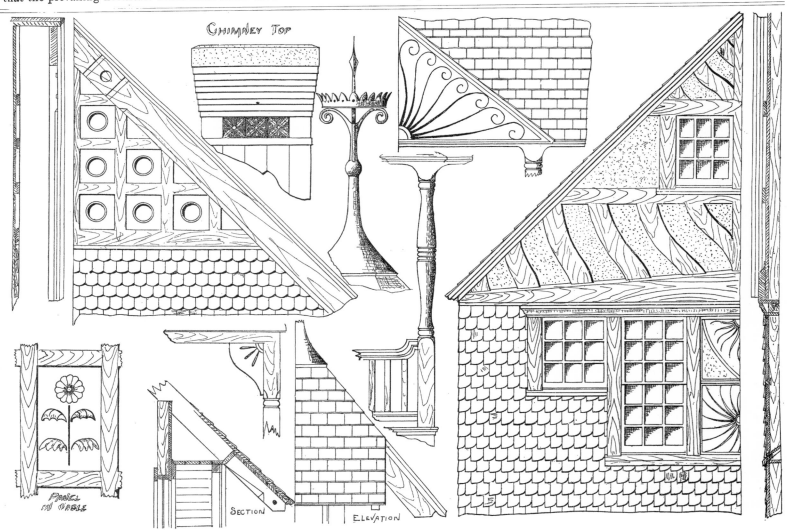

CHIMNEY TOP

PANEL IN GABLE

SECTION

ELEVATION

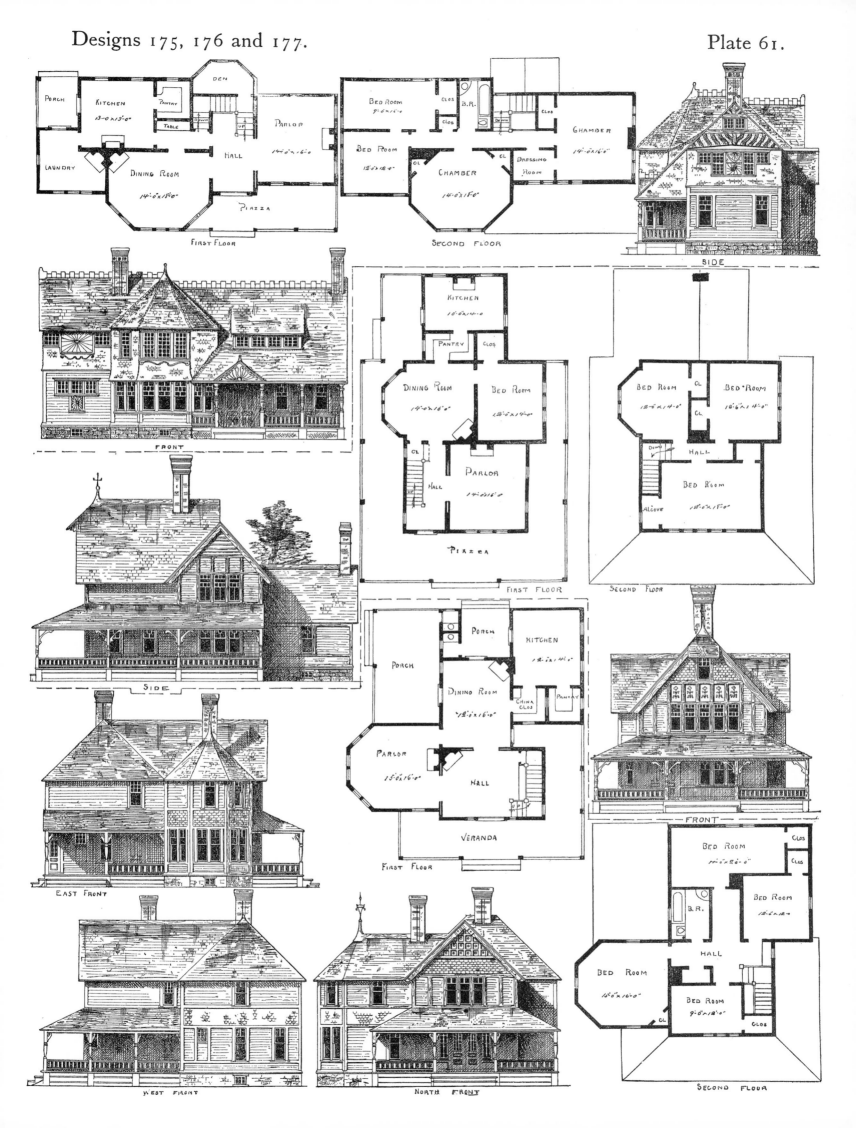

Design 178 is for a suburban dwelling constructed of brick with the window sills of first story windows on a level with the floor; a feature that is seldom carried out in the planning of dwellings in this country. The exterior design is of a plain, substantial kind and well calculated to wear well and give no trouble by way of repairs or expense in the way of painting, and is such as will attract the attention of those who like to possess a house combining such desirable features as they will find this one does, after a careful study of the same.

The interior gives a unique hall, which is entered through a vestibule; an attractive and easy stairs to second floor, toilet-room under stairs, a parlor, drawing-room and dining-room, all of large dimensions and very pleasantly situated and opening up in a most hospitable and useful manner. A study or library, an easy flight of back stairs, a large kitchen with pantries and store-room, and an entrance that will shut out the cold winds of winter. On the second floor is five bed-rooms, dressing-room, bath-room, W. C., and abundance of closets, and on third floor are two bed-rooms and large store-room. Cost, $7,500.

Design 179 is of a perfectly square house, the first story veneered with brick outside of frame and sheathing. First floor has a good arrangement in large hall, parlor, dining-room and kitchen, conservatory at rear of dining-room and veranda extending nearly around the entire house. There are four bed-rooms and bath on second floor.

You will very often hear people talking about a square house and that is the kind they mean to build, and we would say to such here is a model to study and work after without offending good taste. Cost, $2,800.

Objections may be made to some of the plans we have submitted because there is no bed-room marked on first floor and then again some may object to the bed-room on first floor and prefer it upstairs and so on with other arrangements which may be objected to. The answer to these may be, that the bed-room when it is wanted on first floor can be, as a rule, easily obtained there, although not marked and where it is not wanted and is marked, it may be used for other purposes equally as well, and that people's wants, with utility and convenience, are the main objects to be attained in any well ordered dwelling. These requisites attained, the principal one—comfort—is secured.

Cellar kitchens—the most abominable nuisances that ever crept into a country dwelling—might have been adopted, no doubt, to the especial delight of some who know nothing of the experimental duties of housekeeping, but the recommendation of these is an offence which we have no stomach to answer for hereafter. In the country where there is room, it should always be the aim of the intending builder to select a plan that spreads over rather than goes down into the ground and high up in the air. Steep, winding and complicated staircases have been avoided as far as possible, dark closets, intricate passages, cubby holes and all sorts of gimcrackery might have amused our pencil; but we have avoided them as well as everything which would stand in the way of the simplest, cheapest and most direct mode of reaching the object in view; a convenient, comfortably arranged dwelling within, having a respectable dignified appearance without to meet the wants of the people intended for, and such we have endeavored to gather together for presentation in this work.

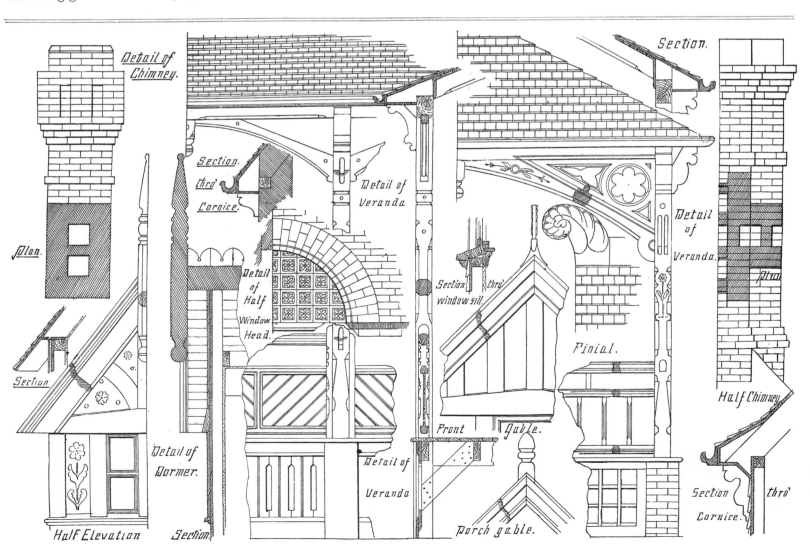

Detail of Chimney.

Plan.

Section.

Section thro' Cornice.

Detail of Half Window Head.

Detail of Dormer.

Half Elevation

Section.

Detail of Veranda

Section.

Detail of Veranda

Section thro' window sill.

Finial.

Front Gable.

Porch gable.

Detail of Veranda.

Plan.

Half Chimney

Section thro' Cornice.

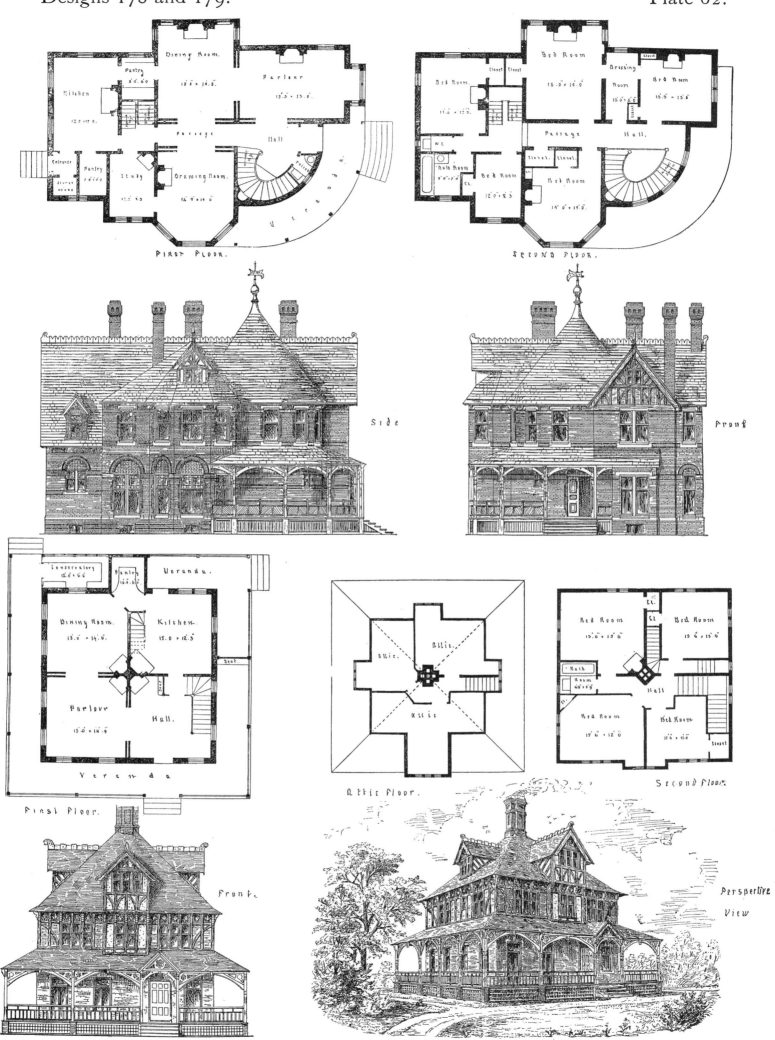

FIRST FLOOR.

SECOND FLOOR.

Side

Front

First Floor.

Attic Floor.

Second Floor.

Front.

Perspective View

Design 180 represents a perfect gem of a suburban or country house, giving a wide hall through the centre, with fire-place and sliding-doors to sitting-room from hall; a piazza at both front and rear, with an entry-way at rear to main hall, away from the kitchen entrance. Main staircase is well back out of the way, yet can be seen sufficiently from main entrance. A toilet room is located under these stairs. The rear stairs are convenient to the domestic offices and continue right up to the attic, and can be shut off from the second floor at pleasure. The dining-room is of good dimensions and good shape for its uses. Some people insist on having a dining-room made 16 or 17 feet wide, which we regard as foolish in an ordinary house, as 12 or 13 feet for the width is all that is necessary or desirable. The second floor gives five bed-rooms, bath-room and closets, all finished up in a very plain, neat manner, painted, with very simple and small mouldings, and the finish of first floor, main rooms and hall is in natural wood, without paint, thus bringing out the natural beauty of the grain of the wood. The exterior is simple, but in good taste; first story of clapboarded finish, and second story shingled with California redwood shingles, all butts rounded. Cost, $4,800.

Design 181 gives a good style, solid and substantial house, built of stone for outside of first story, which is laid around a frame, put up in about the ordinary manner before the stone work is begun to be laid, which is put up in a simple and rough manner, letting the stones run in between the studs inside and working to a face line only on the outside, and then sheathing on the inside of studs with Byrkitt's sheathing lath, making a perfectly substantial, tight and dry job. The second story is of the clapboarded finish, with a roof covered with California red-wood shingle, finished so as to give it the appearance of English tile. The first-floor plan is especially interesting in the arrangement of its hall and the rooms around it, while the second floor contains four chambers, dressing-room and bath-room, with plenty of closets, the woodwork throughout being of California mahogany or redwood. Cost, $7,500.

Among the many objects used for adornment in connection with a dwelling, there is a very pretty one which we would like to see more frequently employed, and which, when properly placed in a gable or on the panel of a brick chimney, with "Tempus fugit," in terra cotta below it, or placed on a summer house by the side of some walk or retired spot, is in itself highly suggestive. It is the sun-dial we refer to. What thoughts this monitor suggests to the mind? How silent, yet how eloquent. His must be a vacant mind who can pass such a teacher without finding in memories of the past something to dwell upon and also hopes of pleasant things for the future. A shadow reminds us of the flight of time, and we learn in the end that we have pursued but shadows. In the words of the poet:

> "This shadow on the dial's face,
>   That steals from day to day,
> With slow, unseen, unceasing pace,
>   Moments and months and years away;
> This shadow which, in every clime,
>   Since light and motion first began,
> Hath held its course sublime—
>   What is it? Mortal man!
> It is the scythe of Time—
>   A shadow only to the eye;
> Yet in its calm career
>   It levels all beneath the sky;
> And still, through each succeeding year,
> Right onward, with resistless power,
> Its stroke shall darken every hour,
> Till nature's race be run,
> And time's last shadow shall eclipse the sun."

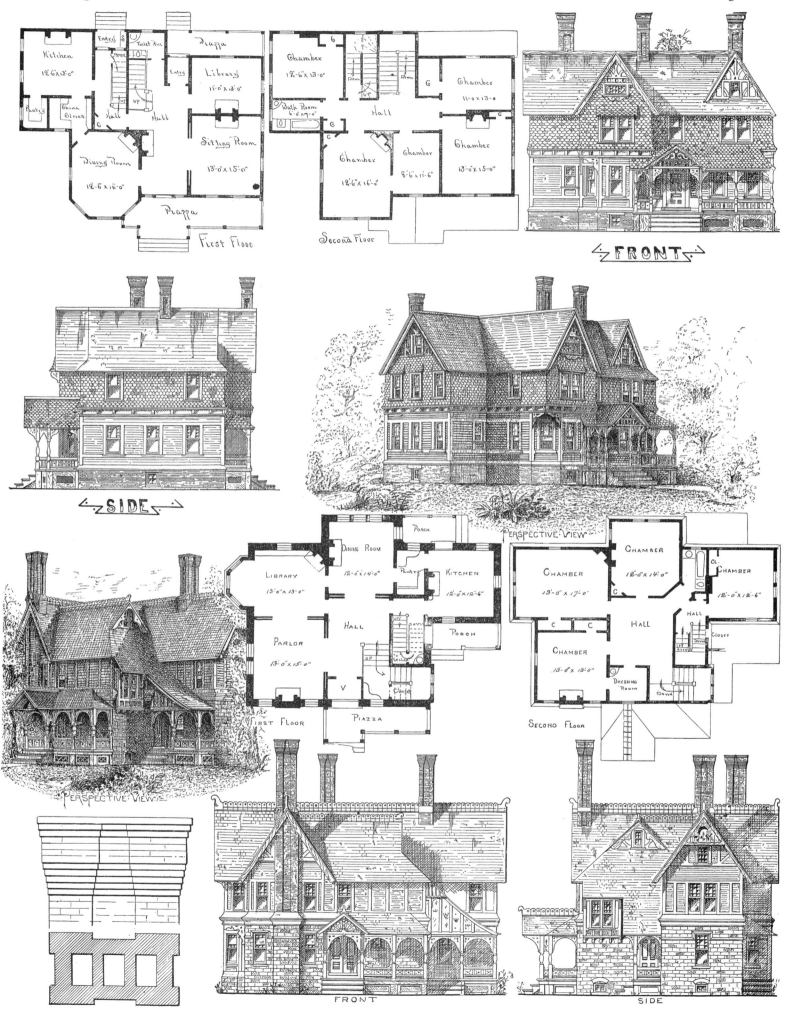

First Floor

Kitchen
12'-6" x 13'-0"

Pantry's

China Closet

Hall

Entry's

Toilet Ans

Piazza

Library
11'-0" x 13'-0"

Dining Room
12'-6" x 16'-0"

Sitting Room
13'-0" x 15'-0"

Piazza

Second Floor

Chamber
12'-6" x 13'-0"

Bath Room
6'-0" x 9'-0"

Hall

Chamber
12'-6" x 16'-0"

Chamber
8'-6" x 11'-6"

Chamber
11'-0" x 13'-0"

Chamber
13'-0" x 15'-0"

FRONT

SIDE

Perspective View

Perspective View

First Floor

Library
13'-0" x 13'-0"

Dining Room
12'-6" x 14'-0"

Kitchen
12'-0" x 12'-6"

Parlor
13'-0" x 15'-0"

Hall

Porch

Piazza

Second Floor

Chamber
13'-0" x 17'-0"

Chamber
12'-6" x 14'-0"

Chamber
12'-0" x 12'-6"

Hall

Closet

Chamber
13'-6" x 13'-0"

Dressing Room

FRONT

SIDE

Design 182 shows a pair of houses with broad front, having four gables on main roof, which is very simple in construction, and at the same time attractive. First and second story are both of shingle finish, and the gables have about them that old-time look which is now coming into vogue so much in the finishing up of the exterior of country houses even to the staining of the shingle to give them that appearance as far as possible. Each house gives 7 good rooms and bath-room. The main hall is just large enough to get an easy stairs with rack and hall stand, door to both parlor and dining-room, and also convenient access to cellar and kitchen, the latter being through two doors, therefore well shut off. Cost, $2,000.

Design 183 gives another pair of houses with entrances well away from one another, and front and back stairs; 3 good living-rooms, all connected on first floor; good dining-room closet under stairs; kitchen and pantry. On second floor, 4 chambers and bath-room, and on third floor 3 bed-rooms. The exterior is after that of some years ago with its gambrel roof, giving good accommodation for rooms on third floor; in fact, these bed-rooms are almost as good as any and are obtained in a very economical manner. Cost, $2,800 a side.

Design 184 gives a house of different type from the two pre-ceeding designs, the halls and entrances being brought together with front piazza in the centre of the house front. This house gives about the same accommodation as the last-mentioned, and can be built on a much narrower piece of ground. Cost, $3,000 a side.

Design 185 is a double house, each side being for a family of six or more persons, gives an immense living-room on first floor, a fine light entrance hall with open fire-place, and seat in corner opposite it, a wash-bowl in passage between front hall and kitchen; cellar stairs are also reached from this passage; kitchen has pantry and large closet, and on second floor there are 3 good bed-rooms with closets, sewing-room or child's bed-room and bath-room. Cost, $1,700 a side.

Those who build double houses like these can easily find tenants or purchasers for them; indeed good large lots of ground in the suburbs of our cities and larger villages, with tasty double houses which can be erected at moderate cost, and with an appropriate amount of landscape embellishment, and a suitable garden, would not remain uncalled for many days. There is a certain steady demand for cosey, comfortable homes, adapted to the means of the great masses that should attract more attention from capitalists. Any convenient locality; and there are plenty of them near all cities where a store, a church, a school-house, etc., can be established, and a number of houses built up and made into an attractive community, that would induce many to leave the crowded town and city tenements, generally so unhealthy, for a home in the open country.

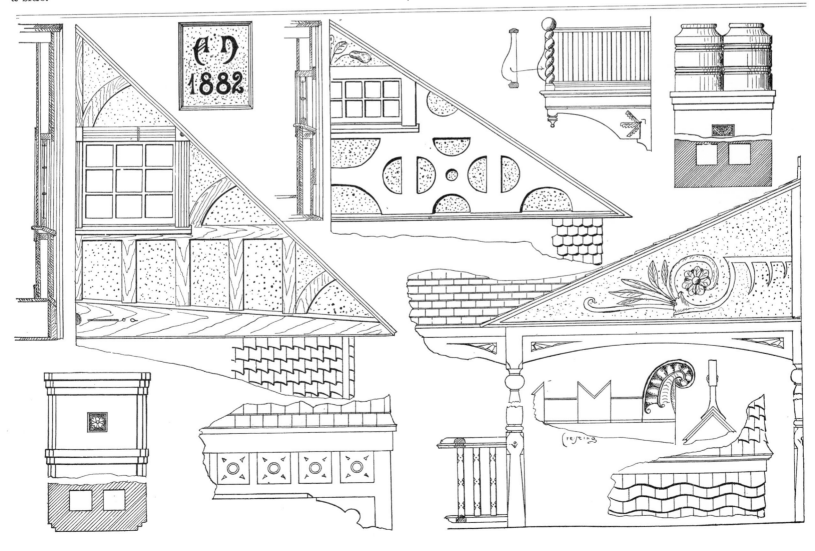

Plate 64.

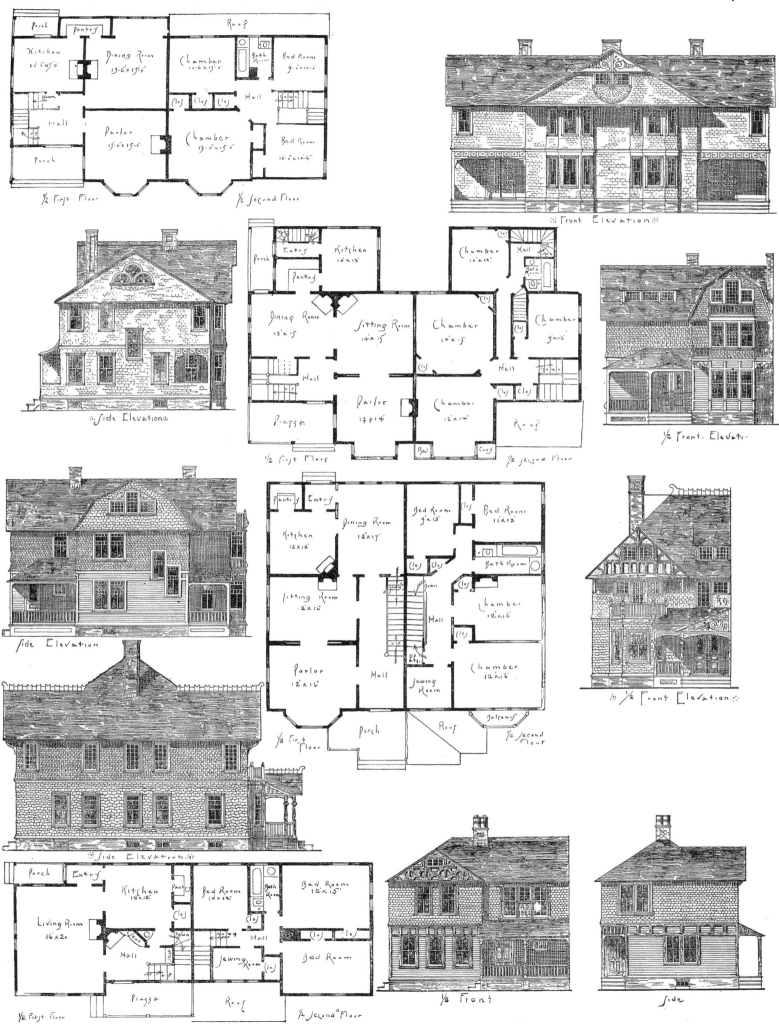

½ First Floor

½ Second Floor

Porch

Pantry

Kitchen 13'6"x13'0"

Dining Room 13'6"x15'0"

Chamber 10'6"x13'0"

Bath Room

Bed Room 9'x10'6"

Roof

Hall

Mall

Clos

Clos

Parlor 13'0"x15'0"

Chamber 13'0"x15'0"

Bed Room 10'0"x10'6"

Porch

Front Elevation

Side Elevation

½ First Floor

½ Second Floor

Porch

Entry

Kitchen 10'x12'

Pantry

Chamber 10'x16'

Hall

Bath Room

Dining Room 12'x15'

Sitting Room 14'x15'

Chamber 14'x15'

Chamber 9'x12'

Hall

Mall

Parlor 17'x14'

Chamber 12'x14'

Roof

Clos

Clos

Piazza

Conv

½ Front. Elevation

½ First Floor

½ Second Floor

Pantry

Entry

Dining Room 12'x17'

Bed Room 9'x13'

Bed Room 11'x12'

Kitchen 12'x12'

Bath Room

Sitting Room 12'x16'

Mall

Chamber 12'x16'

Parlor 12'x16'

Mall

Sewing Room

Chamber 12'x16'

Porch

Roof

Balcony

½ Front Elevation

Side Elevation

½ First Floor

½ Second Floor

Porch

Entry

Kitchen 12'x12'

Pantry

Bed Room 10'x12'

Bath Room

Bed Room 12'x15'

Living Room 16'x20'

Clos

Mall

Bed Room

Hall

Sewing Room

Piazza

Roof

½ Front

Side

PLATE 65

Such designs for fronts of town and city brick street architecture here given if carried out more frequently in the erection of the smaller kind of such houses as they are applicable to, would assist the owner or investor to meet more readily with customers looking for rents or for the purpose of purchasing a snug and attractive home for themselves, but instead of striving to produce something really good and artistic that will be taking with whoever sees them, the builder of blocks of brick houses of moderate cost usually follows a monotonous and unpicturesque, if not an ugly method of building a perfectly straight level top or cornice and an unbroken skyline, and frequently an entirely plain, unbroken front ; in fact it has simply the appearance of a lot of brick boxes all joined together with holes for windows cut symmetrically in them and a flat roof sloping a little to the rear and if one will but take the trouble to watch the life of such houses it will invariably be found that they meet with many trials at the hands of a great army of tenants, and that in the course of eight or ten years they are entirely run down, and the owner has kept reducing the rent and is reducing it still to try and get tenants to occupy the premises, which have gone entirely by the board until they are the dirtiest and meanest of tenements so that no one cares to live in them.

Such houses as these are usually built by investors and speculators, and it is a rare occurrence to find a single individual, building a small brick house in line with a lot of others, and it would be a great deal better for all the parties who are to live in these houses if they could each have their own built to meet their own wants and ideas, and if so, how much more pleasing would be the result of street architecture, as each would vie with the other to put some artistic feature on his front, and therefore, if a box did occasionally creep in, it would only tend to make the others—who had put in a few more dollars for beauty—more prominent, and show that they were wise in doing so, and would therefore teach others a lesson.

Very little, however, can be done with such houses in the city of New York where lots are so costly, run up in price because people have drifted into the manner and custom of living in stuffy tenement houses, four families on a floor of a house of 25 feet in width, with only light to one room in each tenement and in this way a large number of families are squeezed into a single house on a small ground area, and consequently the ground is thus made to yield a fair interest on a large valuation, and as the demand creates the supply, and in this it is for tenements in the city more than for small suburban houses, and we are sorry to see such a state of things, but hope for a movement in the right direction and some one to start the erection of such houses a few miles out of the city where

ground is cheap and plenty, and where people could be very easily induced to come out and live, as there are many who would be glad to go out into the suburbs and live in a house by themselves, and this subject is of vital interest to persons having any consideration for their personal comfort and the preservation of the health of their families. As an investment there cannot be any better one than the building of such houses as these, and we know whereof we speak, as we have superintended the erection of several blocks of such, having from five to eight houses in a block, in some of the smaller cities, and which are rented to mechanics at reasonable rents, and pay the owners over ten per cent. on the investment.

On this plate we give six different styles of fronts sixteen feet in width ; four of double fronts of twenty-five feet ; two of three houses on fifty-foot fronts, and ten fronts of fourteen feet each, all of different design, making in all a grand field for selection, and from which the intending builder can adapt features to meet his case. Cost of such small houses range from $1,500 to $2,500 each.

No pains or expense have been spared in making this work reliable. All designs are of a practical character, can be added to, enlarged reduced and worked from in various ways, and all are well worthy of careful study and attention of the building community, the general public and especially of any one who contemplates building. We mean that it shall supply a want for modern designs of convenient and attractive homes for the million.

We trust that its study will help many a one who does not yet possess a home to strive to own one.

BLESSED ARE THEY WHO HAVE HOMES.

I want to be home when the night comes down—
  When the night comes down and the sun is hid—
And the pale, cold moon lights the glimmering town,
  And is heard the shrill cricket and the katy-did,
Ah me! "There's no place like home."

I want to be home when the night comes down,
  When the storm-king raves and the billows roar,
And the sign-boards creak in the rickety town,
  And the mad waves dash strong ships on shore,
Ah me! what a snug place is home.

With my books, my papers, and my glowing hearth,
  With my wife and children around me there;
With health and love and innocent mirth,
  With a heart content and free from care,—
Ah me! what a heaven is home.

What need I care for the storm-king's wrath?
  What to me is the rain or the lightning's glare?
Though the hurricane sweeps over the doomed ship's path,
  And men lie bleeding, and mangled and bare,
Ah me! what a heaven is home.

Ah! my heart does go out to the homeless band—
  To the homeless and wretched o'er all the earth—
To the wanderer by sea and the wanderer by land,
  And I wish them God-speed from my humble heart;
Ah me! Would that all had a home.

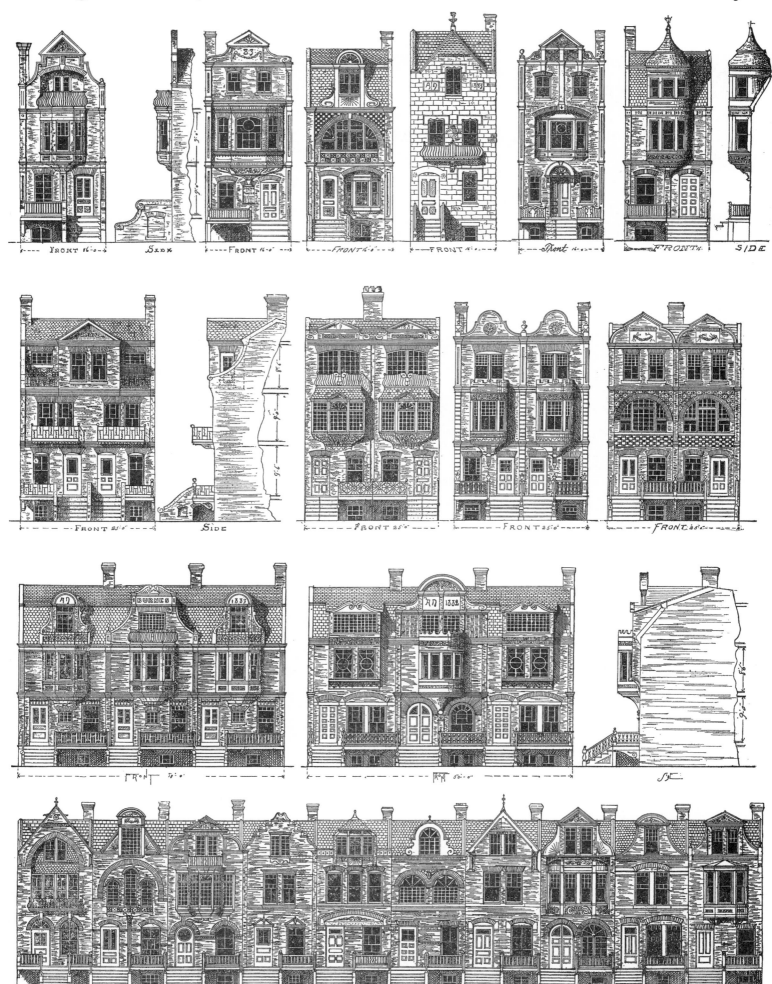

This Conservatory can be found in connection with House on. Plate 27 Design 80

Plan

GLASS GLASS
LARGE SMALL
RAFTERS RAFTERS

WINDOW CORNER
JAMB POST

WELL CURB

Plan

FRONT SIDE

LATTICE WORK OR DOORS

Plan

FRONT SIDE

WELL CURB

SIDE ELEVATION

ONE HALF OF FRONT ELEVATION

Centre Line of Side Elevation

Centre

½ of SIDE

½ of FRONT

Section

ELEVATION

SEAT TABLE PLAN

½ of FRONT ½ of SIDE

PLAN OF ARBOR

TABLE

SEAT SEAT SEAT

SEAT TABLE TABLE PLAN

SIDE FRONT
SUMMER HOUSE

WELL A

ELEVATION

SEAT TABLE SEAT SEAT PLAN

REFRESHMENTS

ELEVATION Centre Line BAR

SEAT TABLE PLAN

PLAN

FRONT SIDE

ELEVATION OF ARBOR

SIDE OF WELL AT A FRONT OF WELL

½ PLAN

LATTICE WORK

EARTH CLOSET

TOOL HOUSE

PLAN

FRONT SIDE CORN CRIB

OPEN OPEN OPEN

PLAN

FRONT SIDE

Conservatory and Outbuildings.

Fences, Gates and Posts.

Doors and Casings.

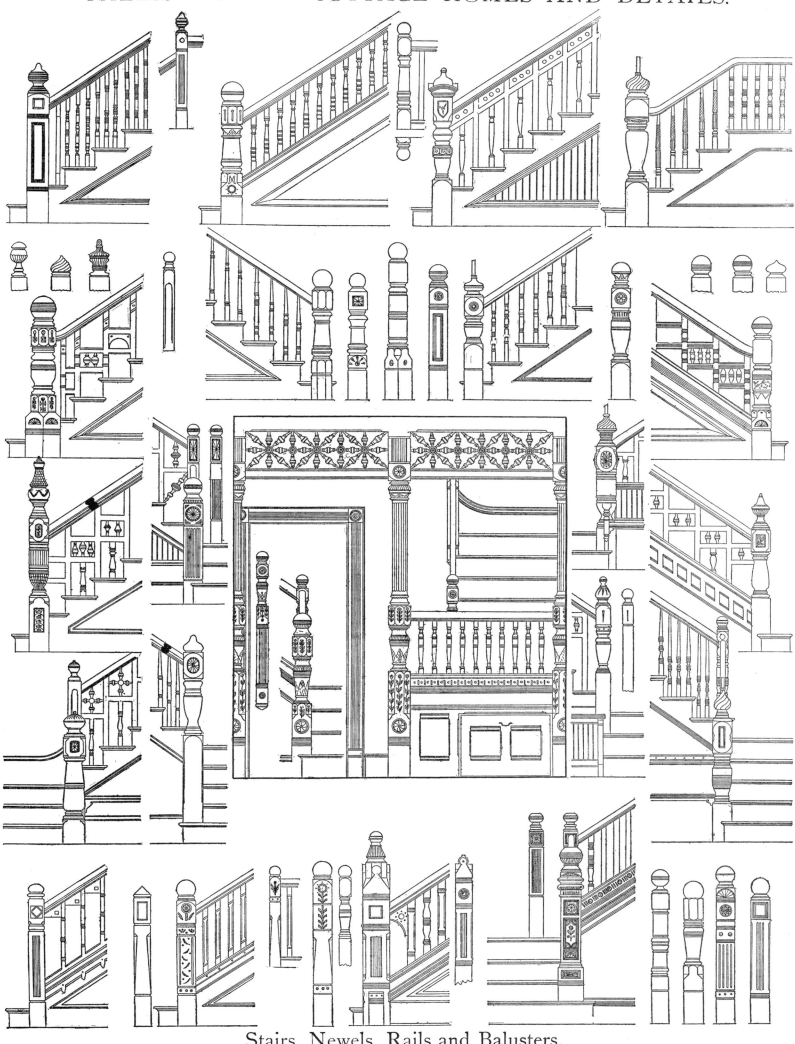

Stairs, Newels, Rails and Balusters.

Mantels.

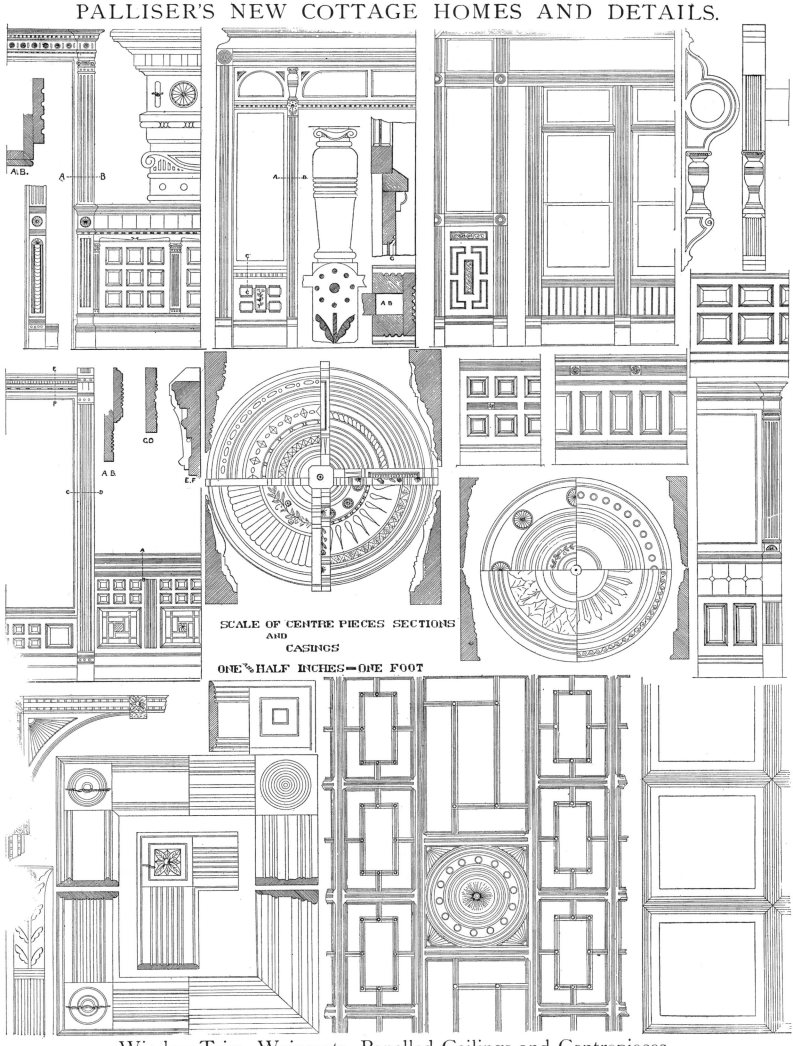

SCALE OF CENTRE PIECES SECTIONS
AND
CASINGS

ONE AND HALF INCHES = ONE FOOT

Window-Trim, Wainscots, Panelled Ceilings and Centrepieces.

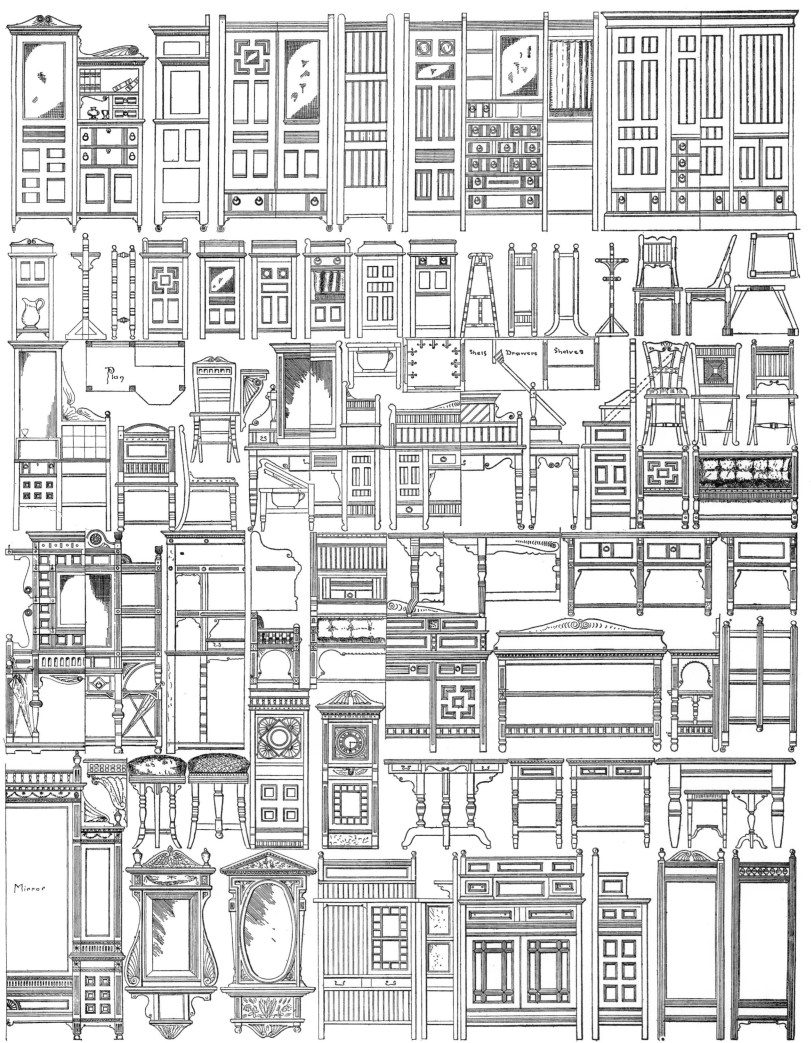

Furniture.

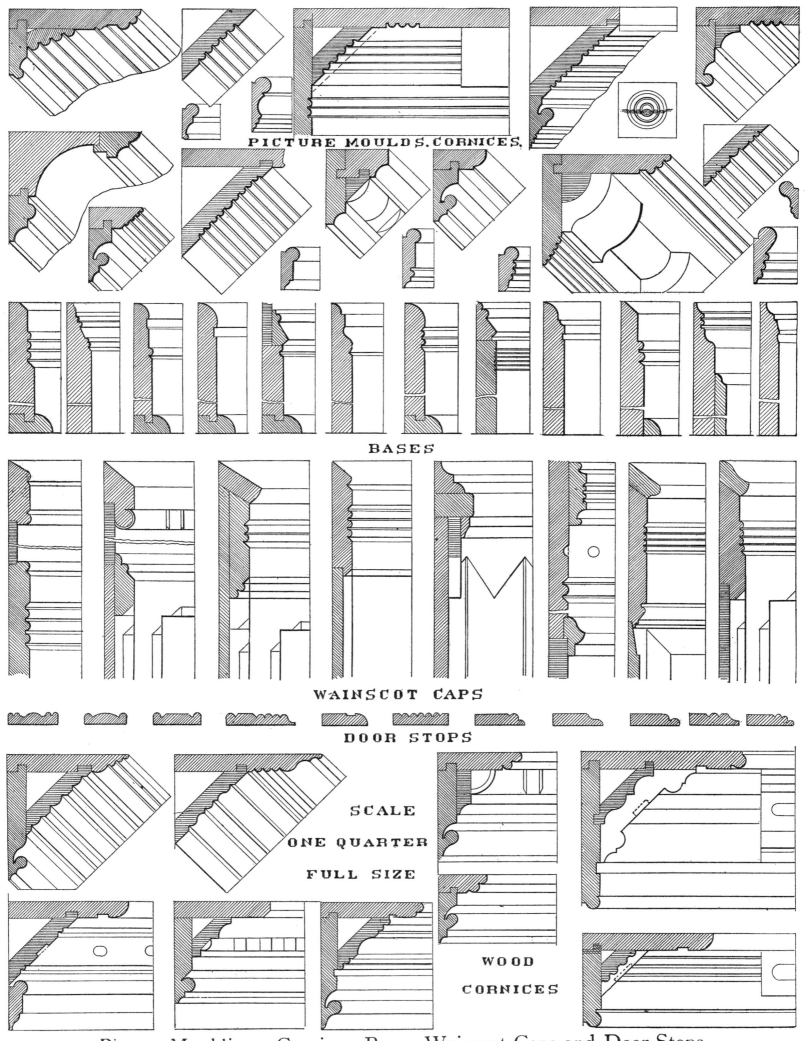

PICTURE MOULDS. CORNICES.

BASES

WAINSCOT CAPS

DOOR STOPS

SCALE

ONE QUARTER

FULL SIZE

WOOD

CORNICES

Picture Mouldings, Cornices, Bases, Wainscot Caps and Door Stops.

Bookcases and Cabinets.

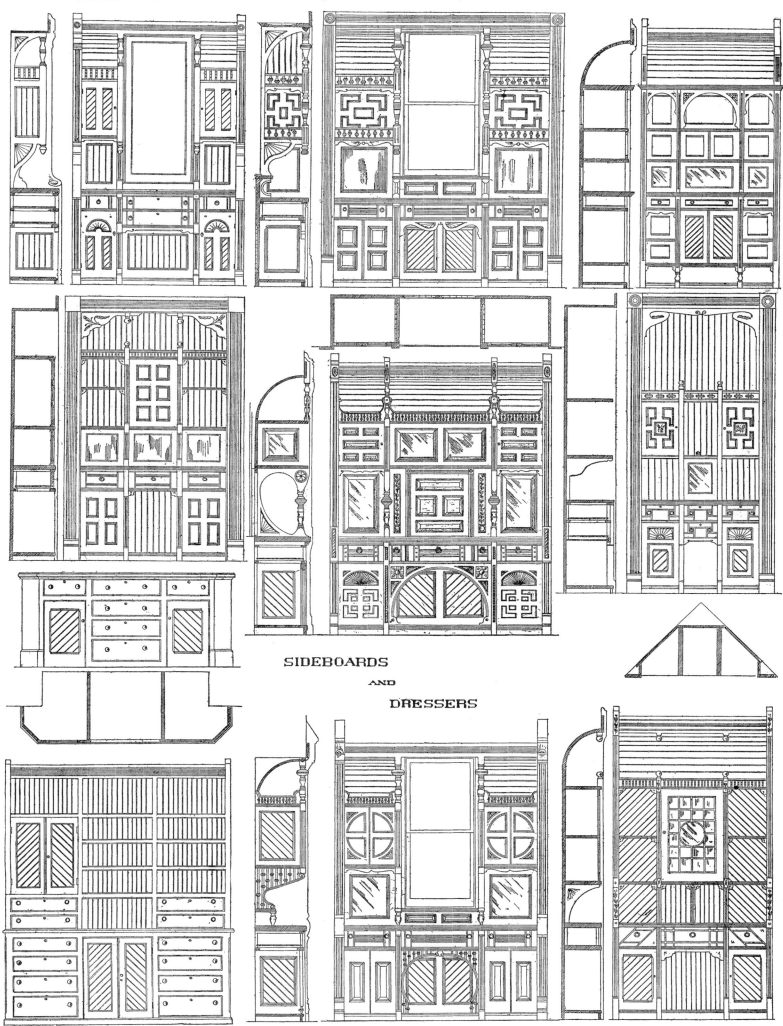

SIDEBOARDS

AND

DRESSERS

Sideboards and Dressers.

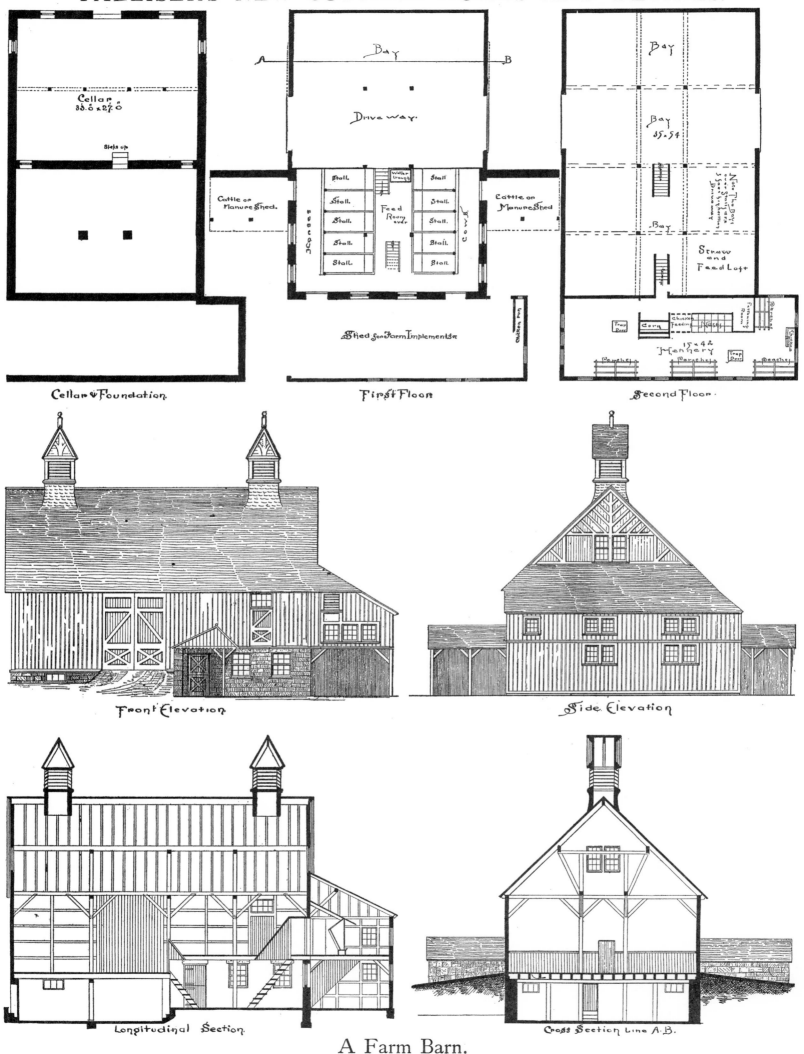

Cellar & Foundation.

First Floor.

Second Floor.

Front Elevation.

Side Elevation.

Longitudinal Section.

Cross Section Line A. B.

A Farm Barn.

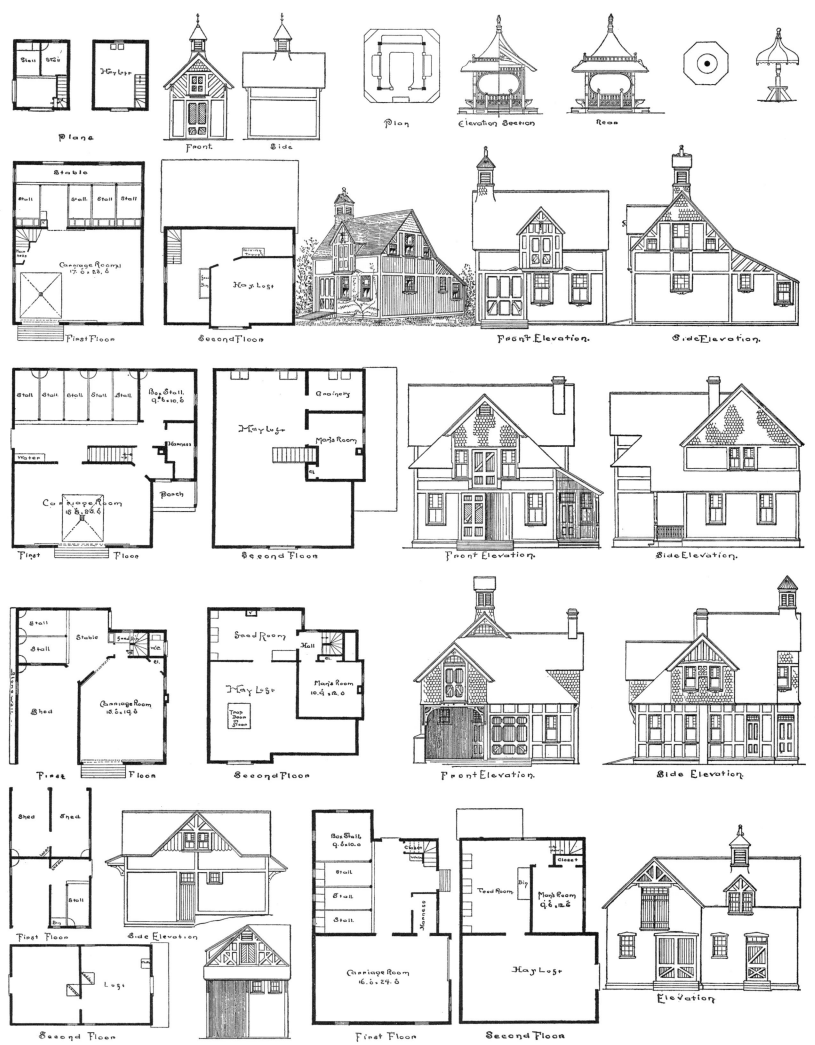

Stall **Stall**

Hay Loft

Plans

Front   Side

Plan   Elevation Section   Rear

Stable

Stall | Stall. | Stall | Stall

Harness

Carriage Room
17.0 x 23.0

First Floor

Mixing Trough

Seed Bin   Hay Loft

Second Floor

Front Elevation.   Side Elevation.

Stall | Stall. | Stall. | Stall. | Stall. | Box Stall.
9.6 x 10.6

Harness

Water

Carriage Room
16.8 x 20.6

First   Floor

Granary

Hay Loft

Man's Room

Porch

Second Floor

Front Elevation.   Side Elevation.

Stall

Stall   Stable   Seed Bin
W.C.

Shed   Carriage Room
16.0 x 19.0

First   Floor

Seed Room

Hall

Hay Loft   Man's Room
10.4 x 12.0

Trap Door in Floor

Second Floor

Front Elevation.   Side Elevation.

Shed   Shed

Stall

Bin

First Floor

Side Elevation

Loft

Second Floor

Box Stall.
9.6 x 10.0

Closet
Water

Stall

Stall   Harness

Stall

Carriage Room
16.0 x 24.0

First Floor

Feed Room   Bin   Man's Room
9.6 x 12.6

Closet

Hay Loft

Second Floor

Elevation

Summer House, Garden Seat and Stables and Carriage Houses.

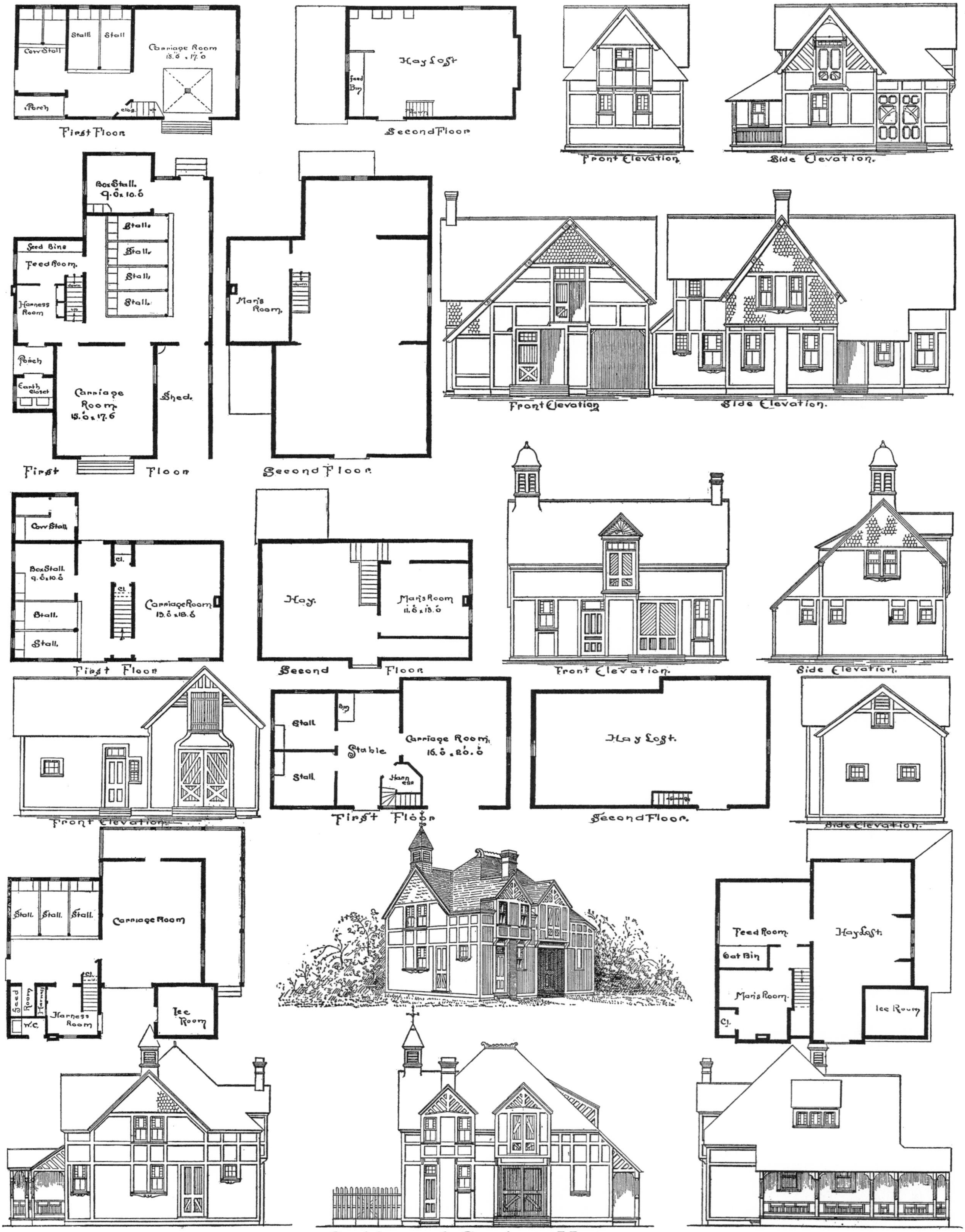

Cow Stall

Stall Stall

Carriage Room
15.0 x 17.0

Porch clos.

First Floor

Feed Bin

Hay Loft

Second Floor

Front Elevation.

Side Elevation.

Box Stall.
9.0 x 10.0

Seed Bins

Feed Room.

Stall.
Stall.
Stall.
Stall.

Harness Room

Porch

Earth Closet

Carriage Room
15.0 x 17.6

Shed.

First Floor

Man's Room.

Second Floor

Front Elevation

Side Elevation.

Cow Stall.

Box Stall.
9.0 x 10.0

Stall.

Stall.

cl.

cl.

Carriage Room
15.0 x 18.0

First Floor

Hay.

Man's Room
11.0 x 13.0

Second Floor

Front Elevation.

Side Elevation.

Front Elevation.

Stall.

Stall.

Bin

Stable

Carriage Room.
16.0 x 20.0

Harness

First Floor

Hay Loft.

Second Floor.

Side Elevation.

Stall. Stall. Stall.

Carriage Room

Seed Room

Harness Room

Ice Room

W.C.

cl.

Feed Room.

Oat Bin

Man's Room.

Ice Room

cl.

Stables and Carriage Houses.

SPECIFICATIONS

(Written to go with Working and Detail Drawings).

Of the works and materials required in the erection, construction and completion of Design No. 10, Plate 4.

DIMENSIONS.—The drawings and details must be accurately followed according to their scale, and in all cases preference must be given to figured dimensions over scale. The building to be in size as shown on plans (figured on drawings). Cellar, 6ft. 6in. ; first floor, 9ft. 0in. ; second floor, 8ft. 6in. in the clear, divided, subdivided, and built in exact accordance with plans and specifications.

MASON WORK.

Excavations.—Do all necessary excavating required for cellar, area and all foundations, to firm and solid ground, and all to be in depth so that foundations will be clear of frost, also excavate for cesspools and dig out space where shown three feet deeper than cellar bottom for cistern. Fill in around all walls and grade off the ground at completion, and remove any surplus earth.

Foundation Work.—Build the foundation walls of good flat building stone, of firm bed, well bonded through the wall, laid up in clean, sharp sand lime and cement mortar, in parts of one of cement to two of lime, laid by and full to a line on the inner face, and flushed and pointed at completion. These walls to be 1ft. 4 in. thick. Put down in like manner foundations under all piers, chimneys and exterior steps, all to be clear of frost.

Underpinning.—From the top of foundation wall, at grade level, extend up 2 ft. 4 in. in height, with stone wall 1 ft. 4 in. thick, laid up with good even colored gray underpinning stone, rock faced, beds and joints worked off with stone hammer to level and plumb and cleaned down and pointed at completion —window sills of blue stone.

Piers.—Build piers in cellar also for support of Porches, as shown, of best hard-burned brick.

Chimneys and Fire Places.—Build the chimneys as shown, using hard-burned brick, the flues to have all mortar joints flushed up close and smooth, and plaster over the brick work in rooms before studding or furring is done—with one good coat. Open fire places to be faced up with buff brick laid in buff mortar. Turn trimmer arches to fire places under hearths, hearths to be of smooth slate properly bedded. Top out the chimneys above the roof, as shown, with selected brick of even color.

Hatchway.—Build the hatchway to cellar as shown on plan, treads of stone walled in, on each end, risers of hard brick, jambs to be of same material as cellar walls and coped with stone on which to secure frame and doors.

Lathing.—All stud partitions, ceilings and work that is furred off, on first and second floors, to be lathed with sound spruce lath and joints broken every tenth lath.

Plastering.—All walls, partitions and ceilings, throughout first and second floors, to be plastered one good coat of brown well-haired mortar, and finish with a coat of soapstone finish. All walls to be finished straight and plumb ; all angles to be maintained sharp and regular in form, and the plastering, in all cases, to extend clear down to the floor.

Whitewashing.—Stop, point and lime whiten twice the whole of mason work in cellar, also whitewash floor joist and timber work overhead.

Cellar Bottom.—Level off the cellar bottom, settle it thoroughly and cover it flush and smooth throughout with cement concrete, three parts of clean, coarse gravel, and one of good cement 2 in. deep and finish with an even surface.

Drains.—To carry off wastes from plumbing, to be of vitrified pipe, size ; as marked, and to run 60 ft. to rear of house and there connect with cesspools to be properly graded and all joints made tight.

Cistern.—Build a cistern as shown under pantry 6 ft. deep, 8 ft. long and 5 ft. wide, inside measurement, lay the walls of hard brick, 8 in. thick, bottom to be laid in two courses of brick laid flat, the whole laid in and smoothly coated on the inside with cement. Connect the cistern with house leaders through 6 in. vitrified pipe. Lay a 6 in. drain overflow connected closely with the cistern near its top, trap it and connect with drain to cesspool.

Cesspools.—Construct a cesspool 5 ft. in diameter and 7 ft. deep in the clear, draw in on top in a substantial manner, leave manhole with cover of flag stone. Build a separate cesspool for overflow from cistern—with stone walls laid dry and 3 ft. in diameter and 5 ft. deep. Cesspools to be located 60 ft. from house.

CARPENTER.

Timber.—All timber not otherwise specified, to be of good seasoned spruce and put together in the most substantial and thoroughly workmanlike manner known to the trade.

Framing.—The frame to be what is known as a balloon frame, well nailed together ; second floor girts to be notched into and well spiked to studs. Do all necessary framing around stairways and chimneys properly mortised and tenoned together.

Frame Timber.—Girders, 6x6 in.; sills, 3x7 in.; posts, 4x5 in ; girts of yellow pine, 1x4 in.; plates, 2x4 in., double and well spiked into ends of studding. First floor timbers, 2x9 in.; second floor, 2x8 in.—16 in. centres ; header and trimmer beams, 3 in. thick ; roof rafters, 2x5 in.—2 ft. centres ; door and window studs, 3x4 in. intermediate studding, 2x4 in.—16 in. centres ; studding in partitions, 2x4 in.—16 in. centres. Porch sills and cross sills, 3x6 in.; floor timbers, 2x6 in.—20 in. centres.

Bridging.—Bridge the floor timbers through centres with 1x2 in. cross-bridging, properly cut in between timbers, and nailed at each end with two 10d. nails.

Furring.—Furr overhead on rafters, using 2x3 in. stuff for ceilings of rooms on second floor, and do any other furring required ; also furnish any other timber, as required by the design, of the requisite sizes and quality.

Sheathing.—Cover all sides of frame with tongued and grooved boards, not to exceed 8 in. in width, nailed through each edge to every stud with 10d. nails.

Lumber.—The lumber to be of white pine, unless otherwise specified, free from knots, shakes and other imperfections impairing its durability and strength.

Water Table to be $\frac{7}{8}$ in. thick, beveled and rabbeted for clapboards.

Corner Boards, casings and bands to be $1\frac{1}{4}$x6 in.; bands to be rabbeted top and bottom for clapboards and beveled on top.

Shingling on sides of second story to be as shown, using shingle 6 in. wide and laid 6 in. to the weather and all laid close and made tight at angles and corners, each shingle nailed with two nails.

Clapboarding.—Cover first story with clear pine clapboards $4\frac{1}{2}$ in. wide, put on with 8d. box nails, to have not less than $1\frac{1}{4}$ in. lap and underlaid with rosin-sized, waterproof sheathing felt, which, also, place under all covering, casings, watertable, etc., so as to lap and make tight job.

Cornices to be formed as shown, gutter formed on same and lined with tin, so as to shed water to points indicated on plan ; all as per detail drawings.

Window Frames to be made as shown ; cellar frames of 2 in. plank rabbeted for sash ; sash hinged to top, and to have suitable fasteners to keep open or shut ; all other sashes to be double hung with braided cotton cord and cast-iron weights, and to be glazed with best American sheet glass all sashes $1\frac{3}{8}$ in. thick, of seasoned pine, window sills 2 in. thick.

Blinds.—Outside blinds to all windows, except cellar, hung in two folds, properly secured.

Door Frames.—Outside door frames of plank, rabbeted, with 2 in. oak sills.

Porches to be constructed as shown by the detail drawings ; steps $1\frac{1}{8}$ in. thick, $\frac{7}{8}$ in. risers, to have cove under nosings ; lay floors with $1\frac{1}{8}$x4 in. flooring, blind nailed to beams, and to have white lead joints ; ceiling ceiled with narrow beaded battens of even width and molded in angles. Columns, rails, newels, panels, etc., all as per detail drawings.

Roofing.—All roofs to be covered with 18 in. sawed pine shingles, laid on 1 x 2 in. strips, nailed to rafters with 10d. nails ; each shingle to be nailed with two 4d. nails, to be well laid, joints properly broken and made tight ; valleys to be lined with tin 20 inches wide and well painted both sides. Put small scuttle in roof and step ladder to same.

Floors.—Lay the floors throughout with $\frac{7}{8}$ in. flooring, not to exceed 6 in. in width, to be well laid, joints broken, and well nailed to every timber ; the best to be selected and laid on first floor.

Partitions.—Set partitions as marked on plans, to foot on girders, and to have 3x4 in. plates to carry second floor ; all angles to be formed solid ; all partitions to be bridged once in their height.

Grounds.—Put up all necessary grounds to skreed plaster to, to be $\frac{7}{8}$ in. thick and left on.

Wainscoting.—Wainscot walls of kitchen 3 ft. high, with beaded battens 3 in wide, and cap with molded and beveled cap.

Casings in front hall, parlor and dining-room to be moulded on face as shown, 1x6in.; all doors and windows elsewhere to be cased with $\frac{7}{8}$ in. casings, and finish with a $\frac{7}{8}$x$1\frac{3}{4}$in, mold ; put down 8 in. beveled and moulded base after plastering ; door jambs to be $\frac{7}{8}$in. thick, and rabbeted for doors and beaded on edges: windows to be finished with neat stool and apron finish.

Doors to be made in size as shown ; outside doors to be sash doors, as shown ; all other doors six-panel, ogee moulded solid.

Finish of first story hall, parlor and dining room to be of ash, elsewhere clean pine for natural wood finish.

Saddles.—Put down neat hard pine saddles to all doors.

Stairs.—Cellar stairs to be of plank, no risers ; stairs to second floor as shown, $1\frac{1}{4}$ in. treads, $\frac{7}{8}$ in. risers, properly put together and supported. Newel to be 6 inches square with turned top, rail $2\frac{1}{2}$ x $3\frac{1}{2}$ in. worked as shown, balusters 2 in. turned and all of ash.

Sink.—Ceil up under sink with narrow beaded battens, to match wainscoting; hang door to form closet under ; ceil up splash back 16 in. high ; also place drip board complete.

Pantry to have counter shelf and four shelves above, also put up one dozen pot-hooks.

China Closet to have counter-shelf with closet under and three drawers and press with doors and shelves.

Clothes Presses to be fitted up with shelves and double wardrobe hooks, 9 in. apart, on neat molded strips.

Knobs and Escutcheons on front door and main part of first floor to be of ash and elsewhere mineral.

Locks to all doors to be mortise locks, brass fronts and keys ; outside doors to be secured with suitable shove bolts. All sash to have a burglar-proof sash lock to match other furniture.

Stops.—Insert hard-wood door stops in base, where requisite.

Hinging.—Hang all doors with loose joint butts of appropriate size ; those on first floor to have acorn-drops and japanned.

Hatchway Doors to Cellar to have a frame well secured and doors made out of 1x6 in. stuff well battened and secured.

Side Board to be constructed of ash as per details.

Mantels to be constructed, as shown, of ash as per details.

Cellar.—Partitions in cellar to be boarded with matched boards ; coal bin to be boarded up 5 ft. high, to have slides complete ; put up two swing shelves in cellar.

Door Bell.—Put a good gong bell on front door with suitable pull, etc., to match other furniture.

Ice Closet.—Line inside with two thicknesses of spruce matched ceiling with air space and paper between and fill in between studs with mineral wool, prepare tank for lining by plumber, fit up shelves and drawers, etc., as directed.

Bath Room.—Fit up with ash, wainscot walls 3 ft. high, ceil up over bath and closet 20 in. high. Case up bath-tub and wash bowl and finish with neat capping. Hang seat and cover to W. C. in most approved manner.

Tank.—Construct of plank and support in a substantial manner, a tank 3x4x3 ft. inside measurement.

Final.—Also do any other carpenter work as shown by and as required to carry out the design.

PAINTING.

All wood-work on exterior, to be painted two good coats of Lucas & Co.'s pure tinted gloss paints in the following colors :

Body of the work, 1st story, No. 241. Body of the work, 2d story, No. 244, Corner boards and casings, No. 258. Sash, No. 240. Blinds, No. 234. Roof. No. 240.

Paint tin work two coats, leaders two coats to match other work. Finish the front door and all interior wood work by filling with Wheeler's filler, and give two good coats of varnish and rub down.

TINNING AND PLUMBING.

Tinning.—Line the gutters with tin, well soldered in rosin ; furnish and put up the necessary number of tin leaders to convey the water from gutters to grade level, and there connect with drains. These leaders to be firmly secured to building, and to be graded in size to suit amount of service required.

Sink to be a 20x30x6 in. steel, supplied with water through $\frac{5}{8}$ in. lead pipe and $\frac{5}{8}$ in. brass drawcock, to have 2 in. cast iron waste, properly caulked at joints, trapped and connected closely to drain. Extend waste pipe above roof.

Pump to be lift and force, and connected to cistern and well, and supply to tank in attic, with tell tale return—line tank in attic with lead.

Boiler to be 35 gallon galvanized iron set on stand and connected to water back of range, and fitted up complete.

Bath Room to have W. C. selected by owner net cost not to exceed $12, to have drip tray and set open. Bath-tub 12 oz. sheet copper planished, and to have combination bibb for hot and cold water. Washbowl of best ware marble top, counter sunk, hot and cold water—all properly supplied with water and wastes to go into 4 in. cast-iron soil down to drain, and this pipe to extend up above roof—put safe wastes under W. C. and bowl. All fixtures to be properly trapped and vented, and the whole to be a first-class sanitary job. Faucets to be nickel plated. Stop-cocks to be provided wherever requisite. Ice tank to be lined with zinc.

Of the works and materials required in the erection, construction and completion of Design No. 22, Plate 7.

DIMENSIONS.—The drawings and details must be accurately followed according to their scale, and in all cases preference must be given to figured dimensions over scale. The building to be in size as shown on plans (figured on drawings). Cellar, 6ft. 6in.; first floor, 8ft. 6in., and second floor, 8ft. 0in. in the clear, divided, subdivided, and built in exact accordance with plans and specifications.

MASON WORK.

Excavating.—Do all necessary excavating required for cellar, area and all foundations, to firm and solid ground, and all to be in depth so that foundations will be clear of frost; grade off the ground as directed at completion.

Stone Work.—Build the foundation walls of good, flat building stone, of firm bed, well bonded through the wall, laid up in clean, sharp sand lime and cement mortar, in parts of one of cement to two of lime, laid by and full to a line on the inner face, and flushed and pointed at completion. These walls to be 1 ft. 4 in. thick. Put down in like manner foundations under all piers, chimney and exterior steps, all to be clear of frost.

Drains.—All drain pipes to be of the first quality cement drain pipe, in sizes as marked on plan and to be connected with sewer in street. These pipes to be properly graded, trapped and the joints cemented tight.

Underpinning.—From the top of stone wall, at grade level, extend up two feet in height with 8 in. brick wall, laid up with best hard-burned brick and clean sharp sand lime mortar; face walls with selected brick of even color, laid in red mortar, close joints, jointed, properly cleaned down at completion, and finished with black joints. Window sills of blue stone.

Piers.—Build piers in cellar, as shown, of best hard-burned brick, laid in clean, sharp sand lime mortar.

Hatchway.—Build the hatchway to cellar as shown, treads of blue stone 3 in. thick, risers of hard brick, jambs to be of stone same as foundation walls and leveled up on top just above grade.

Chimney.—Build chimney as shown, plastered on the inside and outside, furnished with proper stove collars and ventilating covers where required. Top out the chimney above the roof, as shown, with selected brick in like manner to underpinning.

Lathing.—All stud partitions, ceilings and work that is furred off, on first and second floors, to be lathed with sound spruce lath and joints broken every tenth lath.

Plastering.—All walls, partitions and ceilings, throughout first and second floors, to be plastered one good coat of brown well haired mortar and finish with a good coat of white hard-finish. All walls to be finished straight and plumb; all angles to be maintained sharp and regular in form, and the plastering, in all cases, to extend clear down to the floor.

Cellar Bottom.—Clean out all rubbish, level off cellar-bottom and settle it thoroughly.

Whitewashing.—Give all brick, stone and timber work in cellar one good coat of whitewash.

Privy Vault.—Excavate for and stone up a privy vault 3x5 ft. and 5 ft deep and level up on top to receive framework.

CARPENTER.

Timber.—All timber not otherwise specified, to be of good seasoned hemlock and put together in the most substantial and thoroughly workmanlike manner known to the trade.

Framing.—The frame to be what is known as a balloon frame, well nailed together, second floor girts to be notched into and well spiked to studs. Do all necessary framing around stairways and chimneys, properly mortised and tenoned together.

Frame Timber.—Girders, 4x6 in.; sills, 3x5 in.; posts, 4x5 in.; girts of yellow pine, 1x4 in.; plates, 2x4 in., doubled and well spiked to ends of studding. First floor timbers, 2x8 in.; second floor, 2x7 in.—16 in. centres; header and trimmer beams, 3 in. thick; roof rafters, 2x5 in.— 2 ft. centres; door and window studs, 3x4 in. intermediate studding, 2x4 in.—16 in. centres; studding in partitions, 2x3 in.—16 in. centres; also furnish any other timber, as required by the design, of the requisite sizes and quality.

Bridging.—Bridge the floor timbers with 1x2 in. cross bridging, properly cut in between timbers, and nailed at each end with two 10d. nails.

Sheathing.—Cover all sides of frame with tongued and grooved boards, not to exceed 10 in. in width, nailed through each edge to every stud with 10d. nails.

Lumber.—The lumber to be of White pine, unless otherwise specified, free from knots, shakes and other imperfections impairing its durability and strength.

Water Table to be ⅞ in. thick, furred off, 1 in., and capped with a beveled and rabbeted cap for clapboards to lap.

Corner Boards, casings and bands to be 1¼x5 in.; bands to be rabbeted top and bottom for clapboards and beveled on top.

Clapboarding.—Cover sides of first story with clear pine clapboards, 4½ in. wide, put on with 8d. box nails, to have not less than 1¼ in. lap, and underlaid with rosin-sized waterproof sheathing felt, which, also, place under shingling and all casings, water-table, etc., so as to lap and make tight job.

Shingling.—The side walls of second story and gables to be covered with California redwood shingle 6 in. wide with rounded butts and laid 6 in. to weather, to be put close at all angles, well nailed and made perfectly tight.

Cornices to be formed, as shown, gutter formed on same, and lined with tin, so as to shed water to points indicated on plan; and all as per detail drawings.

Window Frames to be made as shown; cellar frames of 2 in. plank rabbeted for sash; sash hinged to top, and to have suitable fasteners to keep open or shut; all other sashes to be double hung with hemp cords and cast iron weights, and to be glazed with best American sheet glass, all sashes 1⅜ in. thick, of seasoned pine, window sills 1½ in. thick.

Blinds.—Outside blinds to all windows, except cellar, hung in two folds, properly secured and painted two good coats of invisible green.

Door Frames.—Outside door frames of plank, rabbeted, and to have 1½ in. oak sills.

Porches to be constructed as shown by the detail drawings; steps 1⅛ in. thick, ⅞ in. risers, to have cove under nosings; lay floors with 1¼ x4 in. flooring, blind nailed to beams, and to have white lead joints; ceiling ceiled with narrow beaded battens of even width and molded in angles. Columns, rails, newels, panels, etc., all as per detail drawings.

Roofing.—All roofs to be covered with 18 in. sawed pine shingles, laid on 1x2 in., nailed to rafters with 10d. nails; each shingle to be nailed with two 4d nails, to be well laid, joints properly broken, and made tight. Valleys to be lined with tin 20 in. wide. Put small scuttle in roof and step ladder up to same in closet.

Floors.—Lay the floors throughout with ⅞ in. flooring, not to exceed 6 in. in width, to be well laid, joints broken, and well nailed to every timber; the best to be selected and laid on first floor.

Partitions.—Set partitions, as marked on plans, to foot on girders, and to have 3x3 in. plates to carry second floor; all angles to be formed solid; all partitions to be bridged once in their height.

Wainscoting.—Wainscot walls of kitchen and dining-room 3 ft. high, with beaded battens 3 in. wide, and cap with molded and bevelled cap.

Casings in front hall and sitting-room to be beaded on face, as shown, ⅞x5 in.; all doors and windows elsewhere to be cased before plastering with ⅞ in. casings, and finish with a ⅞x1¾ in. band mold; put down 7 in. bevelled base in front hall, sitting-room and bed-rooms after plastering; door jambs to be ⅞ in. thick, and rabbeted for doors and beaded on edges; windows to be finished with neat stool and apron finish.

Doors to be made in size as shown; to be six-panel, ogee molded solid.

Saddles.—Put down neat hard pine saddles to all doors.

Stairs.—Cellar stairs, to be of plank, no risers; stairs to second floor as shown, 1¼ in. treads, ⅞ in. risers, properly put together and supported; 2x3 in. rail on side.

Sink.—Ceil up under sink with narrow beaded battens, to match wainscoting; hang door to form closet under; ceil up splash back 16 in. high; also place drip board complete.

Pantry to have counter-shelf and four shelves above, also put up one dozen pot-hooks.

China Closet—In dining-room, to be fitted up with two drawers and four shelves above.

Closets to be fitted up with shelves and double wardrobe hooks, 9in. apart, on neat molded strips.

Furniture to front door to be jet pattern, elsewhere mineral, plain.

Locks to all doors to be mortise locks, brass fronts and keys; outside doors to be secured with suitable shove bolts. Sash to be secured with burglar proof sash locks.

Stops.—Insert hard-wood door stops in base, where requisite.

Hinging.—Hang all doors with loose joint butts of appropriate size.

Mantel in sitting-room to be constructed, as shown, of ash.

Cellar.—Partitions in cellar to be formed with matched boards; coal bin to be boarded up 4 ft. high, to have slides complete.

Privy.—Build a privy 4 ft. 6 in. x5 ft. 0 in. inside, board it with tight matched boards, hang batten door properly secured, small sliding sash in one end, shingle roof.

Hatchway doors to Cellar.—To be constructed out of 1x5 in. stuff, battened and to be properly hinged and secured.

Final.—Also do any other carpenter work as shown by and as required to carry out the design.

PAINTING.

Furnish all materials and perform all labor for the proper painting of the building.

Cover all sap and knots with shellac, putty up all wood-work smoothly and use New Jersey ochre in oil for priming exterior work as put up, and finish with one good coat of Lucas' pure tinted gloss paints in the following colors.

Body of the work, No. 258.

Corner boards and casings, No. 205.

Shingling of sides, stain and oil.

Sash, white.

Front door, grain walnut.

Paint tin work two coats, leaders two coats to match other work.

Paint privy two coats to match house.

Paint all wood work of interior that it is customary and usual to paint two good coats such tints as directed; grain wood work of kitchen and dining-room oak and varnish same and leave all work in a complete state.

TINNING AND PLUMBING.

Tinning.—Line the gutters with tin, well soldered in rosin; furnish and put up the necessary number of tin leaders to convey the water from gutters to grade level, and there connect with drains. These leaders to be firmly secured to building, and to be graded in size to suit amount of service required.

Sink to be a 20x30x6 in. cast iron, supplied with water through ⅝ in. lead pipe and ⅜ in. brass draw cock, to have 2 in. cast-iron waste, properly caulked at joints, trapped and connected closely to drain. Extend waste pipe above roof for vent.

It is desirable for parties who contemplate building to obtain the greatest amount of room, with the best architectural effect for the amount of money expended, and to accomplish this they should secure the services of a competent architect, one who has made such things a study and pursuit for years, and has used every means to become familiar with it in all its detail. The parties for whom the building is to be erected should carefully study their wants, and give their ideas to the architect to be worked out by him; he can then prepare a complete set of drawings, details and specifications. The proprietor knows just what he is going to have before the building is commenced, and he feels the assurance that there can be no misunderstanding with his contractor, as the architect's drawings and specifications serve as a mediator between the owner and contractor, to remind the former what to require, and the latter what his agreement is to perform.

Care should be taken by clients not to place too many restrictions on the architect -how he shall do this or that, and make a mere draughtsman of him; but after stating the price, it would be well to say what room is required, and give him your ideas on the matter; and you may be sure that everything will be added to the building which can be, internally and externally, that will enhance its beauty and usefulness.

When parties communicate with us with a view to obtain our services in preparing plans, etc., they will please give the following particulars and any and all the ideas they have on the subject which they may deem of importance.

1. The amount you will expend on the building to make it complete in every particular. Do not state an amount less than you really intend to spend as by so doing you may be disappointed, as some of our clients have been heretofore on account of their understating the amount they were willing to expend with the idea that it was sure to run up above the amount they named. A lady client of ours instructed us that her house and barn must not exceed $10,000 in cost, and the actual cost by contract was $9,500, and she was disappointed and would have been glad to have had it better finished and more elaborate work and would willingly have paid $15,000 and believed at the start that it would run up to that figure before it was finished, her friends having informed her that architects' estimates were always increased in actual execution by about one half.

2. Prices of labor and materials in your locality for cash; also state how you intend to have your work done, by contract or how, or would you give it proper, personal attention yourself, and sharp business management in buying the material and getting the work done according to advice and suggestions that we could give as to purchase of some of the materials and doing the work; give character and ability of contractors in your locality that you are likely to employ; are they mechanics and workers, thorough, pushing, wide-awake business men and close buyers for cash or are they bound to buy in the local market and pay whatever some one chooses to ask, who gives them credit, and are unable to buy elsewhere.

3. Nature of ground, size and shape of lot, grade of ground and in which direction the building will front, also principal side. The best way is to send a rough draft of the lot, with points of compass, and indicate roughly where building is to be placed, something like this:

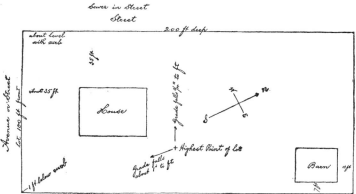

4. What material will be used in construction? Wood, brick or stone? Give full particulars where material can be obtained, and state which can be had most conveniently and economically for the several purposes. What is your preference for foundations and also for underpinning,

5. Particulars of other buildings near it, if any.

6. Number and what rooms are required on each floor; heights of ceilings and number of floors; also give particulars of any special disposition to be made of any of the rooms on account of scenery, views, or otherwise.

7. What the building and rooms are to be used for.

8. From which direction are your most severe winds and storms.

9. Give particulars of locality and character of the grounds and surroundings, and any special circumstances to be considered in the design, and in the location and arrangement of rooms.

10. What improvements are required, such as heating, hot and cold water, bath, gas, water-closets, etc.

11. Out-side finish—Porches, Tower, Bay-window, Verandas, etc., etc.

12. Have you any public water-works? Do you require Cisterns to receive water from roof, or what provision must be made for water service? Also give full particulars of drainage. Can yours connect with a sewer in the street or must a cesspool be provided and state whether the ground has a bottom of sand, gravel, hard-pan or clay.

13. What fence and out-buildings are required?

14. Name any work and materials you wish to do or supply, so that they may be mentioned in specifications.

Write your name and address legibly, giving your post-office, county and state, and write your own name at the bottom of your letters.

After receiving particulars, anything that will interfere with the proper arrangement of the rooms, and the carrying out of a suitable design, will be brought to your notice, and we shall correspond with you until everything will harmonize. We do not wish to send out designs when we think they will not give satisfaction.

Correspondence invited from those who contemplate building, which will always receive our prompt and careful attention.

When we are employed by parties at a distance, we make preliminary sketches of floor plans, and usually with this we send a small free hand-sketch of the Elevations. These we send to the client and they are returned, with whatever alterations, corrections and suggestions he makes. Then we make the changes suggested as far as proper and send again to the client for final approval if necessary and when our sketches show just what is wanted by our client to meet his necessities and desires, we make the working plans, detail drawings and specifications, etc, as required for the builders to work from. Parties who wish to employ us, should not wait until the last moment, but should open correspondence with us two or three months, or even more, before they wish to commence building.

Our charges for services, are for full working plans, all detail drawings for exterior and interior work and fittings, specifications and forms of contract, two and a half per cent. on cost of erecting and completing building, and where parties are unknown to us, one-quarter of said charges usually accompanying the order for preliminary sketches, and as a guarantee of good faith.

In addition to above rates, one per cent. is charged when elaborated sketches and perspective in line or color are required to be made previous to making full working plans; also one per cent. additional when there is a large amount and variety of elaborate interior wood work and fittings to design in detail for first-class dwellings, mansions, etc.

For preparing complete bills of quantities of materials, a charge of three-quarter per cent. is made.

For superintendence, one and one half to three per cent., according to the requirements or by the visit by special agreement for inspecting the work to see whether contractor's payments are due or not, and that he is fulfilling the conditions of the contract.

When required, we furnish our client with a competent and reliable Clerk of Works to be constantly on the ground superintending the construction, and which is very necessary in case of large or intricate buildings.

For designs in detail of Furniture and Interior Decorations, ten per cent. on cost.

For buying material and appliances required in building and furnishing, such goods in all cases being bought at the best wholesale trade rates, a charge of five per cent. is made.

For appraising and valuing, charges are made according to time occupied and circumstances.

Traveling expenses and surveying in all cases are charged in addition to above rates.

Charges are based on the total cost of actual execution and payment of full value, but previous to ability to arrive at the proper and full cost, the approximated intended cost is used as the base on which to reckon charges.

It is our constant aim to please our clients, and we usually succeed. Our long practice has convinced us that it is quite as easy to satisfy parties with our designs when we never see them, as in any other way. When parties correspond with us in regard to procuring designs, we are always prompt in answering their inquiries; but oft-times people have written us simply to get our ideas and not pay for them. To all such we would say that our time is valuable, and we sincerely wish they would not trouble us. We mention this fact, because we have received scores of letters, and answered them, when the parties really never intended to employ us, but simply steal our ideas. Now our ideas are for sale, and by this means we live, and it is a pleasure as well as a livelihood, to assist people to build artistic, convenient and comfortable homes. Perhaps if architects were rich—they seldom are—it would be sufficient compensation to them to assist people as far as possible with ideas; but as they are not, they are obliged to combine pleasure and profit in a way it is seldom done, except in architecture.

When you want a lawyer do you ask all the attorneys you know to make a "bid" and then employ the cheapest? Do you not rather look for the attorney whose skill, knowledge of the law, and personal character insure thorough and honest effort in your interest? Level-headed business men seek the best legal talent; in their judgment the best is the cheapest and it should be just the same in regard to the employment of architects, yet many think that the least they can get a design for is so much made. This is a great mistake and is admitted by all intelligent men. It is impossible to get anything for less than its value, and at the same time have it prove satisfactory. It is but a very small design that will occupy a week's time in its study, and the proper preparation of the drawings and specifications.

We shall be very glad to hear from all persons who intend to build, and wish our services, and we will serve them faithfully.

Our aim is to please our clients and to give just as much for their money as possible.

It may seem a curious fact, but to design a small cottage, and get the most for a limited cost, is a much harder study than to design a house to contain so many rooms, and have this and that, where we are not limited to cost.

Our drawings are made on vellum, so that they will stand wear and tear; are thoroughly lettered, figured, and made plain as daylight. Also, any one can understand our full-size working drawings. The specifications are always made complete in every particular, and are furnished in duplicate, for builder and proprietor, as are also our forms of contract; and all instructions are given our clients in the most complete way to enable them to have the design properly executed, and their building affairs satisfactorily conducted.

To those who need our services, we would say that our aim at all times is to produce what will in every way give satisfaction, and our services, advice, etc., are rendered in full confidence that they will do so.

You will do us a favor by showing this book, or speaking of it to your friends and any one in your locality who intends to build or is otherwise interested.

We have the honor to be yours most respectfully,

PALLISER, PALLISER & CO.,

ARCHITECTS.

SPECIFICATIONS.

Of the works and materials required in the erection, construction, and completion of Design 16, Plate 6.

DIMENSIONS.—The drawings must be accurately followed according to their scale, and preference given to figured dimensions over scale. Detail Drawings will be furnished; any work constructed without such drawings must be removed if required, and work replaced at contractor's expense. The building to be in size as shown and figured on drawings. Cellar, 7 ft. 0 in.; first floor, 10 ft. 0 in.; second floor, 9 ft. 0 in.; all in the clear, divided, subdivided, and built in exact accordance with plans and specifications.

MASON WORK.

EXCAVATOR.—Excavate in depth for the cellar, area, foundations, and footings of all the walls and chimneys, also for all drains, cistern and cess-pools. Dig trenches for footings of all walls 8 in. below level of cellar bottom; fill in around walls as laid; grade the excavated earth around the building as may be directed. Lay aside the top soil at commencement, and replace over the graded surface at completion.

STONE WORK.—Build foundation walls of good building stone, of flat bed and firm build, laid in clean, sharp sand, lime and cement mortar, in parts of one of cement and two of lime. Lay down footings under all the walls of the building of flat stones, not less than 20 in. long and 6 in. thick, bedded crosswise of the walls on the natural, undisturbed earth; build the walls from thence to grade level, by and full to a line on the inner face, and flush and point at completion. These walls to average 1 ft. 6 in. in thickness, the greater breadth at the base. Lay down substantial foundations under chimneys and piers in cellar; put down clear of frost, solid foundations under piers supporting porches and verandas, also under all exterior steps. Area copings and steps to be of blue stone, steps properly walled in on each end.

UNDERPINNING.—Build the underpinning walls 16 in. thick from grade level, and extend up 2 ft. 4 in. in height, with good underpinning stone, level beds, plumb joints; all angles and jambs to have chisel draft, and to be properly pointed and penciled with a red joint at completion. Window sills to be of blue stone; such portions of walls as are covered up with veranda to be rough work.

CESS-POOL.—Stone up cess-pool 3 feet in diameter and 8 feet deep, covered with rough flag, provided with man-hole, etc., complete; make the necessary connections with the cistern to receive the overflow through vitrified pipe of the required size. Also stone up, in like manner, cess-pool, to receive wastes from house, and connect with 6 in. vitrified drain-pipe.

BRICK WORK.—To be laid up with best quality hard-burned brick and clean, sharp sand, lime mortar.

PIERS.—Build piers in cellar 16 in. square, as shown, and cap with flat stone, size of piers; piers supporting porches and verandas 12 in. square.

CHIMNEYS.—Build the chimneys as shown on plans; carry up the flues of uniform size, to be well plastered, furnished with proper stove collars and ventilating flues where required; turn arches to all fire-places, and turn trimmer arches under all hearths; top out above the roof, as per detail drawings, with selected brick laid in red mortar, close joints, jointed and cleaned down, stained and oiled. Face the throat, breast and jambs of kitchen fire-place with selected brick, laid in red mortar, provide with cut stone shelf, to have blue stone hearth as shown on plans. Build fire-places with buff brick, laid in buff mortar, as per details, also furnish the necessary brick, mortar and plaster for setting the range. Clean out all flues and test the draught of flues and fire-places, hearths to fire-places of slate.

CISTERN.—Build a cistern where directed, 10 ft. diameter and 10 ft. deep, with 8 in. walls laid in and smoothly coated on the inside with cement; cover man-hole in neck with flag-stone, connect to leaders with 4 in. and 6 in. vitrified pipe.

LATHING.—Lath all walls, ceilings, and work that is furred off, throughout first and second floors, and three rooms in attic, with sound, seasoned lath, securely nailed to each stud, and joints broken every tenth lath.

PLASTERING.—All walls and ceilings throughout to be plastered with one good coat of brown, well haired mortar, and finished with one coat of white hard-finish. All angles to be sharp and regular in form, walls to be straight and plumb, and in all cases to extend clear down to floors.

FINAL.—Whitewash walls in cellar and do all necessary mending of walls after other craftsmen, and deliver the mason work up in thoroughly good order at completion; make the floors broom-clean from time to time as required; also remove all mason's waste materials and rubbish accumulated during the progress of the works, from off the premises and leave everything in a perfect, complete and satisfactory state.

CARPENTER.

TIMBER.—The whole of the timber used in and throughout this building to be the best of their several kinds, well seasoned and free from sap, shakes and other imperfections impairing its durability and strength.

FRAMING.—The frame to be what is known as half balloon, the studs to be tenoned into sills and plates, to be braced with long angle braces cut in barefoot and well spiked. The girts to be of yellow pine, notched into and well spiked to studs. Do all necessary framing around stairways and chimneys, all properly mortised and tenoned together, and all to be done in a thoroughly workmanlike and substantial manner.

FRAME TIMBER.—Sills and girders, 6 in. x 6 in.; posts, 6 in. x 6 in., with inside angle cut out to make them 4 in. from faces. Girts, 1¼ in. x 4 in.; plates, 4 in. x 5 in.; first-floor timbers, 2 in. x 10 in.; second-floor, 2 in. x 8 in.; attic, 2 in. x 6 in.—all 16 in. centres; header and trimmer beams, 3 in. thick, all floor timbers under partitions running same way to be 4 in. thick, roof rafters, 2 in. x 6 in.—2 ft. centres; hip and valley rafters, 3 in. x 8 in. Door and window studs, 3 in. x 4 in. intermediate studding, 2 in. x 4 in.—16 in. centres; long braces, 2 in. x 4 in. All main partitions to be set with 2 in. x 4 in. studding—16 in. centres, to be set as the frame is raised, and foot on girders, to have 3 in. x 4 in. plates on which to foot second-story partitions and carry floor timbers; other partitions set with 2 in. x 3 in. studs—16 in. centres, and all partitions that are directly over each other, to be set in like manner to above, all to be well braced and spiked; all angles to be formed solid, and all partitions to be bridged once in their height. Porch and veranda sills, 4 in. x 6 in.; floor timbers, 2 in. x 6 in.—16 in. centres; plates, 4 in. x 5 in.; rafters, 3 in. x 5 in.—2 ft. centres.

BRIDGING.—All the floor timbers to be bridged through centres with 2 in. x 2 in. cross-bridging, properly cut in between timbers and nailed with two 10d. nails at each end; also furnish any other timber of the required size and necessary to fully complete the works.

FURRING.—Studd off 3 rooms in attic, properly support and furr under stairs, furr for arches, and do any other furring required by the design, as grounds, etc., etc.

SHEATHING.—Cover the entire frame with tongued and grooved boards, not to exceed 10 in. in width, nailed through each edge to every stud with 10d. nails; this includes all roofs.

LUMBER.—The lumber to be of white pine, unless otherwise specified, well seasoned and dry, and free from shakes, loose knots and other imperfections. Sashes, panel work and inside casings to be perfectly clear lumber.

CLAPBOARDING.—Cover first story with clear pine clapboards, put on with 8d. box-nails, with not less than 1¼ in. lap. These boards to be underlaid with rosin-sized, waterproof sheathing felt, which also place under corner boards, casings, etc., so as to lap and make a tight job. Second story shingled with California redwood shingles, with paper under, and made tight.

CORNER BOARDS, casings and bands, 1¼ in. x 6 in.; bands to be rabbeted top and bottom for clapboards.

WATER TABLE.—To be furred off from frame, and to have beveled cap 1½ in. thick.

CORNICES.—To be formed as shown by drawings; barge boards and gable to be as shown. Brackets, as shown, and all as per details. Gutters to be lined with tin, graded to shed water to points indicated on plan.

LEADERS.—Furnish all the required leaders of sufficient size to convey the water from the gutters to the cistern and the tank in attic; said leaders to be firmly secured to building.

CRESTING.—To be of iron, as per details, to have galvanized iron cover base and securely put up on wrought-iron rods.

WINDOW FRAMES.—To be made in the ordinary manner; cellar frames to be made out of 2 in. plank, rabbeted for sash; sash hinged to top and to have suitable fasteners to keep open or shut; all sash to be of seasoned pine, 1½ in. thick, and double hung with best cotton cord, iron weights, and 1¾ in. sham axle pulleys, and to be glazed with Chances English sheet-glass, all to be well bedded, bradded and puttied; top sash leaded and diamonds of Cathedral glass; stair-case sash filled with art glass, cost $2 a sq. foot; window sills 2 in. thick.

BLINDS.—Inside blinds of cherry to all windows on first and second floors hung in folds about 7 in. wide, with bronze hinges, and secured with best style fasteners and filled with Pratt & Lambert's filler, and finished with two coats Pratt & Lambert's No. 110 Cabinet varnish.

DOOR FRAMES.—Outside door frames to be of plank, rabbeted, and to have 2 in. oak sills.

VERANDAS.—Construct veranda and porches, as shown, and as per detail drawings; steps, 1¼ in. thick, risers 1 in., to have cove under nosings;

lay the floors with 1⅛ in. x 3½ in. flooring, blind nailed to beams, and to have paint joints; narrow beaded ceiling of even widths. Columns, rails and brackets, to be as shown; cornices formed as shown; panels formed under floor as shown. Roofs to be covered with tin.

DEAFENING.—Deaden the floors throughout the first and second stories by laying diagonally a rough floor, surfaced and ⅞ in. thick, well nailed through top edges to each bearing; on this lay all-wool heavy deadening felt properly lapped, then place ½ x 2 in. strips over each joist, and well nailed through, on which to nail flooring.

FLOORS.—Lay the floors of kitchen part with yellow pine, ⅞ in. x 3 in., blind nailed to every beam; all other floors lay with white pine, not to exceed 5 in. in width, to be well laid, joints broken, and blind nailed in a thorough manner. Lay front hall floor with oak, to have neat border of oak and cherry strips.

WAINSCOTING.—Walls of kitchen to be wainscoted 3 ft. high, with beaded battens ⅞ in. x 3 in., and to have neat beveled molded cap.

CASINGS.—Case all doors and windows throughout with ⅞ in. casings, hall, parlor, dining-room and library finish of oak and cherry, elsewhere finish of ash and white pine; windows in main rooms to be finished down to floor with framed and molded panel-backs to match doors; other windows to have neat stool and apron finish; door-jambs to be 1 in., beaded on edges, and stop for doors.

BASE.—Put down 9 in. molded base in principal rooms, first floor; 9 in. plain beveled elsewhere.

DOORS.—To be made in size and thickness as marked on plans, and all as per details.

SADDLES.—Put down molded hard-wood saddles to all doors.

STAIRS.—Stairs to cellar to be of plank, no risers, to have slat rail on side; main stairs as shown, 1 in. risers, 1¼ in. treads, to be well supported and rough bracketed, steps housed into strings; newel, posts, rails and balusters to be of oak, as per details. Back stairs, and stairs to attic to be box stairs.

WASH TUBS.—To be constructed out of 2 in. plank, rabbeted and put together with white lead joints, and to have hinged lids—these tubs to be 14 in. deep.

SINK.—Ceil up under sink with narrow beaded battens; to have door properly hung; ceil up splash-back 16 in. high, and cap same as wainscoting; also place drip board complete.

WASH BOWLS.—Ceil up under with narrow beaded ash battens, and hang door to form a closet under.

BATH-ROOM.—Wainscot walls of bath-room, 3 ft. high, with narrow beaded ash battens, and cap with neat cap; water-closet to be fitted up with seat, riser and mitre-clamp flap, hung with brass butts.

BATH-TUB to be cased in most approved manner, all of ash.

TANK.—Construct out of 2 in. plank, a tank in attic, 7 ft. long, 5 ft. 6 in. wide and 3 ft. deep, framed, braced and supported in a substantial manner.

PANTRY.—To have counter-shelf and four shelves above, closet for barrel of flour, with lid in counter-shelf; also put in two dove-tailed drawers, and put up one dozen pot-hooks.

PASSAGE OR CHINA CLOSET.—To have table with closet under, and three dove-tailed drawers; also shelves in closets as shown.

CLOSETS.—To have shelves on neat strips, and double wardrobe hooks, 8 in. apart, on neat molded strips.

FURNITURE.—To front doors and main rooms 1st floor to be bronze; other doors jet, sash fasteners to correspond; all small closets to have suitable catches; all drawers to have suitable pulls, locks, etc., complete.

LOCKS.—All doors throughout to be secured with mortise locks, of best make, bolts and keys; outside doors to have suitable shove bolts.

STOPS.—Put rubber-tipped door-stops in base where required.

HINGING.—Hang all doors with loose joint butts, of appropriate sizes; all doors over 7 ft. 6 in. high to have three butts each. Sliding doors to run on track overhead and adjustable hangers.

BELLS.—Front door to have bell connected with kitchen and annunciator with four other connections.

NIGHT-LATCH to front door, combined with lock, and supplied with four keys.

COAL BINS, and partitions in cellar, to be boarded up with matched boards, as shown; doors in cellar to be batten doors.

MANTELS.—Construct mantels of oak, cherry and pine, as per details furnish of best cabinet work and finish and set complete.

SIDE BOARD.—To be of oak as per details, best cabinet work furnished and finished into recess as shown.

CORNICES AND CENTRE PIECES.—To be as per details, and corresponding with other wood.

FINAL.—Any other work that is shown by the drawings, and necessary to fully complete the work, to fully complete the same to the true intent and meaning of these particulars, is to be done without extra charge.

SLATER.

Cover all roofs with best Franklin Tunnel black slate, of small size, laid with a lap of at least 3 in. of the third over the first; each slate to be nailed with two galvanized iron nails; lay under slate heavy tarred felt paper; cover the ridges with zinc, also flash valleys and chimneys with heavy zinc and secure with slater's cement. To be a first-class job, and warranted tight for two years.

PLUMBER.

IRON SOIL-PIPE.—Furnish and connect with drain, a 4 in. cast iron soil-pipe, extend up and connect with water-closet in bath-room through 6 lb. lead trap; soil-pipe to be properly secured and the joints calked tight with lead, and extend up above roof and cap with ventilator. All traps to be anti-siphon.

SUPPLY-PIPE.—Furnish a ¾ in. B lead pipe, connect with the attic tank, and run to and connect with boiler in kitchen; tank to be lined with 4 lb. lead, and to have 2 in. overflow run through outside wall.

BOILER.—To be a 35-gallon, copper, of the best construction, connected to water back of range, through double A lead pipe and brass couplings; these pipes to be left ready for connection.

SINK.—To be 20 in. x 30 in. x 6 in. steel, supplied with hot and cold water through ⅝ in. B lead pipe, ⅝ in. brass draw cocks, to have 2 in. waste, properly trapped and connected.

PUMP.—Put in a combination lift and force pump, to cost $12; connect the same with cistern and well through 1¼ in. B lead pipes, provided with stop cocks, one on each pipe, placed beneath the pump, connect with tank in attic through 1 in. B lead pipe and run tell-tale back from tank to sink.

WASH TUBS.—Supply the two wash tubs in laundry with hot and cold water, through ⅝ in. B lead pipe and brass thimble tray draw cocks, to have 2 in. main waste and 1½ in. branch wastes, properly trapped and connected.

WASH BOWLS.—To be of best ware, and to have marble counter sunk tops and surbases, supplied with hot and cold water through ½ in. B lead pipe and compression double nickel-plated draw cocks, and plated plug and chain; to have 1 in. lead wastes, properly trapped and connected; lead pans to each with ½ in. lead waste run down to underside cellar ceiling.

WATER-CLOSET to be a Sanitas closet, with cistern, to be set and fit up in a perfect, tight and complete manner.

BATH TUB.—To be 14 oz. sheet-copper tub, well tinned and planished, supplied with hot and cold water through ⅝ in. B lead pipe and nickel-plated draw cocks; also to have plated plug and chain; also rubber hose shower-bath attachment; waste, 1½ in. lead, properly trapped and connected.

COCKS.—Put in the necessary stop-cocks over the boiler to shut the water off from the upper part of the house; also put in a lead branch connected with drain with stop-cock for emptying the boiler; also put in one draw-cock in cellar and all other stop and draw-cocks necessary to make a complete and first-class job; all pipes to be graded, so that if the water is shut off they will drain dry, and the whole of the work to be done in the very best and workmanlike manner, and delivered up in a complete and perfect state at completion.

PAINTER.

Properly stop and otherwise prepare for and paint all wood-work that is customary and usual to paint, on the exterior.

Paint finials and crest green, and gild the tips with gold leaf.

All interior wood-work to be properly filled with Pratt and Lambert's filler and finished with two coats of Pratt and Lambert's No. 110 cabinet varnish, properly applied and rubbed down smooth.

Stain and oil the shingles.

Paint clapboards No. 244; paint corner boards, casings, etc., No. 246; pick out all sunk and cut work in red, paint sash, No. 245; Veranda ceilings, No. 217; and do any other painting as required by the design, and necessary to fully complete the same. Tin work two coats metallic paint.

HEATER.

FURNACE.—Furnish and set complete a No. hot-air furnace in cellar, as indicated on plan, to be properly enclosed in galvanized iron, and to be connected with cold-air duct; to have the required man-hole door, and evaporating pan to hold 5 gallons, supplied with ⅜ in. pipe and ball-cock; to have all required mason work in setting, and for ash pit, etc.; all necessary fire tools, and smoke flue connection, ready to start fire.

Hot-air pipes to be connected to top of heater as shown, and in size as marked on plans, and extend up to registers with pipes 8 and 10 inches in size, made of XX. bright tin, joints soldered, and all properly connected, and wood-work to be protected by tin linings, and where plastering will be over face of heater pipes to be lathed with iron lath. The registers to have boxes, to be fixed properly, those in floors to be black japanned, and in side walls convex enameled, and to be in sizes as marked on plans.

All cutting for the pipes will be done by the Carpenter; any beams, etc., cut by the Heater man will be replaced at his expense.

HEAT REGULATOR.—The draughts on the heating apparatus to be automatically controlled by the Johnson Heat Regulating Apparatus, from a thermostat placed in the main hall, said thermostat to be adjustable to any temperature desired, and to control both the door over and the door under the fire; closing the lower and opening the upper door when the house warms to point at which the thermostat is set, and reversing them when the house cools one degree.

FORM OF CONTRACT.

In some States, according to law, it is important that within 48 hours after a Contract is made for Building, it be put on file or record at the Town Clerk's Office by the party of the second part, for his proper and legal protection. Several cases might be quoted where Proprietors have had to pay money twice over, to the amount of several hundred dollars, on account of omission to put on record the Contract.

AGREEMENT FOR BUILDING.

Articles of Agreement, MADE and entered into this _____ day of _____ in the year One Thousand Eight Hundred and _____

By and Between _____ of the _____ of _____ County of _____ and State of _____ as the part _____ of the first part, hereinafter called the Contractor :

And _____ of the _____ of _____ County of _____ and State of _____ as the part _____ of the second part, hereinafter called the Proprietor :

Witnesseth, first.—The said part _____ of the first part do _____ hereby, for _____ heirs, executors, administrators or assigns, covenant, promise and agree to and with the said part _____ of the second part, _____ heirs, executors, administrators or assigns, that _____ the said part _____ of the first part, _____ heirs, executors, administrators or assigns, shall and will, for the consideration hereinafter mentioned, on or before the _____ day of _____, in the year One Thousand, Eight Hundred and _____ well and sufficiently erect, finish and deliver in a true, perfect and thoroughly workmanlike manner, the _____ work required in the erection and completion of _____

or the part _____ of the second part, on ground situated _____ in the _____ of _____ County of _____ and State of _____ agreeably to the Plans, Drawings and Specifications prepared for the said works by _____ Architect , to the satisfaction and under the direction and personal supervision of _____ Architect , and will find and provide such good, proper and sufficient materials, of all kinds whatsoever, as shall be proper and sufficient for the completing and finishing all the _____ and other works of said building mentioned in the _____ Specifications, and signed by the said parties, within the time aforesaid for the sum of _____ _____ Dollars.

Second.—The said part _____ of the second part do _____ hereby for _____ heirs, executors, administrators or assigns, covenant, promise and agree to and with the said part _____ of the first part, _____ heirs, executors, administrators or assigns, that _____ the said part _____ of the second part, _____ heirs, executors, administrators or assigns, will and shall, in consideration of the covenants and agreements being strictly executed, kept and performed by the said part _____ of the first part, as specified, will well and truly pay, or cause to be paid, unto the part _____ of the first part, or unto _____ heirs, executors, administrators or assigns, the sum of _____ Dollars, lawful money of the United States of America, in manner following :

First payment of $ _____

Second payment of $ _____

Third payment of $ _____

Fourth payment of $ _____

Fifth payment of $ _____

when the building _____ is all complete, and after the expiration of _____ days, and when all the Drawings and Specifications have been returned to _____ Architect

Provided, That in each case of the said payments, a certificate shall be obtained from and signed by _____ _____ Architect , to the effect that the work is done in strict accordance with Drawings and Specifications, and that he _____ considers the payment properly due ; said certificate, however, in no way lessening the total and *final responsibility of the Contractor ; neither shall it exempt the Contractor from liability to replace work, if it be afterwards discovered to have been done ill, or not according to the Drawings and Specifications, either in execution or materials ; and, Provided further, that in each case a certificate shall be obtained by the Contractor, from the clerk of the office where liens are recorded, and signed and sealed by said clerk, that he has carefully examined the records and finds no liens or claims recorded against said works, or on account of the said Contractor ; neither shall there be any legal or lawful claims against the Contractor, in any manner, from any source whatever, for work or materials furnished on said works.*

AND IT IS HEREBY FURTHER AGREED, BY AND BETWEEN THE SAID PARTIES :

First.—That the Specifications and Drawings are intended to co-operate, so that any works exhibited in the Drawings, and not mentioned in the Specifications, or *vice-versa*, are to be executed the same as is mentioned in the Specifications and set forth in the Drawings, to the true intent and meaning of the said Drawings and Specifications.

Second.—The Contractor, at his own proper cost and charges, is to provide all manner of labor, materials, apparatus, scaffolding, utensils and cartage, of every description, needful for the due performance of the several works ; must produce, whenever required by Superintendent or Proprietor, all vouchers showing the quality of goods and materials used ; and render all due and sufficient facilities to the Architect, Superintendent or Clerk of Works, for the proper inspection of the works and materials, and which are to be under their control ; and they may require the Contractor to dismiss any workman or workmen who they may think incompetent or improper to be employed ; the workmen and Contractor being only admitted to the ground, for the purpose of the proper execution of the works, and have no tenancy. The Contractor shall deliver up the works to the Proprietor in perfect repair, clean and in good condition, when complete. The Contractor shall not sub-let the works, or any part thereof, without consent in writing of the Proprietor

Third.—Should the Proprietor, at any time during the progress of the said works, require any alterations of, deviations from, additions to or omissions in the said Contract, Specifications or Plans, he shall have the right and power, to make such change or changes, and the same shall in no way injuriously affect or make void the Contract ; but the difference for work omitted, shall be deducted from the amount of the Contract, by a fair and reasonable valuation ; and for the additional work required in alterations, the amount based upon same prices at which Contract is taken shall be agreed upon before commencing additions, as provided and hereinafter set forth in Article No. 6 ; and such agreement shall state also the extension of time (if any) which is to be granted by reason thereof.

Fourth.—Should the Contractor, at any time during the progress of said works, become bankrupt, refuse or neglect to supply a sufficiency of material or of workmen, or cause any unreasonable neglect or suspension of work, or fail or refuse to follow the Drawings and Specifications, or comply with any of the Articles of Agreement, the Proprietor or his Agent, shall have the right and power to enter upon and take possession of the premises, and may at once terminate the Contract, whereupon all claim of the Contractor, his executors, administrators or assigns, shall cease ; and the Proprietor may provide materials and workmen sufficient to complete the said works, after giving forty-eight hours' notice, in writing directed and delivered to the Contractor, or at his residence or place of business ; and the expense of the notice and the completing of the various works will be deducted from the amount of Contract, or any part of it due, or to become due, to the Contractor ; and in such case no scaffolding or fixed tackle of any kind, belonging to such Contractor, shall be removed so long as the same is wanted for the work. But if any balance on the amount of this Contract remains after completion in respect of work done during the time of the defaulting Contractor, the same shall belong to the persons legally representing him, but the Proprietor shall not be liable or accountable to them in any way for the manner in which he may have gotten the work completed.

Fifth.—Should any dispute arise respecting the true construction or meaning of the Drawings or Specifications, or as to what is extra work outside of Contract, the same shall be decided by Architect, and his decision shall be final and conclusive ; or in the event of his death or unwillingness to act, then of some other known capable Architect, or a Fellow of the American Institute of Architects, to be appointed by the Proprietor ; but should any dispute arise respecting the true value of any works omitted by the Contractor, the same shall be valued by two competent persons, one employed by the Proprietor, and the other by the Contractor, and these two shall have power to name an umpire, whose decision shall be binding on all parties.

Sixth.—No new work of any description done on the premises, or any work of any kind whatsoever, shall be considered as extra unless a separate estimate in writing for the same, before its commencement, shall have been submitted by the Contractor to the Superintendent and the Proprietor, and their signatures obtained thereto, and the Contractor shall demand payment for such work immediately it is done. In case of day's work, statement of the same must be delivered to the Proprietor at latest during the week following that in which the work may have been done, and only such day's work and extra work will be paid for, as such, as agreed on and authorized in writing.

Seventh.—The Proprietor will not, in any manner, be answerable or accountable for any loss or damage that shall or may happen to said works, or any part or parts thereof respectively or for any of the materials or other things used and employed in finishing and completing the said works ; or for injury to any person or persons, either workmen or the public, or for damage to adjoining property, from any cause which might have been prevented by the Contractor or his workmen, or any one employed by him against all which injuries or damages to persons and property, the Contractor having control over such work must properly guard against, and must make good all damage from whatever cause, being strictly responsible for the same. Where there are different Contractors employed on the works, each shall be responsible to the other for all damage to work, to persons or property, or for loss caused by neglect, by failure to finish work at proper time and preventing each portion of the works being finished by the several Contractors at date named in this Contract for completion, or from any other cause ; and any Contractor suffering damage shall call the attention of the Proprietor or Superintendent to the same, for action as laid down in Article No. 4.

Eighth.—The Contractor will insure the building to cover his interest in the same from time to time, as required ; and for any loss of the Contractor by fire the owner will not, under any circumstances, be answerable or accountable ; but the Proprietor shall protect himself by insurance to cover his interest when payments have been made to Contractor

Ninth.—All work and materials, as delivered on the premises to form part of the works, are to be considered the property of the Proprietor, and are not to be removed without his consent ; but the Contractor shall have the right to remove all surplus materials after his completing the works.

Tenth.—Should the Contractor fail to finish the work at or before the time agreed upon, shall pay to or allow the Proprietor, by way of liquidated damages, the sum of dollars per diem, for each and every day thereafter the said works remain incomplete.

In Witness Whereof, *the said parties to these presents have hereunto set their hands and seals the day and year above written.*
Signed and sealed in presence of

Witnesses : _____

Part of the First Part. _____ { SEAL. }
_____ { SEAL. }

Witnesses : _____

Part of the Second Part. _____ { SEAL. }
_____ { SEAL. }